THE MOST SHOCKING, BIZARRE, AND HISTORIC DEATHS OF PERFORMERS ONSTAGE

JEFF ABRAHAM AND BURT KEARNS

CHICAGO REVIEW PRESS

An A Cappella Book

Jeff Abraham

To my amazing mother and father, who inspired me in so many ways. I am a better person today because of them!

Burt Kearns

For Alison, Sam, Sally Jade . . . and Brian. *Prima la famiglia.*

Copyright © 2019 by Jeff Abraham and Burt Kearns
All rights reserved
Published by Chicago Review Press Incorporated
814 North Franklin Street
Chicago, Illinois 60610
ISBN 978-1-64160-217-4

Library of Congress Cataloging-in-Publication Data
Names: Abraham, Jeff, 1962– author. | Kearns, Burt, author.
Title: The show won't go on : the most shocking, bizarre, and historic
   deaths of performers onstage / Jeff Abraham and Burt Kearns.
Description: Chicago : Chicago Review Press Incorporated, 2019. | Includes
   index. | Summary: "The first comprehensive look at a bizarre show
   business phenomenon: the actors, singers, musicians, magicians,
   comedians, and others who died while performing onstage"—Provided by
   publisher.
Identifiers: LCCN 2019011885 (print) | LCCN 2019980914 (ebook) | ISBN
   9781641602174 (trade paperback) | ISBN 9781641602181 (pdf) | ISBN
   9781641602198 (kindle edition) | ISBN 9781641602204 (epub)
Subjects: LCSH: Entertainers—Biography. | Entertainers—Death.
Classification: LCC PN2205 .A37 2019 (print) | LCC PN2205 (ebook) | DDC
   791.0922 [B]—dc23
LC record available at https://lccn.loc.gov/2019011885
LC ebook record available at https://lccn.loc.gov/2019980914

Cover design: Preston Pisellini
Typesetting: Nord Compo

Printed in the United States of America
5 4 3 2 1

Contents

Prologue

This project began with an Elvis Presley tribute concert in 2004. Elvis's announcer, Al Dvorin, the man who'd say, "Elvis has left the building" at the end of shows back when Elvis was alive, spoke the phrase into a microphone after the performance by Elvis impersonator Paul Casey. Al got a standing ovation, then signed autographs in the lobby. One of us was there at the Trump 29 Casino in Coachella, California, that night, when some fan suggested to Al that he write his autobiography. "I know, I keep putting it off," Al replied. "But I will one day. I have time." He set off for home in Las Vegas the next morning, only to be killed in a car crash in the desert.

This unfortunate Elvis-related event led to a discussion that turned into an exploration that was even more ambitious and unwieldy than the one you're about to read. It was a study of performers who died after a show. These were the show people who took their bows, wiped off the greasepaint, put on their top hats, and made it to the car or plane or back to the hotel room—and then, like poor Al Dvorin, wound up "leaving the building." Next came an accounting of the troupers who didn't quite make it to the stage or set, because death stuck out its bony foot and tripped them up along the way.

That exploration became an investigation that landed on an even more surprising and devastating show business phenomenon that has gone, for the most part, unexamined until now: the ones who died onstage, while performing.

The investigation took us to Broadway shows, nightclubs, dinner theaters, amphitheaters, playhouses, arenas, concert halls, auditoriums, studios, tents, movie sets, and televised events and introduced us to an illustrious group that includes actors, singers, musicians, magicians, comedians, deejays, chorus girls, models, journeymen, and social media stars—people who are remembered as much for the way they left the building as for what they did inside. (We didn't include athletes, fighters, toreadors, race car drivers, or others who enter the field, arena, or ring, accepting that death is always a potential outcome.)

Initially, we chronicled every recorded death of a performer onstage. Our research led to hundreds of incidents, dating back centuries, and a project that turned out to be more comprehensive than any study previously attempted. Urban legends were debunked, long-held assumptions contradicted, Wikipedia-style misinformation corrected, new details from well-known stories unearthed, and the obscure stood (or were laid) shoulder to shoulder with the legendary. As the work continued and the pages flew from the calendar, however, we discovered a phenomenon just as compelling and even more frustrating: performers keep dying onstage. Every month or so, a singer would collapse mid-song, an act of violence would shatter the tranquility of a recital, or one of the new breed of social media personalities would expire live on camera before millions of fans. The number of performers who die onstage is always growing, too many and too often to be contained within the pages of a single volume.

So we boiled it down to the onstage deaths that really stood out among the rest. These are performers who died in front of an audience, grouped roughly into the categories of their specialties, with nods to additional related onstage passings that bring the total well into the three-figure range. These are our picks. The reader can debate if others deserve equal attention.

To die onstage—is it a curse? Could it be a gift? Is there any consolation in knowing that these performers died doing what they loved? And was it *really* the way they'd have wanted to go? Some answers, and much more, will be found in the pages to follow.

1

The Guinness World Record

Jane Little

Jane Little stood four feet, eleven inches tall and weighed less than a hundred pounds. Yet she played the double bass, the largest instrument in the Atlanta Symphony Orchestra, and one that stood a good foot taller than she did.

She was Jane Findley and sixteen years old when she joined the Atlanta Youth Symphony Orchestra in 1945. She made her debut that February 4 wearing a pastel evening gown, and she remained with the group when it began to admit adults and grew into the Atlanta Symphony.

Jane married the symphony's principal flutist in 1953. Warren Little was six foot two and would carry his little flute and her big bass. Even after he retired, he'd drive her to and from Atlanta Symphony Hall in their big baby-blue Chevrolet Caprice Classic station wagon. During her career, Jane played for conductors such as Igor Stravinsky, Leopold Stokowski, Aaron Copland, and James Levine. In 1996 she performed at the opening and closing ceremonies of the Atlanta Summer Olympics with conductor John Williams.

The highlight of her symphonic career came on February 4, 2016, two days after she celebrated her eighty-seventh birthday. Jane wasn't in the best of health that day. She'd been undergoing chemotherapy treatment for multiple myeloma and had suffered a cracked vertebra the previous August, but after months of rehabilitation she was ready to play the double bass once more. The *Washington Post* reported on the occasion: "On Monday, Jane Little got her weekly chemo shot. Thursday, she gulped down five green steroid pills and reported to Symphony Hall to fight her way back to the stage. And that she did, all 98 pounds of her, stroking a D chord at 8:04 p.m. to make her comeback official."

With that stroke of the bow, Jane Little became holder of the Guinness World Record as the musician with the longest tenure with an orchestra. With seventy-one years, she passed the record set by Frances Darger, the violinist who'd retired in 2012 after seventy years with the Utah Symphony. Indeed, the prospect of taking the title was one reason Jane decided to return to the symphony for one last season, despite serious illness and injuries.

"I'd thumb through the Guinness book and say, 'Wouldn't it be neat?'" she told the *Post*. "A lot of people do crazy things like sitting on a flagpole for three days. I just kept on. It was just me and the lady in Utah. So finally, I said, 'I'm going to do this.'"

To Michael Kurth, who joined the bass section in 1994, Jane's accomplishment was less inspirational than mythical. Kurth tells us, "You'd have to be really ambitious to be inspired, because it was such an unattainable record. To spend that many years on the job, it's almost inconceivable. She was certainly a great musician. Nobody can stand in that job for long unless they have real intuitive and innate musicality. And her technique was amazing. Her hands were so flexible. I would sit behind her, and her thumb would bend in angles that I didn't think human thumbs could bend."

Jane and her double bass were onstage on the afternoon of Sunday, May 15, 2016, for an Atlanta Symphony pops concert. *Broadway's Golden Age* was a great, rousing show. For an encore, the program called for a tune from Irving Berlin's classic musical *Annie Get Your Gun*.

The players were about thirty seconds from the final measures of the encore number when Jane stopped playing. Michael Kurth was playing bass right beside her, sharing her music stand. "There were maybe ten measures left in the last piece of the last program of the year," he says. "And I suddenly saw, out of the corner of my eye, her falling. Her bass teetered over and crashed into my bass—there's still a gouge in my bass from it. And she just collapsed over, unresponsive."

Kurth and tuba player Michael Moore (a mere forty-nine-year veteran of the orchestra) carried the tiny double bassist off the stage while the rest of the orchestra went on with the show and completed the number. A physician who was a member of the chorus and a nurse from the audience worked to revive her, but Jane Little never regained consciousness.

After the paramedics took Jane away, Michael Kurth joined most of the orchestra backstage behind the bass section. There were tears and hugs. "We weren't calculating and assessing the momentousness of the occasion. We were just reacting and trying to—I mean, it's our Jane. We all loved Jane," he says.

That night, Kurth told the *Washington Post*, "She seemed to be made of bass resin and barbed wire. She was unstoppable. I honestly thought I was going to retire before she did."

The Atlanta Symphony Orchestra announced on Facebook that it would dedicate the following weekend's performances to the late Jane Little. One commenter on the site said she was "still shakened" after witnessing her collapse but added, "RIP dear lady; you are an inspiration!" Another called that final concert at Atlanta Symphony Hall "harrowing" but added that Jane Little died "doing what she loved." "What an amazing way to go," orchestra fan Amanda Turner wrote.

Senior orchestra manager Russell Williamson marveled at the timing. "For her to go out at the end of a concert, the golden age of Broadway, and it was during the encore!" he told the *Post*.

Michael Kurth points out that "when she played her last note, she was doing what she loved, surrounded by people she loved, in a place that was like home to her.

"It was a pretty spectacular exit, frankly," he says, "for a really spectacular lady. I mean, you really couldn't write a better Hollywood ending."

Had the actual ending been scripted by a Hollywood screenwriter, reviewers would say it was too obvious. The song that Jane Little was performing when she collapsed to the stage was "There's No Business Like Show Business."

2

Theater

CORPSING IS BRITISH THEATRICAL SLANG for unintentionally breaking character by laughing. The origin of the term has never been nailed down, but it most likely arose from a laughing fit by an actor portraying a corpse. Another, far more literal interpretation of *corpsing* would be to actually become a corpse onstage, by dying. This has happened many times in many venues over the years. If there's a stage on which to act, there's a public platform on which to drop dead.

Some onstage deaths are more obvious than others. The seventeenth-century French actor and playwright Jean-Baptiste Poquelin, known to the world as Molière, was fifty-one and suffering from tuberculosis on February 17, 1673, when he performed in the title role in his play *Le malade imaginaire* ("The Hypochondriac") for King Louis XIV at the Théâtre du Palais-Royal in Paris. Already so ill that he was forced to perform while sitting in a red velvet chair, he was seized by a violent coughing fit and began hemorrhaging from the mouth. "Don't be alarmed! I am not dead!" Molière announced, insisting on going on with the show before he collapsed after an even more copious hemorrhage. They carried him offstage in his red velvet chair. No hypochondriac, he was indeed dead within a few hours.

Then there was Emil Hasda, the comedic actor who in 1904 starred in a Berlin touring company production of Ludwig Fulda's play *The Twin Sister*. When the show opened at the Municipal Theatre in Nimptsh,

Poland, on March 24, he had the crowd roaring with laughter through the first act and received half a dozen curtain calls. On the sixth, he drew a revolver from his hip pocket, placed it to his temple, and, in front of the entire audience, pulled the trigger and blew out his brains. One wire service reported that "when the blood was seen to flow, women fainted and men fought their way to the stage to get a glimpse at the suicide." Apparently one of the actresses had rejected his proposal of marriage. (If Hasda's suicide seems an overreaction, consider Ludwig Heinle. On October 26, 1926, the actor ran onstage and stabbed himself to death with a dagger during a performance of *Peer Gynt* at the Municipal Theatre in Strasbourg, France. He was upset that the stage manager gave him a hard time for showing up late!)

Despite such histrionics, the most memorable deaths onstage are ones in which an actor recites a line and then takes his or her leave from the stage and mortal coil, as if on cue. The "exit line" often serves as all-too-perfect set-up for the ultimate punchline. Most of the time, the audience thinks it's part of the show.

Joe Greenwald

After three weeks of rehearsals in Los Angeles, Homer Curran's road production of *Golden Boy* rolled north in March 1938 for two tryout performances at the Lobero Theatre in Santa Barbara. The show, starring Francis Lederer, would be a hot ticket. Clifford Odets's acclaimed play about violinist-turned-prizefighter Joe Bonaparte was a smash hit on Broadway and still running at the Belasco Theatre on West Forty-Fourth Street, where it had opened the previous November with Luther Adler in the title role and Frances Farmer as his love interest.

The only omen of any potential problems was that the first road performance was scheduled for April Fools' Day. Twenty-one-year-old future movie star Glenn Ford had the job as stage manager (and two lines in the third act: "Knockout!" and "Lombardo's stiff"). "Actors are a very superstitious breed," he told his son Peter, as noted in the latter's biography, *Glenn Ford: A Life*, "so there was already some feeling of uneasiness among some in the cast. The curtain went up and everything went smoothly, until we got to the second scene."

In the second scene of the first act, Joe's father, Mr. Bonaparte, shows off the expensive violin he plans to give his son the next day for his twenty-first birthday. "The actor playing the boxer's immigrant father in the play, Joe Greenwald, said his line—'A good life ah, is, ah, possible . . .'—and suddenly collapsed dead of a heart attack," Ford remembered. "I rushed onto the stage immediately. He was lying in the arms of one of the other actors." The trade journal *Variety* reported a different line in the *Golden Boy* script as the sixty-year-old actor's final words: "He had just concluded his line, 'This is the moment for which I have waited,' when he collapsed." The *New York Times* offered its own version: "Mr. Greenwald had just uttered the opening lines of a speech, 'All my life . . .' when he crumpled to the floor." So there's some confusion:

> *A good life ah, is, ah, possible . . .*
> *This is the moment for which I have waited . . .*
> *All my life . . .*

Any of those reported last words would suffice, as Joseph Greenwald's body lay motionless and Sam White, the only other actor on the stage at the time, called frantically for the curtain. The curtain was dropped, the capacity audience was eventually dismissed, and everyone got refunds. The Santa Barbara Fire Department's pulmotor squad tried to revive Greenwald, to no avail. "He was already dead," Glenn Ford said. "God, what an experience."

There was no understudy for Joe Greenwald, so the show was shut down for a week until a replacement was found. The producers brought in Lee J. Cobb, from the original Broadway production.

Edith Webster

Edith Webster died onstage every night. For eight years, she'd played the role of the grandmother in community theater productions of *The Drunkard* at the Moose Lodge in Towson, Maryland. In each performance, the role called for her character to sing a song, then collapse to the floor, dead.

That's what she did on Saturday night, November 22, 1986. "There was tremendous applause. Hearing that, she died," the director, Richard Byrd, told United Press International. The applause was the last thing Edith Webster would ever hear.

When the other actors called for a doctor and phoned paramedics, most of the two hundred people in the audience thought Edith's exit was part of the show. When the performance was stopped and they realized Edith had died of a heart attack, most of the audience sat quietly for almost an hour. Some of them prayed.

Edith Webster was sixty. Her daughter, Merri-Todd Webster, told the UPI reporter that the way she went was "not a bad thing . . . a lot of people have been saying it."

"Night after night, she died and she died," director Byrd observed, "and last night she died and she really did."

By the way, what was the name of Edith's show-stopping song? "Please Don't Talk About Me When I'm Gone."

Kent Stork

Kent Stork was a community theater actor whose death was notable not only for his dedication as an amateur thespian but also for the name of the last play in which he starred.

Kent was already well known to a certain audience long before he stepped onto a stage. For thirty-nine years, he and his wife Joyce ran a flower shop in Fremont, Nebraska, and over time became leading experts on the African violet. Kent won a dozen major awards at national flower shows. He and Joyce traveled as far away as Russia and Hong Kong to speak to growers. They wrote a column for *African Violet Magazine* that was turned into the book *YOU CAN Grow African Violets*. One Amazon reviewer called the book "My AV bible."

After Kent and Joyce hit sixty-five, they decided to retire. They closed Kent's Flowers in August 2016 and began packing for a move to Henderson, Nevada, a suburb of Las Vegas. There, they'd be close to their son Zach and his family, and Kent could follow his passion— not African violets but show business. Kent had been bitten by the acting bug several years earlier, when he and Joyce had attended a play in Omaha and he was invited onstage. He won his first role playing the superintendent in an Omaha Community Playhouse production of *The Drowsy Chaperone*. He'd appear in four more productions, including one in which he acted while inside an iron lung.

"It would have been January 2017 when they arrived in Henderson," Zach Stork tells us. "They rolled into town at like, 6:00 or 7:00 PM. And my dad had been looking at his phone on the way in, and there was a tryout for a play that was happening that night. He'd been in the car all day, and everyone's exhausted, and he's leaving at nine to go try out for a play somewhere. So that was definitely going to be his retirement hobby."

Kent didn't get that part but within months won a starring role at Henderson's community theater company, Theatre in the Valley. The dark comedy opened on Friday night, April 21, and was set to continue for eight more weekend performances.

On Sunday, April 30, Kent and Joyce attended church and Bible class before Kent took the stage for the 2:00 PM matinee. Joyce was in the audience.

"When he first comes out onstage, it was supposed to be like he had just gotten out of a shower," Zach says. "So he came out soaking wet, and my mom could just tell that he seemed a little off, and she knew the script well enough that she could tell that he missed a line."

"He didn't look right," Joyce later told the *Fremont Tribune*. "His coloring wasn't right. He was panting and I kept waiting for the panting to stop and it didn't. Then I realized he was having trouble standing."

"They completed part of a scene, and he exited," Zach explains. "The funny part, the story that I tell people, is that my mom was there, and she saw him not looking well. And then he kissed another woman, put a gun into his robe, exited the stage, and that was kind of the last she saw him fully conscious. The director came and got my mom. My dad was backstage, trying to fight to the bitter end, saying that he just needed to catch his breath. Then it was like, 'No, we need to call 911.'"

The show was stopped. Paramedics arrived and rushed Kent Stork to St. Rose Dominican Hospital.

Zach posted on Facebook from the hospital the following day:

> Great and sad news from the last 24 hours. This morning Janna
> and I were blessed with the birth of our beautiful daughter Lydia,
> and they are both doing well. The sad part is that my dad Kent
> Stork suffered a heart attack yesterday afternoon and died in this
> very same hospital less than 9 hours before his granddaughter
> was born. Circle of life.

"It's kind of interesting how things line up like that," Zach says. "We
were preparing for my daughter to come . . . and then a surprise heart
attack that happened less than twenty-four hours before. It's actually good
that he was pronounced dead a little bit before midnight, so he and my
daughter don't share the same date of departure and arrival."

Kent Stork had died two days before his sixty-seventh birthday.
Zach's mother Joyce, a devout Lutheran, told the *Tribune*'s Tammy Real-
McKeighan that she was comforted knowing that her husband was "safe
in the Lord's hands," and "that when that last day comes, that I'll be
there, too, and that we'll see the Lord together."

How about Zach, the eldest of Kent Stork's two sons? Did he take
comfort knowing his father died doing what he loved?

"You know what?" he replies. "I do, because he had gone from
working fifty, sixty hours a week for four decades, and then retired, and
six months later, he was gone. But he was able to go, doing something
that he was interested in.

"Honestly, my dad was somebody who liked attention. And the day
he died, for at least a couple of hours, he was trending. When you went
to the main website of the *Las Vegas Review-Journal*, his death story was
above the story about the new Raiders stadium being built. He would've
been kind of tickled to know that his passing garnered such attention."

There was another reason that Kent Stork's death got attention:
the name of the play was *Art of Murder*. Zach is able to laugh about
that. "When the newspaper posted the link to the article to Facebook, I
couldn't help but read through some of the comments," he says. "Some
were like, 'Sounds like a bad episode of *Murder, She Wrote*.' That's kind
of funny."

He continues, "When he was brought to the hospital, he had this
stage gun in his pocket. I think the hospitals here are used to having real

guns come into the emergency room. And my mom actually got a call late that night from the coroner's office to see if she thought this was a suspicious death that needed to be investigated. No, not because of the name of the play. I think it was just because of the odd circumstances, where he died while performing."

David Burns

Broadway star David Burns was singing, dancing, and acting his heart out on Friday, March 12, 1971. He was onstage at the Forrest Theatre in Philadelphia, in an out-of-town tryout for John Kander and Fred Ebb's latest musical, *70, Girls, 70.*

Kander and Ebb had written the songs for *Cabaret.* They'd go on to musicals like *Chicago* and *Fosse* (and write "New York, New York," the Liza Minnelli showstopper that became Frank Sinatra's anthem), but this show was a bit more risky in concept. The plot concerned the residents of a retirement hotel, and seventy was the average age of the cast members. Each night, producer Arthur Whitelaw had to worry about whether the entire cast would survive to make it to Broadway. In fact, Burns, best known for his long-running role as Horace Vandergelder in *Hello, Dolly!*, had signed on to play Harry the Desk Clerk only weeks earlier. He was sixty-eight and had replaced Eddie Foy Jr., who couldn't remember his lines at sixty-six.

Onstage on this night, everyone was doing just fine: the show was getting laughs, and the musical numbers were boffo. Then, around 10:00 PM, near the end of the second act, David Burns literally sang and danced and acted his heart out. In the middle of the number, he exclaimed, "How about this move!" He did a double take and spun around. The audience roared with laughter. Burns then clutched his chest and fell to the stage. It was a heart attack.

During the confusion that followed, Burns's understudy, Coley Worth, helped drag his body offstage. Backstage, Worth tried to revive him, to no avail. David Burns was dead.

Producer Arthur Whitelaw did his best to put a positive spin (no pun intended) on the death of his star: "He went, I guess, the way he would have liked to have gone. He died the way he lived. He died after one of the biggest laughs of the evening."

Whitelaw later told Coley Worth to prepare to take over the role of Harry the Desk Clerk for the Saturday matinee. Worth's life had led to this moment. He was born Coleman Rothmund sixty-two years earlier and first took the stage as a kid, performing in his father's minstrel show before running away to join a vaudeville circuit. He made his Broadway debut in 1927 in a show called *A la Carte*, and in the decades since had been in countless productions. He'd understudied for David Burns in *A Funny Thing Happened on the Way to the Forum* and *Hello, Dolly!* but had never been given a chance like this.

He managed five hours of sleep that night and was back on the Forrest Theatre stage at 9:00 AM Saturday morning, rehearsing for the 2:00 PM show. He went over the book, piece by piece. This early in the process, there were many scenes he hadn't yet studied. He knew he'd have to wing it and do the best he could.

That's what Coley Worth did. He learned what he could and when he hit the stage for the show, he let instinct handle the rest. When he missed a cue or flubbed a line, he improvised. He invented. He adlibbed. The audience was never the wiser. Arthur Whitelaw and the other backers stood at the back of the house and knew they were witnessing something very special.

After the show, Whitelaw came backstage and embraced the actor.

"Well, we got through it," Worth said.

"It was fine, fine," Whitelaw assured him. "You did a wonderful job!"

Teary-eyed costars congratulated him, whispered a "bravo," and patted him on the back. Someone asked Coley Worth if he thought he'd wind up taking over the leading role on Broadway. Coley smiled wistfully, sadly, knowingly. "They'll probably bring in a star," he said.

He was correct. After the evening performance, Arthur Whitelaw closed the show and announced that the play was heading back to rehearsals in New York. When *70, Girls, 70* opened at the Broadhurst Theatre on April 15, 1971, Hans Conried was starring in David Burns's role. The show ran for nine previews and thirty-five performances before it closed a month later.

Coley Worth lived to seventy-nine. He died of pneumonia in Port St. Lucie, Florida.

In a remembrance of David Burns printed in the *New York Times* two weeks after his death, *Hello, Dolly!* star Carol Channing recalled their reaction to President John F. Kennedy's assassination: "The evening's performance had been canceled due to the tragedy and, while I cried, Davey handed me Kleenex and fed me lines. We decided then and there that the lucky ones 'died with their boots on.' The only way to go, we agreed, was in the line of duty. . . . I cannot think of any way that Davey would rather go."

Interlude

Bad Night for Green Day

Pedro Aunión Monroy

With his performance company, In Fact Aerial Dance, Pedro Aunión Monroy was at the cutting edge of theatrical presentations, combining acting, dancing, acrobatics, harnesses, and bungee cords to create a new kind of entertainment.

"Aerial dance-theatre is a language that brings a unique 'tempo' to a performance as a result of constantly shifting perspectives and dramatic movement," he explained on the company's website. "The audience is drawn into the performance through its captivating sense of wonder and risk."

In Fact had presented many productions around the world since it was established in 2001 in Brixton, the rough and diverse neighborhood in south London where Pedro had settled. The company also operated (under the name Ciadehecho—which translates to "In Fact") in Madrid, Spain, where Pedro was born and was still a popular figure on the cultural scene. Pedro had studied at Madrid's Royal Conservatory of Dance and since the late 1990s had acted and done stunt work in films—including *Cyrano de Bergerac*, starring Plácido Domingo—and was a senior choreographer for the 2008 Spanish television reality show *Circus*.

In 2017 he was forty-two, athletic and handsome, with a trim beard, and he lived outside London in the seaside resort of Brighton. He had a good life there, making ends meet as a massage therapist at the posh Grand Hotel, and had a British boyfriend named Michael Sells. Pedro was popular among the Brits, who got a kick out of his accent; some even called him "Peter."

Pedro performed across Europe with In Fact and conducted workshops for aspiring aerial dancers. He was invited to return to his hometown in July to perform at a major festival—Mad Cool, Spain's answer to the Coachella Valley Music and Arts Festival in Southern California. Like Coachella, Mad Cool's inaugural lineup in 2016 had featured a mix of artists and genres: classic rock stars the Who and Neil Young; alternative favorites Jane's Addiction, the Prodigy, and Garbage; and contemporary acts like Flume and the Kills. The several outdoor stages also featured Spanish bands and local artists. The three-day lineup in 2017 was equally impressive. The first day was to be headlined by the Foo Fighters, the last by Kings of Leon. On the middle day, Friday, July 7, the main act was Green Day, the punk rock band turned Broadway musical stars.

After a day of music that included sets by Spoon, Rancid, Ryan Adams, and many others, Pedro had a premier spot on the main stage, following the British rockers alt-J and immediately before the entrance of Green Day. Of course, Pedro would actually be performing above the stage. He'd dance in the sky in an illuminated cage as it was hoisted a hundred feet in the air by a crane. His image would be projected on the big screen onstage, so everyone in the audience could get a close look.

On Thursday, the day the festival opened with the Foo Fighters, Pedro logged on to Facebook and tagged Michael Sells on a treated photo of the couple together. He wrote, "I can't wait to see my beautiful boyfriend. Love, come to my arms!!!!!" It would be his last Facebook post.

———————————

By the time alt-J left the stage just before 11:00 PM on Friday night, there were more than thirty-five thousand people waiting for Green Day. The stage went dark, and the opening chords of Prince's "Purple Rain" rang from the sound system.

This was Pedro's moment, a tribute to the rock idol and musical genius who'd died unexpectedly and tragically in April 2016. All eyes were on Pedro inside the white box, with clear sidewalls but without a floor, as it rose from the stage. Prince's voice rang from the loudspeakers. Heads craned to see Pedro moving gracefully as he danced and spun in 360-degree turns. Others watched his breathtaking movements on the big screen. Many held up cell phones to record the image of the figure inside the illuminated cube. Though he was suspended by various straps and harnesses, he seemed to be floating in midair.

Pedro was lifted a hundred feet into the air. The crowd sang along with the recording of Prince:

> *Purple rain, purple rain*
> *I only wanted to see you bathing in the purple rain*
> *I never wanted to be your weekend lover—*

At that moment, Pedro dropped like a stone.

His harness had snapped. The figure inside the cube was now a man plummeting a hundred feet to the hard earth. Thousands of people—the ones looking up at the box—saw him fall with their own eyes: feet first, and extending his arms at the last second, as if to prepare for a landing on his feet. Others watched the shocking image flash by on the big screen, when, even more vividly, Pedro plunged toward and past the camera trained on him from below. Still others would, moments later, watch again what they thought they'd seen while recording cell phone videos.

Many people screamed. Others cried or were sickened. Among those in the crowd was Michael Sells, watching his partner perform for the very first time.

The big screen showed images of the aftermath at the side of the stage, including the paramedics gathered around the broken aerial dancer. Anyone who'd assumed the fall had been part of the show, or that a dummy had been dropped, could see that wasn't the case. The medical team went through all the motions of trying to save a life for half an hour, before giving up. Pedro Aunión Monroy was dead.

Meanwhile, as thousands of fans waited in the humid field, festival organizers debated what to do. There was no announcement, but a decision was made: at least for security reasons, to prevent any panic or disruption, the show would go on.

Green Day took the stage about forty-five minutes late and performed their show, the last of their European tour. There was no mention of Pedro. A sense of disgust rippled through the audience. Even before their final encores, social media was already aflame with outrage that these American idiots would perform as usual after their opening act had died onstage.

Shortly after the show, the band tweeted:

> We just got off stage at Mad Cool Festival to disturbing news.
> A very brave artist named Pedro lost his life tonight in a tragic accident
> Our thoughts and prayers go out to his family and friends

Many people reacted angrily. One post included the accusation "You lie!"

The next day, the Green Day organization issued a long statement in the name of the band's forty-five-year-old frontman, Billie Joe Armstrong. The statement claimed that members of Green Day were in an artists' backstage compound a half mile away from the stage when the tragedy occurred. Armstrong wrote that the band was warming up and ready to hit the stage at 11:25 PM but fifteen minutes before showtime was "told by local authorities to wait to go on stage because there was some sort of security issue. . . . We had no clue there was any such accident." The band took the stage around midnight, played two and a half hours and, he wrote, "everything seemed normal." It was only after the show, he insisted, that the band was informed of what happened to Pedro:

> All of us were in disbelief. I don't know why the authorities chose not to tell us about the accident before our concert. . . . If we had known prior to our performance we most likely would not have played at all. We are not heartless people. The safety and well

being at any of our concerts absolutely comes first. What happened to Pedro is unthinkable. Once again we are heartbroken
for his friends and family. We are also shocked and heartbroken
for anyone that had to witness this tragedy.

Pedro's sister announced his death on Facebook. Estefi Chaje wrote
that she and her family were devastated. The post also included this line:
"Estaba haciendo lo que más le gustaba, un espectáculo en el mad cool."
"He was doing what he loved, performing in Mad Cool."

3

Comedy

COMEDIANS DIE ONSTAGE EVERY NIGHT. Not literally, but if you ask one of them, he or she would probably say that a real death is preferable to the figurative kind, when the audience is an oil painting and the clinking of glasses, coughing, and the plinking drips of flop sweat are all that can be heard amid the dead silence of a failing routine.

But an actual death onstage, a real, live, heart-stopping death amid the hilarity, is something else altogether. And it often takes the audience a few minutes to get the joke—the big cosmic joke, that is. There are a few onstage comedy deaths that have made their marks in show business history.

Harry Einstein, a.k.a. Parkyakarkus

One of the comedy death stories most told is that of dialect comedian Harry Einstein, known for his pseudo-Greek character Nick Parkyakarkus (as in "Park yer carcass! Sit down!"). Parky, as he was called by fans and friends alike, was the father of future comedians Bob Einstein and Albert Brooks (né Albert Einstein—not necessary to explain why he changed his name to "Brooks"). In the 1930s and '40s, he appeared in films and on the Eddie Cantor and Al Jolson radio shows; for three seasons, he had his own radio program, *Meet Me at Parky's*, in which Parkyakarkus was running a lunch counter.

In 1958, at fifty-four, Harry "Parky" Einstein was in poor health with heart and back problems, living off investments, and, with the exception of a role on the television anthology series *Playhouse 90*, limiting his appearances to dinners and roasts hosted by the Friars Club, the private show business club whose membership boasted top comedians and entertainers of the day.

———————

A gala Friars Club event took place on Sunday night, November 23. Twelve hundred people packed into the International Ballroom of the Beverly Hilton hotel, paying up to $200 a plate to attend a testimonial dinner honoring Hollywood comedy power couple Lucille Ball and Desi Arnaz. Art Linkletter was master of ceremonies, and the featured stars included Dean Martin, George Burns, Danny Thomas, George Murphy, Sammy Davis Jr., and Milton Berle.

Parky was the only comic on the dais who didn't have a regular gig on the tube or in clubs, and, Linkletter recalled, "on this particular night he was making his big comeback." When it was his turn at the podium, Parky went into a routine that poked fun at the exclusivity of the Friars Club.

Audio from the big night reveals uproarious laughter from the crowd: "These two people we are honoring tonight—Danny Arnaz and Lucille Bowles—have met every requirement of our screening committee. But you must not think that the Friars Club is an easy club to get into. Quite to the contrary, it is most difficult. Before a prospective candidate is even issued an application he must first satisfy us, beyond any question of a doubt, that he is either a resident"—that gets the laughs rolling—"or a nonresident of the state of California." A huge wave of laughter shakes the room. "He then must be proposed by and then vouched for by at least two men . . . who are listed in the phone book." A torrent of laughter. The Friars Club membership, he says, includes "many prominent businessmen, several fine judges, and quite a few defendants."

Years later, Linkletter, Berle, and Friars entertainment chairman Barry Mirkin relived the evening for the Friars tribute documentary

Let Me In, I Hear Laughter. "He was," Art Linkletter recalled, "up there knocking them dead."

"It was the most hilarious routine I have . . . ever stolen—ever heard," said Berle. "And he actually was the hit of the show."

"He did a monologue that lasted ten minutes [that] under normal circumstances might have lasted six minutes," Mirkin, who'd opened the show with the Friars song "Here's to the Friars," remembered. "But the laughs were so great, so impossible to believe, that as a result it just stretched."

"He got a standing ovation," Berle recalled. "While he was standing up and bowing, he said, 'Thank you, thank you,' and they were cheering."

As Parky made his way back to his seat, Linkletter asked the room, "How come anyone as funny as that isn't on the air?"

Parky settled back next to Berle and said, "Yeah, how come?"

"And then suddenly he put his head over on Milton Berle's lap and shut his eyes and apparently slumped down," Linkletter said. "And everybody stopped laughing and applauding because he had apparently fainted—or worse."

Parky's wife, the actress Thelma Leeds, was sitting in the audience with Ed Wynn to her right. Moments earlier, she'd bragged to him that Parky wrote all his own material. Now, while all around her looked confused, she knew immediately what was wrong with her husband. She bolted onto the dais and reached into his pocket for the pillbox. She opened it and plucked out a nitroglycerin tablet that would increase blood flow through his coronary arteries. But when she tried to put the pill in his mouth and under his tongue, she couldn't. His teeth were clenched tight.

Meanwhile, Wynn was shouting advice in his giggly voice: "Put his head down, put his head down!"

Berle screamed shrilly, "Is there a doctor in the house?"

Audience members, caught up in the excitement, called by name the doctors they knew would be in the room. Friars roasts and banquets are traditionally benefits for hospitals (this one benefited a Burmese leper colony), so there was no shortage. Five top specialists jumped from their seats.

Linkletter recalled, "I said, 'Ladies and gentlemen, we have a little medical accident here for the moment. We wonder if anyone happens to have any nitroglycerin—nitro tablets.' Well, the surprise of my life, big producers, writers, stars came forward with vials. Apparently half the people in the room had heart problems."

"Everybody was frozen in the room," Mirkin added. "The drama is unbelievable because they knew what was happening. And I tried to get Lucy to unleash her fingers from the table to come back, and I couldn't get her. I couldn't move her hands."

Amid the ruckus, Berle waved to singer Tony Martin. "'Get up, stall, do something to get their mind off it. Do something—sing a song, sing a song!' He says, 'All right.' Tony Martin, quickly, it wasn't his fault—improv, ad lib—he got up and sang . . . 'There's No Tomorrow.'"

Said Linkletter: "There were probably a couple of sympathetic heart attacks when 'There's No Tomorrow' rang out."

Berle, George Burns, and others carried Parky's carcass backstage. Within seconds, one of the doctors had sterilized a pocketknife, sliced open Parky's chest and was holding his heart in his hand, massaging it. Another doctor yanked the cord from an electric lamp and placed the live ends against the heart muscle like a MacGyver defibrillator, shocking it into beating again.

One of the doctors said that Parky had probably died on the dais, but the hand massage brought him back to life. The five doctors took turns massaging—and got a faint beat going from the right side of the heart. The left side only fluttered. Firemen and police arrived with plasma and a pulmotor—a device to inflate the lungs and possibly get him breathing again.

As they worked behind the curtain, the show went on—for a while. The Associated Press reported that "the off-key singing of George Burns and the audience's laughter could be heard over the pulsations of the pulmotor." There were several announcements that Parky would be fine, but everyone on the dais knew better. When it was his turn to address the crowd, Desi Arnaz was ashen-faced and barely audible. "This is one of the moments that Lucy and I have waited a lifetime for, but it's meaningless. They say the show must go on. But why must it? Let's close the show now by praying for this wonderful man backstage who made a world laugh." He took the award that Linkletter had presented him and crammed it in his pocket.

Lucy stepped to the microphone and through her tears said, "I can say nothing."

As the proceedings were wrapped, they cued Sammy Davis Jr. for one last number. He decided not to perform.

"And then everybody just sat there," Mirkin said. "A few people left, but there were a thousand people in the room. Everybody wanted to know what the outcome was. Parky's wife went up to the dais and she sat at the very end and when she saw the five doctors leave with their sleeves rolled up, very glum, she knew. And, oh God, she let out a screech."

Dr. Alfred Goldman of City of Hope hospital pronounced Parkyakarkus dead at 1:10 AM, about eighty minutes after he was stricken.

When it was over, Ed Wynn spoke to a reporter. "This is ample proof that the old saying 'The show must go on' is a lot of baloney," he said. "The show doesn't have to go on, and it does not, as you saw tonight."

Al Kelly

It turns out that Harry "Parkyakarkus" Einstein wasn't the only funny-talking comic to die at a Friars Club function after slaying the crowd. Time has forgotten Al Kelly. The man born Abraham Kalish was a vaudeville and Borscht Belt comic with a fifty-year career that included stooging on *The Ernie Kovacs Show* and appearances on Ed Sullivan's *Toast of the Town*. He was also a dues-paying Friar.

For years, Al Kelly had worked the same angle as Harry Einstein, often hired at events under an assumed name and title, stringing the crowd along before revealing himself to be a gagman. Whereas Einstein might have appeared at a function in the guise of a foreign dignitary and insulted the honored guest in a convincing accent (that's how he was discovered by Eddie Cantor), Al Kelly would be introduced as an expert in a particular field and then would cause confusion—and eventually laughter—with his double-talk routine.

What is double-talk? As explained by comic legend Joey Adams in his book *Here's to the Friars*, "fractured English is what it is. If you should find someone who introduces himself with something that sounds like 'I am Charley Imglick and I'd like to javlin with my liebst. Can you get me a rabinat or a flang?' . . . you have just been introduced to double-talk!"

Al Kelly was the king of double-talk. He was once hired to speak at a doctors' convention, where he began by explaining a study in a technical field and spoke intelligently for a few minutes before going into a double-talk routine that left everyone stunned, too embarrassed to ask what he meant: "We've been able to rehabilitate patients by daily injections of triprobe into the right differenarium, which translucentizes the stoline, producing a black greel, which enables you to stame the klob."

"One thing disturbing me," Kelly recalled, according to the *New York Times*, "was when I said that—some of the doctors were agreeing with me."

On September 6, 1966, Al Kelly was sixty-nine years old and living with his wife, Mary, in Forest Hills, Queens. After fifty-two years in show business, he was known to a new generation thanks to his occasional appearances on *The Soupy Sales Show*. That Tuesday evening, he and Mary were at the Friars Club at 57 East Fifty-Fifth Street for a black-tie dinner honoring and toasting comedian Joe E. Lewis.

Kelly's grandnephew ("he was my uncle Lenny's uncle"), comedian, actor, and Friar Bob Greenberg, grew up hearing the story. "It was held in the dining room," Greenberg tells us. "Usually when we do a roast or a very big event, it's at the Waldorf, so this was an in-house event. It was a toast, a tribute."

Radio personality William B. Williams and comic Alan Gale served as emcees, and the lineup of speakers included Frank Sinatra, Buddy Hackett, Soupy Sales, Henny Youngman, Nipsey Russell, and Pat Henry. In the early hours of September 7, Al Kelly took to the podium and did his double-talk routine. According to the Associated Press, he "massacred the Gettysburg Address." According to Joey Adams in *Here's to the Friars*, he killed: "The beloved little double-talker was the hit of the night."

Kelly returned to his seat amid gales of laughter and rose to acknowledge a standing ovation. Seconds later, he collapsed. "William B. took him in his arms," wrote Adams, "but in the twinkling of an eye that it took Bill to cradle him, he was gone."

"Frank, the maitre'd, saw what happened and wanted to get him out of there right away," Greenberg says. "He got a busboy to hold him by the legs and they brought him to the Round the World Bar, which is what the Billy Crystal Bar used to be called, and laid his body on the bar."

Amid the commotion, seventy-five-year-old vaudeville singer Blossom Seeley made her way unsteadily to the microphone. She was going to serenade Joe E. with "It Had to Be You" but announced she was feeling "a little weak." A few bars in, she became faint. Somebody yelled that Blossom may be having a stroke.

Joey Adams wrote memorably of the scene: "The handsome silver-haired William B., who could attribute some of his gray hairs to this evening, thought it was a doubleheader for a moment."

Blossom Seeley hadn't suffered a stroke, after all. She made it out alive. Meanwhile, Dr. Milton Reder and Saul Meylackson, two Friars who happened to be physicians, were in the Round the World Bar, inspecting Al Kelly.

"He was pronounced dead on the bar," Greenberg recounts. "I don't know if they held a mirror under his nose or what, but they say he was gone."

It was left to the guest of honor, Joe E. Lewis, to offer a toast of his own, a toast to Al Kelly. "If you have to go, that's the way to do it," he said. "Leave with the cheers ringing in your ears." Even so, all agreed it was a shame that the doctors failed to triprobe Kelly's right differenarium, translucentizing the stoline and producing a black greel that possibly could have stamed the klob.

Dick Shawn

I don't wanna die in front of you. Hey, comics don't like
to die. That's why we act like children. In our minds, if
we stay as children, we'll never get old and die.

—Dick Shawn
The 2nd Greatest Entertainer in the Whole Wide World

Why isn't Dick Shawn held in the same high regard as his contemporary
comedians, including Lenny Bruce, Jonathan Winters, and Dick Gregory?
Why hasn't his influence on comics like Robin Williams, Andy Kaufman,
and Garry Shandling been more celebrated? Perhaps it's because he was
so versatile, so much more than a stand-up, with talents spread across so
many other genres: Broadway plays and musicals, movies, and television
among them. Maybe it was because of his unpredictability, or simply the
circumstances of his exit, that this comedic genius is remembered mainly
for the way he died.

More than three decades later, his son Adam Shawn has a theory
of his own. "I think part of it is that he really didn't care," he says.
"He did his own thing. He wasn't commercial. He didn't play the game.
He went into stand-up, and he kind of killed it, but he was already off
into something else. He wanted to be more diverse."

He was born Richard Schulefand in Buffalo, New York, in 1923.
Growing up, his greatest ambition was to be a major league baseball
player. He tried out for the Chicago White Sox and walked away
with a contract. "He was wild, but he threw hard," Adam says, in
a good description of the life to follow. Within days of the baseball
offer, Richard was drafted into the US Army and sent the Philip-
pines, where he worked in USO shows and learned he had a knack
for making people laugh. After the Army, he attended the University
of Miami, and left early to pursue a career as Dick Shawn, stand-up
comic.

Shawn emerged from the same 1950s New York City hipster comedy
and cabaret scene as Lenny Bruce. His first break on the *Arthur God-
frey's Talent Scouts* television show led to performances in nightclubs,
The Ed Sullivan Show, Las Vegas, Broadway, and ultimately films, in

which he was known for playing counterculture beatniks and weirdos. He was a genie in *The Wizard of Baghdad*, the surfing son in *It's a Mad, Mad, Mad, Mad World*, and, in Mel Brooks's *The Producers*, hippie actor Lorenzo St. DuBois (LSD), who's hired to play the lead role in the Broadway show *Springtime for Hitler*.

It was onstage, though, in his one-man show, that Dick Shawn really shined. *The 2nd Greatest Entertainer in the Whole Wide World* was a collection of free-association bits, non sequiturs, singing, dancing, absurdities, drama, pantomime, gags, and stream-of-consciousness monologues—with an apocalyptic undercurrent born in the Cold War atomic era from which he sprang.

In a typical performance, the audience would enter the theater to see a bare stage with a pile of newspapers at center. When the show began, the pile would shake and Shawn, who'd been underneath all along, emerged, like a bum awakened from a period of sleeping off a hangover. Sometimes, he'd be eating a banana. It was an opening tour de force that required great concentration, discipline, and breath control. The slightest movement from the pile would have blown the surprise. Later in the first act, Shawn would talk himself into a "coma," or collapse on his back and lie onstage throughout intermission. He'd rise for the second act, portraying that "2nd Greatest Entertainer," a Vegas showman named Fabulously Fantastic Jr. ("Fabby Fanty Jew" for short—not too far a throw from Freddy Funky, Shawn's old Elvis Presley parody that inspired Charles Strouse and Lee Adams to write the 1960 musical *Bye, Bye Birdie*.)

"It is an entertainment piece," he told a reporter for the *New York Times*, "even though the thrust of the humor is serious. I've always taken chances with my work. In my club act, for example, I always ended up pretending to die onstage, rather than taking bows. Two guys would come in with a stretcher and carry me out. I like that. I feel life is a game of opposites." You can see how this might not end well if Dick Shawn ever needed real medical assistance during a show.

Dick Shawn was widely regarded as brilliant, wildly entertaining, and unpredictable—wildly unpredictable. What would turn out to be his second most notorious and outrageous incident was the one on May 6, 1974, that supposedly, legendarily, got him banned from *The Tonight Show Starring Johnny Carson*. The fog of pop culture history has him guest-hosting while Johnny Carson was away on vacation, but it was celebrity impersonator Rich Little behind the desk, demonstrating less of a controlling hand than Johnny might have when Shawn came out as a guest and went crazy.

"He just decided to tear the set apart," Little told Mark Malkoff on *The Carson Podcast*. "And he turned the plants over, he turned the sofa over, he turned the desk over. We got in the desk and started rowing like we're going across the Potomac. You know, like George Washington. I was out in front with the oar. And we wrecked the set, totally wrecked the set. The people were in hysterics, so Freddie de Cordova and all the staff were all just standing around, going, 'Well this is awful. He's ruining the set but at the same time, this is the funniest thing we've ever seen.'"

Little continued, "Carson wasn't there to see the humor—'cause it was funny. All Carson saw when he came back was the set was ruined."

Johnny Carson was offended that his set, desk, and plants had been violated, but in fact, perhaps because of his affection for the comedian, Dick Shawn was invited back to *The Tonight Show* many times over the next dozen years—though he appeared only with guest hosts like David Brenner. Carson eventually reconciled with the comic in 1985, and Shawn made two appearances with him that year. When Carson introduced Shawn on the show in November 1986, he said, "He can be very brilliant."

———————

That all led to Good Friday, April 17, 1987. Dick Shawn had two films in the can. He had been appearing on network television in guest roles on shows like *St. Elsewhere* and Steven Spielberg's *Amazing Stories*, and he was featured in Disney theme parks around the world as Michael

Jackson's boss, Commander Bog, in Francis Ford Coppola's new 3D short film, *Captain EO*. His real joy was his one-man show. *The 2nd Greatest Entertainer in the Whole Wide World*, which he'd been touring on and off for the past decade, had wrapped a long run—close to three hundred performances—at the Canon Theatre in Beverly Hills.

On this Friday afternoon, twenty-eight-year-old Adam Shawn, the show's stage manager and technical director, drove his father from his home in Santa Monica to a performance at the University of California San Diego's Mandeville Auditorium. Shawn was going to try out some new material, with plans to take the show to the Kennedy Center in Washington, DC.

The performer carried reel-to-reel tapes containing music and audio tracks that Adam would cue up and play during the show. "He doesn't want to lose them, so he shoves them under his seat in the car," Adam says. "We get there three hours later, now it's five o'clock, six o'clock. It's getting close to when they're going to let the people in. You've got to have a run-through with the crew. You've got a whole crew there.

"So we get there, and he can't find his tapes. He forgot he put them under the seat. So everybody's looking for the tapes, all over the theater, all over the car—he was almost resolved to just doing his stand-up without the data. Finally, he finds his tapes under the seat, where he hid them so he wouldn't lose them—typical.

"We do a quick run-through with the crew and then half an hour before the show starts, I always got this from my dad: 'I need some time to get my head together,' which was his way of saying, *I need to be alone before I go on*. He gave me a plate of fruit that they had for him because 'he's a big star.'

"'I'll see you after the show.' That was it."

Dick Shawn took the stage shortly after 8:00 PM—part of him did, at least—as a disembodied head appearing out of a table. "It was a very funny comedy routine about how you don't have to be a *stand-up* comic," Adam recalls. "He was a 'heads-up comic.' You don't need your body or to be physical to be a comic. It just takes ideas to be funny."

After that bit, in which another actor came out and carried on as if he was eating dinner at the table, the stage lights went dark. Shawn reappeared for a vignette in which he was "out of rhythm to some dance music," Tim Wartelle, who was in the audience, told the *Los Angeles Times.* "He was obviously moving around and didn't seem to be having any trouble."

About twenty-five minutes in, Shawn put aside his microphone and asked if he could be heard without it. Satisfied with the audience response, he began talking about the end of the world. He imagined a nuclear war in which nobody would survive—nobody, he said, except the five hundred people in this theater! He shouted, "And I would be your leader!"

He fell forward.

As he'd done for close to three hundred shows, Adam Shawn was running audio and lighting cues from the booth at the rear of the auditorium, and communicating via headset with a stagehand at the side of the stage. "He starts talking about what would happen if everybody else in the world were destroyed by a nuclear bomb, and they were the only ones left. And he would be their leader," Adam tells us. "I honestly believe that's when he went down. There was this move, and it wasn't a move I'd ever seen before, and it looked like it hurt. He went down on a knee, and then fell forward, on his face—and a little bit hard."

Dick Shawn remained motionless, prone on the stage.

Of course, the audience thought the face-plant was part of the act. Not only was it seamless with the routine, it had been part of Dick Shawn's act for decades. So many times he showed off that impressive breath control, remaining stock-still under the pile of newspapers. So many times he'd worked himself into a frenzy and dropped to the stage. *But face first?* Maybe it was a signal that intermission had begun. The crew knew not to interfere or interrupt him should he wind up sprawled out. One never knew if a routine would take him there.

The audience laughed. There was some applause. Someone yelled out, "Take his wallet!" There was more laughter—uncomfortable laughter now. Everyone waited.

"So we're waiting, and a minute goes by, maybe longer," Adam recalls. "I tell the guy on the headset to go out and see if he's OK. So he goes out. He checks on him, he kinda shakes him, and he comes back onto the headset. I'm like, 'Well, what did he say?' He's like, 'He didn't say anything. He just kinda grunted, you know? He didn't say anything.' So I said, 'Well, go back out and get a response! Make sure he's OK!' So he went back out, came back to the headset, said there was no response. That's when the chaos started."

As it happened, Scripps Memorial Hospital was on the UC San Diego campus. Several doctors and their wives were seated in the first few rows when the stagehand asked, "Is there a doctor in the house?"

"A doctor came from back of the wings, felt for his pulse, and realized something had happened," audience member Wartelle said. "He flipped him over. The audience reaction by then was, 'Boy, this is out of taste.'"

Meanwhile, Adam Shawn was making a dash from the booth. He scrambled down the stairs and was heading through the lobby when he was stopped dead in his tracks. "Standing in the lobby was my dad's second cousin, with his wife and infant. They couldn't get a babysitter, so they brought the child, and they were standing there. Mind you, this is about half an hour into the show. They're standing in the lobby. And he's a heart surgeon.

"I tell him what's happening, and he runs down the aisle in the middle of the house, onto the stage. By then, some other doctors were already tending to him. They were giving the CPR. I don't even know his name—'Dr. Cousin' continued it for like twenty, thirty minutes or whatever it was, until the paramedics came. There was a defibrillator. The defibrillator was out of power. It wasn't charged.

"And the whole time he's lying there, the audience is still there. So there's that interaction between the audience. They might be hurling something, and then there are people on the stage, asking everybody to leave: 'This isn't part of the show.' And there were people that wanted their money back. It was a ten-dollar ticket. My dad's working for a ten-dollar ticket. And they didn't get their money's worth. They came to see a comedy show."

Adam Shawn could only watch. "One of the doctors' wives was telling me, one, he can still hear you. Two, he's gonna be OK. She kept telling me that, so I kept yelling. Oh, my God. I just kept yelling, 'Come on, Dad! Come on, Dad!'"

When the paramedics finally arrived, one of them mentioned they'd had four or five calls that evening. It was a busy night. As Adam Shawn remembered, they gave up on his father in the ambulance.

Dick Shawn was pronounced dead at 9:55 PM. His second cousin the heart surgeon signed the death certificate. There would be no autopsy. "I didn't want an autopsy," Adam says. "It didn't really matter to me. I didn't care if I knew what he had or what he didn't. Everybody thinks it's a stroke or a heart attack, and we just kind of left it at that."

Adam Shawn remained in the hospital until 3:00 AM, after all the reporters had gone. "Then a few of us went back to the lifeless, dark theater before our drive back to Los Angeles without my best friend and father. For me, it truly was the night the comedy died."

Dick Shawn did manage to get one last laugh on the world—and an extra six years of life—that Saturday, when the *Los Angeles Times* reported that he'd died onstage at fifty-seven. Dick Shawn was actually sixty-three.

———————

"Someone once told me to like put it down on paper, and I eventually started," says Adam. "It started off like this: 'Good Friday, a funny day for a Jew to die.'" Decades later, Adam Shawn is still trying make sense of what happened that Easter weekend: "He'd been to the cardiologist only about a week or two before. The doctor was shocked because he really thought everything was fine there. Our family was shocked. After it happened, trying to make sense of what went down, I called some of his *supposed* close friends. To me, they seemed tight-lipped and even agitated that I called—as if they were privy to something, and I didn't want to go there.

"But you never know," he says. "If somebody takes something that speeds his heart up a little bit—nicotine from his cigarettes with no filters, caffeine from coffee, maybe something that might have been illicit back in the day—if he's working hard . . . we'll just never know."

Adam says he takes cold comfort knowing his father died doing what he loved. "As cliché as it sounds, he didn't necessarily want to go onstage, doing what he loved. He wanted to be able to do what he loved forever until he went—but he didn't want to be infirm.

"What was really sad is that he was so happy and so happy about the way he was working. And that was really his main thing, his work. Doing what he loved? It's so overshadowed by the place he was at and what he was aspiring to do. He'd finally worked all those years, and he took all the knocks and paid his dues, and he was finally making it again. So there's this ironic twist, where even though you're doing what you love, it's like, man, he still had a lot in him and a lot to do."

4

The Tommy Cooper Effect

SURE, BRITISH THESPIANS CAME UP with the term *corpsing*, but when it comes to dying onstage, no one does it quite like British comedians.

Tommy Cooper

When I die, I hope it's like Tommy—on stage, surrounded by laughter.

—Magician Gordon Williams, before he died onstage

Tommy Cooper, six-foot-four, bulky, knob-nosed, and easily identified by the red fez that topped his lumpish head, leaves a double legacy of perhaps the best-known onstage death of a comedian as well as onstage death of a magician—though comedy took preference right up until his truncated final performance, witnessed live by millions, and viewed more than a million times on video posted on the Internet.

Born in 1921 in Glamorgan, Wales, Cooper spent his childhood practicing magic tricks, got into show business as a comic monologuist after serving in World War II, and got his break in 1947 when booked to tell jokes in a show starring the sand-dance act Marqueeze and the Dance of the Seven Veils. Cooper followed the gig with two years of touring, including a stint in pantomime, playing one of Cinderella's ugly sisters—take note of that, as it will come into play later—and went on to three decades of success on British television with a combination of silly jokes ("Two cannibals were eating a clown. One said to the other, 'Does he taste funny to you?'" One more? "I bought some pork chops and told the butcher to make them lean. He said, 'Which way?'"), a catchphrase ("Just like that!"), and tricks that intentionally failed, even though he was a respected member of Britain's elite magician's association, the Magic Circle.

Cooper became such a part of British popular culture that he received a mention in the final verse of John Lennon's song "Give Peace a Chance":

> *Everybody's talking 'bout John and Yoko, Timmy Leary,*
> *Rosemary, Tommy Smothers, Bobby Dylan, Tommy Cooper,*
> *Derek Taylor, Norman Mailer, Allen Ginsberg, Hare Krishna,*
> *Hare Hare Krishna . . .*

Tommy Cooper ventured stateside for a run at the Flamingo Hotel in Las Vegas in 1954 and made several appearances on *The Ed Sullivan Show* in the 1960s. Though he was not a household name in the United States, Americans were familiar with his brand of shtick through the work of Carl Ballantine. Ballantine, a.k.a. the Great Ballantine, master of incompetent stage tricks and wiseacre patter, has been cited by Steve Martin as a major influence on him and magicians like David Copperfield. He's probably familiar to the Baby Boomer generation as sailor Lester Gruber on the 1960s TV classic *McHale's Navy*. Like Tommy Cooper, he'd been doing a comedy magic act since the Second World War. Ballantine, however, was the original. His act first clicked at the State-Lake Theatre in Chicago in 1942. He died in 2009, at home in Hollywood, at age ninety-two.

Tommy Cooper was sixty-three when he died in the homes of millions of Britons on the evening of Sunday, April 15, 1984. He was performing on *Live from Her Majesty's*, a Sunday-night entertainment show that the British television network ITV aired live, as advertised, from Her Majesty's Theatre in London's West End.

The show offered variety entertainment for the whole family, hosted by family comic Jimmy Tarbuck, a primary schoolmate of John Lennon who fronted many variety and quiz shows on the telly. Tarbuck went on to be awarded an OBE and was beloved in the UK until 2013, when, in the wake of the Operation Yewtree police investigation into sexual abuse (primarily involving children) allegations against British media personality Jimmy Savile and others, he was arrested for the alleged sexual assault of a young boy in the 1970s. Police would investigate six separate claims of abuse before the charges were dismissed a year later, on the grounds of insufficient evidence.

———————

By the time a wheezing and unsteady Tommy Cooper arrived that Sunday in 1984 at Her Majesty's Theatre, decades of drink and cigars had most definitely caught up with him. Along with alcoholism, his maladies included lumbago, sciatica, bronchitis, circulation problems, and the lingering effects of a heart attack he'd suffered while performing in Rome in 1977. His appearances in the past two years had been rare, and the production staff had been alerted to his fragile condition. They'd even constructed a makeshift dressing room for Cooper in the wings so he wouldn't have to climb any stairs. In any case, the show would go on.

That night, Jimmy Tarbuck was not only emcee but also a participant in part of Cooper's act: the famous "Magic Cloak" routine. Tarbuck would hide behind the curtain, waiting to pass Cooper props that the magician would appear to pull out of his flowing gown: a paint pot, a plank of wood—props that got bigger and bigger, until finally Tarbuck would walk onto the stage carrying a stepladder, complaining he couldn't fit it through Cooper's legs. Only they never made it to the punchline.

Sandie Lawrence, playing the pretty blonde assistant, walked onstage to help Tommy Cooper into his magic cloak. "It was all very normal, to be honest. I was waiting there with the cloak, and Tommy was his usual self. And the audience were in raptures of laughter," she recounted in the documentary *The Untold Tommy Cooper*. "I wrapped the cloak round his shoulders and I then came round the front and sort of done up the bottom, and went to move away the mic, and literally within seconds of me moving away, he fell. He sort of slumped backwards."

Cooper fell backwards onto the floor, dropped to his haunches, and sat against the curtains, gasping for breath. "I actually thought, 'This isn't right,'" Lawrence said. "The audience was still laughing, but there was something not right. And I remember looking back, thinking, 'I wonder if he's all right,' because, I mean he was a big chap, so you could hear him fall."

Tarbuck waited for his cue behind the curtain. "We all thought he'd just stuck another physical gag into his set," he told *Wales on Sunday*. "He was a real terror for introducing new bits and pieces without warning. But as time ticked on, we realized something terrible had happened."

Tommy Cooper remained onstage, on camera, knees bent beneath him. He took seven or eight halting breaths before falling backwards with a snoring grunt. His fez dropped over his face. A hand poked from behind the curtain, leading to more laughter as Cooper's body twisted under the big cape, emitting another snoring sound as his legs twitched. There was a longer, more awkward pause, enough time for the director to realize that this had not played out in dress rehearsal and that something was terribly wrong. He cued the orchestra to play into an unscheduled commercial break. Forty-nine seconds after Tommy Cooper's collapse, viewers at home saw the screen go blank for several seconds.

That's the story everyone knows and can watch online. The story *behind the story* continued during that commercial break, as Jimmy Tarbuck and the stage crew struggled to maneuver Cooper's six feet, four inches, and 215 pounds of dead weight into the darkness behind the curtain and provide him with medical attention.

Tommy Cooper wasn't the last act in the *Live from Her Majesty's* lineup, and the show did not end on that tragic note. A troupe of dancers, Howard Keel, and Donny Osmond were all waiting to fill the rest of the hour.

"I was standing behind the curtain, waiting to go on next, when Tommy fell down," Osmond told the *Daily Mail.* "The audience thought it was part of the show. So did I! Then everyone stopped laughing and he didn't get up and the backstage people said, 'The joke's over, Tommy. Tommy! Tommy!' then, 'He's dead! Pull the curtain over him.' So they did. I was going to do a song. They said, 'We've got a commercial, we'll be right back.'"

With Cooper's body splayed behind the curtain, it wasn't possible to reset the stage for Osmond's musical number. Tarbuck stepped away from the medical scene, grabbed Les Dennis and Dustin Gee, and informed the comedy impressionist duo that they were going on as soon as the show returned from the break. When the red light on the camera blinked on, they were to perform in front of the same curtain shielding the noisy efforts around Tommy Cooper.

Dustin Gee, the senior member of the team, said they'd need more room on the stage. "Well, you ain't gonna get it!" Tarbuck barked. "You're professionals. Just get on with it!"

So they did. The program returned live from the commercial break, and in the grand show-must-go-on tradition, the two unfortunate blokes in tuxedos hauled out impressions of stars of the day, from David Bowie and Mick Jagger to John Cleese as Basil Fawlty (with prosthetic forehead and fake mustache, Gee was regarded as the world's foremost Cleese impersonator). Then they pulled on wigs and put on the voices of two old birds, Vera Duckworth and Mavis Riley from the soap opera *Coronation Street*; it was Dennis and Gee's signature piece. They went through the motions, trying to get laughs while they could hear the noise of Cooper's groaning corpse as people thumped on his chest behind the curtain a few feet upstage.

There was no mention of the tragedy until after the credits rolled and a news bulletin announced to the country that Tommy Cooper had died in the ambulance on the way to the hospital. Witnesses who were backstage disputed that report, insisting that the big man was dead when he hit the curtains. The production company stayed silent on the matter, allegedly aiding in the cover-up because of fear that an onscreen death might put an end to live television productions. Worse, the company might be found liable for Cooper's death (that makeshift dressing room was seen as evidence).

The death of Tommy Cooper and the events of that traumatic evening seemed to haunt Les Dennis and Dustin Gee in the years to follow. In May 1985, Gee was a hair's breadth away from dying onstage on opening night of a summer season at the North Pier in Blackpool. He fell ill onstage but, determined not to end up like Tommy Cooper, carried on. He was taken to the hospital afterward and diagnosed with a minor heart attack. Doctors told him to take at least six months off, but he returned to complete the run barely a month later, on June 24. That was his forty-third birthday. It would be his last.

On New Year's Day, 1986, the Vera and Mavis team was appearing as the ugly sisters in a pantomime version of *Cinderella* in Southport, Merseyside. (Callback! Remember, one of Tommy Cooper's first roles was an ugly sister in the same pantomime.) After a scene in which they got laughs with tongue-in-cheek naughty humor and local references, Dennis and Gee were rushing offstage to a costume change in their dressing room when Gee suddenly clutched his left arm. "I think I am dying," he said.

At that, he collapsed from another heart attack, this one massive. Basil Soper, the show's company manager, managed to revive him. Gee's production assistant Roger Edwards accompanied the comic to Southport General Hospital. Gee remained there, unconscious until 8:00 AM two days later.

Doctors feared that Dustin Gee may have sustained brain damage, but that morning he sat up, asked for a cup of tea, drank it, and then asked for ice cream. Family members who were with him said he was "quite chatty" and "lucid." He thanked them for coming and insisted they must see him in pantomime when he recovered. He asked if anyone had seen his wristwatch. Later that morning, he fell into a deep sleep and died at 12:45 PM.

In the days to follow, many British comics blamed the pressure of the industry for the death of Dustin Gee. Surviving partner Les Dennis mentioned the Tommy Cooper incident as some kind of omen. "After the show Dustin told me, 'That's the way I want to go! With my boots on!'" he told the tabloid the *Mirror* in 2016, after the character he played on the soap opera *Coronation Street* died onscreen of a heart attack. "And now I think, 'Be careful what you wish for.'"

Dustin Gee's funeral took place on January 9 at St. Oswald's Church in Fulford, York. John Cleese sent a wreath.

Though Les Dennis's 2008 autobiography was titled *Must the Show Go On?*, his partner Dustin Gee really did want to go the way Tommy Cooper went: performing, onstage, doing what he loved best. That may have been Tommy Cooper's greatest contribution to the comedy magic community, for, in coming years, other performers would vow that when they went, they wanted to go like Tommy.

Gordon Williams of the UK comedy magic duo Ziggy Cooper suddenly sat on the stage and died in the middle of a charity show in Sheffield, Yorkshire, on April 25, 1997. His widow Pam told London's *Daily Mirror*: "He had met Tommy Cooper and absolutely idolized him. He always told me he wanted to go just like him." Williams was fifty-three.

The ghost of Tommy Cooper did more than usher fellow magicians into the afterlife. The funnyman's spirit also intervened with one performer who died onstage—and helped bring him back to life! The incident took place at the Manchester Arena on January 31, 2015, opening night of the *Phoenix Nights Live* tour. The show featured stars of *Peter Kay's Phoenix Nights*, a British sitcom about a working men's club in Greater Manchester.

The second half of the show had just gotten under way when actor Ted Robbins, who played series villain Den Perry, made a surprise appearance. It truly was a surprise for the audience because earlier in the show, Peter Kay, in his role as wheelchair-bound Phoenix Club owner Brian Potter, told the crowd that the Perry character was serving time in Strangeways prison after setting fire to the club. So people were chuffed when Robbins emerged from beneath the stage floor, as if he'd tunneled out of prison, and performed a tongue-in-cheek rendition of the Prodigy's "Firestarter."

Robbins, fifty-nine years old, overweight, and sweaty, was perfect for the role. He was also a walking heart attack waiting to happen, and the heart attack did indeed happen a few moments later, when, in the middle of his routine, he suddenly clutched his chest and fell backwards onto the stage, flat on his back.

The audience, of course, wasn't sure what to make of the display. Many thought it was part of the act. Jeers—aimed at the character, not the performer—echoed through the venue. Lucky for Ted, as soon as he fell, his costars and family thought of one thing: Tommy Cooper.

"We were watching him on the screen [backstage] and I noticed his hand shaking and I just thought he was nervous but he just collapsed," costar Paddy McGuinness told Jonathan Ross on his ITV chat show. "It happened to Tommy Cooper, but when you see it, it is horrendous."

Robbins's wife, Judy, was in the audience with their daughter and his sisters. "He just fell backwards. I knew straight away that something wasn't right," she was quoted as saying in the *Mirror*. "People were laughing as they thought it was part of the act. I heard someone say: 'Oh, he's doing a Tommy Cooper impression,' because Tommy Cooper died on stage. But I just knew it wasn't right. Unbeknown to me, a paramedic was sat behind me who knew by the way Ted fell that it wasn't a joke. Thank God we were near the stage because we just flew straight up there and the paramedic started working on Ted straight away."

They dropped the curtain quickly and went to work on saving Robbins's life. "Talk about luck," said McGuinness. "Richard Curtis was in the audience that night and the guy next to him happened to be a heart specialist and he turned round to Richard and asked if he could go on stage."

The heart specialist joined the paramedic and the pair performed CPR in tandem on the stage. Fifteen thousand spectators could only watch and shout encouragement. "It was the most bizarre, surreal experience," Judy Robbins recalled. "I was watching Ted fight for his life in front of fifteen thousand people."

The paramedic continued to pound hard on Robbins's chest. He pounded so hard he cracked twelve of Robbins's ribs and his sternum. Medics who worked for the arena brought out a defibrillator. Fifteen minutes had passed without a response. "He actually died, his heart stopped on stage," said McGuinness.

Ted Robbins was most definitely dead. Then, the defibrillator charged, the paramedic placed the paddles on Robbins's heart, and— *ZAP!* Ted Robbins was jolted back to life! He was drenched in blood, because he'd bitten his tongue when he collapsed, but he had a heartbeat. He was stuffed into an ambulance and taken to Wythenshawe Hospital.

Costar Justin Moorhouse addressed the crowd. "We are very sorry," he said. "This is not part of the show. I'm afraid we're going to have to postpone the show tonight, as obviously we have more important things to do."

Ted Robbins died onstage, and lived to tell the tale. A month later, with a new lease on life and on the way to a fifty-pound (3.57-stone) weight loss, he told the BBC, "I was looking forward to the show, although bizarrely I had a sense of foreboding on the day. I remember coming up the ladder on stage and the crowd booing Den Perry. I did a couple of gags and then I remember feeling kind of peaceful and calm, thinking 'let's have a little sit down for a minute.' I did my Tommy Cooper impression—God rest him."

———————

At least one comedian was not impressed at all with the way Tommy Cooper made his exit. Eric Morecambe of the long-running British comedy team Morecambe and Wise was a contemporary of Cooper's and said publicly that he'd hate to go in that manner.

Exactly six weeks after Cooper's death, Morecambe flew solo, without partner Ernie Wise, in a charity show at the Roses Theatre in Tewkesbury, Gloucestershire. Morecambe's wife Joan was in the audience and recalled he was "on top form." At the close of the show, Morecambe ran onstage six times to clown with jazz musician and multi-instrumentalist Alan Randall. Finally, Morecambe announced, "That's your lot!" and left the stage. He joked, "Thank goodness that's over!" He then took a half-dozen steps and collapsed from a heart attack—his third. Morecambe died at Cheltenham General Hospital just before 4:00 AM on May 28, 1984. He was fifty-eight. If it's any consolation, he did at least make it into the wings.

Kenneth Horne

Kenneth Horne, the last of Britain's great radio comedians, was in noticeably shaky health on February 14, 1969, when he entered the grand ballroom of London's Dorchester Hotel. The star of three of the most popular radio shows in UK history had already suffered a stroke in 1958 and a heart attack in 1966. He'd been prescribed an anticoagulant to ward off future coronary unpleasantness, but on the advice of his new medical adviser, he had stopped taking his medicine. His new medical adviser was a faith healer.

Horne had arrived at the Dorchester to host the annual Guild of Television Producers and Directors Awards dinner, a ceremony that was being filmed for broadcast on BBC1 later in the evening. Horne was a solid choice for the role. He'd been a fixture in British comedy since 1944, and his latest radio show, *Round the Horne*, was about to kick off its fifth series (or "season" to the Yanks).

As the show got under way, none of the 740 telly bigwigs or their dates had any idea that the sixty-one-year-old, bushy-browed, bald-headed comic was in anything but tip-top condition. Horne kept them laughing as he announced the award winners. At his side handing out the trophies was Earl Mountbatten of Burma, uncle to Prince Philip and Queen Elizabeth II's second cousin once removed (while you attempt to figure out that incestuous math, keep in mind that ten years later, the Earl would be blown up on his boat by an IRA bomb).

It was midway through the ceremony when Horne announced the award for best comedy script of 1968. The winners were Barry Took and Marty Feldman for their television series *Marty*. Horne was especially tickled to see Took and his hyperthyroid partner take the prize. They were the team that created *Round the Horne*.

The writers headed back to their table and Horne leaned into the mic: "These chaps got an award last year for *Round the Horne*, which is coming back on Sunday, March 16, with a repeat the following day. So don't forget to listen!" The audience got a good laugh at the plug. Horne had moved on to announcing the award for Best Scientific Program when he began to sway. Then he stumbled. Then he fell, three feet off the podium, and crashed onto the ballroom floor.

Several women in the audience fainted. Someone yelled for a doctor, and BBC chairman Lord Hill scrambled from his table to give aid. Hill seemed the right man for the job: he was an MD, who during World War II was popular for his broadcasts as the Radio Doctor, discussing health problems in the language of the simple folk. Could he save Kenneth Horne, though?

Barry Took and Marty Feldman set down their awards and helped carry Horne's body into the nearest room, which happened to be the bar. They laid him on the carpeted barroom floor and Lord Hill tried artificial respiration. Another doctor who was in the house attempted mouth-to-mouth with the star. Kenneth Horne did not respond to the kiss of life.

The ambulance arrived, and Horne was carted off to St. George's Hospital, just a short ride down Park Lane. He was quite obviously cold and dead long before they wheeled him into the emergency room.

Meanwhile, the clock was ticking until airtime and there was an awards show to complete. Guild chairman Peter Morley (a documentarian and director acclaimed for his coverage of Winston Churchill's funeral and for conducting the only interview with Adolf Hitler's younger sister Paula) stepped to the podium and assured everyone that Kenneth Horne would have wanted them to carry on. Lord Mountbatten took over hosting, minus the comic asides, and presented the remainder of the awards. The award for TV Light Entertainment Personality of the Year went to Marty Feldman. His bulging eyes welled with tears.

After the ceremony, there was dancing—it was a ballroom, after all. Peter Morley stepped in once again to stop the music and spoil the party to announce that Kenneth Horne had passed away. In tribute to Kenneth Horne, the dancing stopped for five minutes. Then the party continued.

The awards ceremony did air as scheduled, at 11:15 PM on BBC1, though Kenneth Horne's collapse and tumble were edited out of the program. At the point of disruption, the film jumped to a shot of Mountbatten in Horne's position. An announcer intoned, "Mr. Horne was taken ill at this point and has since died."

Death was attributed to a massive heart attack. According to Horne's biographer, Barry Johnston, his doctor blamed the faith healer, saying, "Poor silly fellow! If only he'd listened to me, he could have had another ten years!"

On the brighter side, Horne's writer Barry Took said, "He went the way he would have liked to, on top of a big laugh."

Sid James

Comic actor Sid James was one of Britain's biggest comedy stars of the 1950s and '60s. Everyone knew him for his big laugh, or more accurately, his "dirty laugh." The *Daily Express* newspaper described the chortle as "the most distinctive laugh in the history of British comedy," an "unforgettable gravelly cackle [that] embodied all the warmth, lechery and cheekiness which made Sid James so cherished by the British public." The craggy-faced star of nineteen films in the very bawdy, very naughty, very British *Carry On* series was born Solomon Joel Cohen in South Africa and had been a fixture in British films, on television, and on stages since 1947.

In the spring of 1976, Sid James was sixty-two and starring as Sid Abbott, husband, father, and traveling stationery salesman in the popular television sitcom *Bless This House*. To coincide with and cash in on the start of the show's fifth series, he set off on a theater tour of a play called *The Mating Season*. The play was a smutty, leering farce by Irish playwright (and *Carry On* screenwriter) Sam Cree, really not much more or less than a stage version of a *Carry On*, with its seaside postcard humor and a chance for audiences to see old Sid James laugh his familiar "Yak! Yak!" in the crumpled flesh.

James had toured Australia with the play to some success. This time around, the theaters were a bit threadbare, the audiences didn't pay more than a couple of pounds for the best seats, and Sid wasn't in the best of health.

The curtains opened on the tour on March 8 at the Grand Theatre in Wolverhampton, and the show carried on its theatrical death march through grand old theaters in need of refurbishment. It was eight shows a week as the company moved around England, to Wimbledon, Birmingham, Richmond, and, on Monday, April 26, the Empire Theatre in Sunderland. It was all a bit depressing. The theater that could hold twenty-two hundred people boasted four hundred patrons on opening night.

The play had proceeded fifteen minutes into the first act. The audience cheered and hollered at the sight of Sid James when he entered the living room stage set. The laughs kept coming as comic actress Audrey Jeans held an aerosol spray and, referring to another woman's perfume, said, "I can't bear the smell of cats!" She sprayed the bottle under Sid's nose. He gasped for breath and fell backwards onto a sofa. The audience laughed. Even the cast thought he was doing it all for show.

Actress Olga Lowe entered the scene. She was another *Carry On* veteran and James's childhood friend, who'd helped him get his start in pictures when he first arrived in England. "I came on, said my first lines and he answered as normal," she was quoted as saying in the *Sunderland Echo*. "Then I sat on the sofa with him. I said my next line and he didn't answer. His head had slumped and his eyes had gone back into his head. I thought it was a gag. Well, you would with Sid. He was such a rascal."

When James didn't respond to her ad-libs, Olga Lowe realized something was very wrong with the star and called to the crew to bring down the curtain. The audience laughed when the technical director stepped out in front of the curtain to ask, "Is there a doctor in the house?" The doctor who stepped forward laughed as well.

Stagehands ran over to James, whose head was now lolled back as he gasped for breath. Tour manager David Jackley attempted the kiss of life. The doctor saw that it was no laughing matter and helped as James was carried offstage and rushed by ambulance to the Royal Infirmary. Sid James, who'd suffered a heart attack in 1967, was stricken with a fatal one this time around. He was dead before the ambulance completed its journey.

All four hundred members of the audience got their money refunded. The remainder of the run in Sunderland and the rest of the *Mating Season* tour was canceled. How could it not be? Sid James was its raison d'être.

As word of his death spread, the tributes poured in. Sid's third wife and widow, Valerie, looked for a silver lining. "Sid died making people laugh," she announced. "I suppose, for him, it was the perfect way to go."

Not so fast. Barbara Windsor, Sid James's costar in all those *Carry On* movies—and a woman with whom he'd carried on a well-publicized ten-year affair while he was married to Valerie—told the *Sunderland Echo* that Sid would roll over in his grave if he realized he died touring run-down theaters in the provinces. "It was everything Sid hated," she insisted. "He liked his films and his television. The only time he did theatre was if he could have some lovely location.

"Everyone said to him: Don't go up to Sunderland. He looked so ill, so unhappy. He went up to Sunderland and the rest is history."

"Don't go up to Sunderland." Sunderland in northeast England had a reputation as a "graveyard" for comedians, where many died a death onstage. In fact, when the theater manager called the show's producer, Bill Roberton, to tell him that Sid James had died in Sunderland, the producer replied, "Don't worry, everybody dies in Sunderland."

Sid James's unhappiness may be eternal. More than one person, including comedian Les Dawson, has claimed to have seen his ghost haunting the Sunderland Empire Theatre.

5

Magicians & Escape Artists

MAGIC! NOWHERE ARE THE FUNDAMENTAL rules of nature defied more spectacularly than on the magician's stage. Beautiful women are sawed in half. Men are impaled in boxes lined with razor-tipped spikes. People literally disappear! Yet, when you get right down to it, magicians are entertainers who perform tricks. Tricks don't require extraordinary, mysterious powers; they require practice. Despite their stage names or advertising, magicians are only human and subject to the same causes of mortality as the rest of us—all too often, onstage.

Washington Irving Bishop

Stage mentalist Washington Irving Bishop professed no special powers when it came to reading people's minds. A leading "anti-spiritualist," he said his "thought reading" was actually "muscle reading," achieved through analysis of a person's body movements. Whatever his methods, Bishop was regarded as one of the top mentalists of the late nineteenth century. He was also known for his ability to drive a horse-drawn carriage blindfolded and the trick in which he'd find a hidden object by holding the hand or wrist of the person who hid it while asking the person to think of the location.

Impressive as it sounds, that description only gives a hint of the wild, insane exhibitions that the slight, curly-bearded, cocaine-addicted forerunner to the Amazing Kreskin would career through in front of audiences, performances like the one reported by the *Kansas City Star* in 1889:

> During his most important tests, the "thought reader" frequently used stimulants and drugs. Hypodermic syringes filled with morphine were an invariable part of the outfit of his famous "driving" tests in which, with his eyes tightly blindfolded and his ears and nostrils plugged with cotton, he drove a team of horses through the streets in a search for a pin or other small articles previously concealed by committee.
>
> During his regular performance he frequently drank wine and sometimes resorted to the morphine.

As for those regular performances in clubs and theaters:

> While performing his feats of "thought reading," his pulse would sometimes run up to 170 beats a minute and a condition of great physical exhaustion followed. His manager, John G. Ritchie, was accustomed to sit in the audience every evening and watch Mr. Bishop closely. At the first indication of fatigue, he would imperatively stop the performance, then and there, even in the middle of an experiment.

Manager Ritchie had good reason to stop the performance before Washington Irving Bishop was too far gone. The thirty-four-year-old performer was afflicted with catalepsy, a condition that begins with a seizure and results in a trancelike state accompanied by body rigidity, a slowing of bodily functions like breathing, and decreased sensitivity to any kind of pain. In Bishop's case, that meant he would often suddenly seize up onstage, fall down, apparently stop breathing, and soon be stiff as a board, as if rigor mortis had set in. He would be unresponsive to kicks, tickles, or needle pokes. He would, in short, appear to be very dead or, to paraphrase John Cleese, an ex–human being. He could remain in that state for as long as fifty-two hours.

So it was wise that he carried a note in his jacket pocket, warning anyone who found him in that condition not to use electricity in an attempt to revive him and definitely not to perform an autopsy on him, because he'd probably wake up soon enough.

———————

That brings us to Sunday, May 12, 1889. Bishop was performing in New York City at the Lambs Club, the exclusive social club for actors, songwriters, and other theater folk, located in a brownstone at 34 West Twenty-Sixth Street. Bishop was in the middle of his very hyperkinetic act when a seizure struck and he collapsed to the floor. It all seemed part of the routine. After a short spell, Bishop recovered and insisted on carrying on with the show. He returned to the thought reading, but only for a few minutes before seizing up and collapsing again.

This time, the mentalist did not rebound. He was taken to an upstairs room at the club, where he was believed to be in a coma. He remained in that state the following day.

Three doctors were called in. They examined Washington Irving Bishop and used electricity to try to revive him. At ten minutes after noon on May 13, they declared him dead. Bishop's body was removed from the Lambs Club and taken to William Hawks's undertakers shop at 8 Sixth Avenue.

When Bishop's mother and wife heard the news, they rushed to the funeral home, expecting he'd soon awaken and they could take him home. So they were more than a little shocked to find out that not only had the doctors already performed an autopsy but also Washington Irving Bishop's head had been cut open and his brain removed!

The doctors who pronounced him dead claimed they never saw the note he carried. Bishop's mother and wife immediately went on the attack. They said Bishop obviously was in a cataleptic state and that an autopsy should never have been performed without their permission—especially an autopsy conducted while he was still alive!

J. A. Irwin, the doctor who declared Bishop dead at the Lambs Club and who led the autopsy, had known Bishop for more than a decade and had been anxious to study his brain. As the scandal kicked up, he issued a statement insisting that the mind reader "died hours before the post-mortem" but added, "The brain changes more quickly after death than any other portion of the body, and had we waited longer the benefit of the autopsy would have been lost. For the trouble I have taken in this case, I have received no thanks, but have been called murderer and other vile names."

Bishop's mother was not about to offer any thanks. She convinced the Manhattan district attorney to file manslaughter charges against Dr. Irwin and two others.

Despite the testimony of expert witness Dr. Edward C. Spitzka, who said he'd seen cataleptic rigidity last as long as two months in a patient, it took a jury an hour and a half to rule that Bishop was dead by coma when he was brought to the undertaker, and that the doctors acted in good faith. They did note that Dr. Irwin, "through overzealousness," was hasty in getting the autopsy underway.

"Amazing Joe" Burrus

Some people regarded Joe Burrus as just another ex-con and recovering drug addict. Joe Burrus saw himself as something more—much more. "I consider myself a master of illusion and escape artist," he said. "I believe I'm the next Houdini and greater."

So on Halloween night in 1990, the sixty-fourth anniversary of Harry Houdini's death, thirty-two-year-old "Amazing Joe" Burrus attempted an escape that even his hero had failed at accomplishing: being buried alive. "To me, that is what an escape artist is: to put myself in an impossible situation and get out of it," Joe declared.

A year earlier in Salem, Oregon, Joe had escaped from a casket buried under dirt. On this night, at Blackbeard's Family Fun Center in Fresno, California, in front of a crowd that included trick-or-treaters and his own young sons Joseph and Joshua, he'd do himself, and every other escape artist in history, one better. Amazing Joe would be handcuffed, shackled, and locked in a homemade, see-through plastic-and-glass coffin; lowered into a seven-foot-deep grave; and then covered in not only dirt but also a layer of freshly poured cement. Then he would escape from the coffin and make his way to the surface.

He'd perform this amazing escape to raise money for the Third Floor drug rehab clinic in Fresno. Joe said he saw the stunt as a metaphor for his own escape from drug addiction.

If he did manage to make the escape, Joe would actually be able to say he did Harry Houdini one better. Houdini spent years trying to master the buried-alive stunt. When he attempted the feat near Santa Ana, California, in 1915, he almost died. Houdini was buried under six feet of dirt (without a casket) and was left to dig his way out. He panicked and managed to get a hand to the surface before he called for help. He was yanked out, unconscious, by his assistants. His conclusion, as written in his diary, was "the weight of the earth is killing." Houdini did pull off an aboveground variation of the stunt—"the Mystery of the Sphinx," featuring a glass-fronted coffin lowered into a vault and covered in sand—just weeks before his death in Detroit.

––––––––––

"He wasn't a drug addict," Joe Burrus's eldest son insists almost thirty years after Halloween 1990. "He was an alcoholic. The only drug he used to do was marijuana. I guess back then you were considered an addict. And he did some time in prison, and while he was there, he kind of realized, 'I gotta do something different when I get out. I love magic. I gotta do something with this.' And so that's what he did."

Joseph Burrus has vivid memories of his father. Not all of them are magical. "When I was probably five years old and my brother was three, he and my mom were going through a separation," he tells us. "Now, they were never married, but they were going through a separation. He was a drunk, and he was abusive, so she was gonna take the kids and everything else, and he didn't want to leave us. He ended up kidnapping us, and took us all the way to Tennessee. I remember every bit of it. I remember being on the road. I remember calling her on the phone. I remember when the police broke in and arrested him in Tennessee, and us having to stay in a foster home until my mom was able to come get us. That was basically why he was in prison, that he had kidnapped us, and he was there for a couple years. And when he got out, he said, 'I got to change things.'"

The key to the change was magic, an art Amazing Joe had first played around with as as teen. "He loved doing magic, because he loved amazing people and seeing the look on their faces," says Joseph. "So he did a lot of close-up magic, but he also had a lot of stage magic. And probably about five years or so before he died, he decided, 'OK, I've got magic down. Now I want to get into stunts. I want to perfect that, and take my show into the big time.' And so he did a lot of stunts. He did a stunt where he was locked into a box and the box was set on fire. And a car would come racing down the track and smash into the box—and he was the one driving the car."

After performing the buried-alive stunt in Salem in late 1989, Joe decided to move to Fresno, where his sons and their mother now resided. "He moved back here January of 1990. He wasn't around in my life a lot, because he was in prison, then he got out and lived in another city, so beginning in 1990, I was with him every day, and I was getting close to him and helping him plan. He pretty much had almost the entire year planning and promoting. And then when October rolled around, he was performing at one of the local pumpkin patches here. He had the coffin out there on display, and he was doing magic tricks for about a week or two before the event. And when he was out there, he would stand on the coffin to show people how strong it was.

"I think a few days before the show, the lid ended up cracking, and he didn't have time to fix it, and he said, 'Ah, it'll be all right.' And that was another factor into everything that happened."

———

As showtime approached on Halloween night, more than 150 people were on hand to watch Amazing Joe's amazing escape, which was to be videotaped, projected live on-screen, and broadcast live on radio. "We all got picked up in a limo, and then got a seat in the front row, and then the limo left, picked him up, brought him," Joseph recalls. "The show kind of started late. I had an opportunity to go backstage and talk to him and say, 'Hey, good luck. I love you,' all this stuff. I chose not to, because I've seen my father and I'll talk to him afterwards. My brother went back. I didn't, and that was a huge regret on my part."

The escape artist appeared at the burial site in a white tuxedo with a shiny purple bow tie and cummerbund, his blond mullet tied into a ponytail and his handlebar mustache pointing down toward his thick goatee, forming a simulated Vandyke beard. He looked every inch the magician—if not the escaping kind, at least one who pulls a rabbit out of a top hat. A police officer cuffed, shackled, and chained Amazing Joe's wrists, while the escape artist provided play-by-play commentary for a bemused radio reporter holding a microphone and recorder near his face. "Through the chains, through the shackles, through the handcuffs," Joe explained, "I'll burrow my way through three and a half feet—" He winced in an exaggerated display of pain as the police officer tightened the cuffs and then continued, "—of dirt and get through all this before the cement hardens."

"You realize that cement starts to harden first at the lower elevation," the reporter warned. "So it's going to be hard—" He gestured toward the ground.

"You mean it hardens at the lower part?" Joe looked around in feigned surprise. "I thought it starts at the top!"

"No, it hardens at the bottom!"

"No, no, no," Joe said. "In fact, I shouldn't even kid. This is very serious. This is no magic trick."

The reporter had one last observation while Joe's assistants secured his leg shackles. "You know, Houdini failed at this, and he was only using dirt." With that, Amazing Joe climbed into the coffin. The coffin was locked, and his aides began to lower it into the seven-foot-deep grave.

Joe was about halfway down into the hole when he began knocking on the sides of the box. The assistants pulled him back to the surface. One of them was Sean Henderson, a resident of the Third Floor clinic. "He said the chain was too tight and was choking him," Henderson would tell the *Los Angeles Times*. "We gave him time to slip the chain from his neck. After he got that done, he wanted the locks back on and asked us to start burying him again."

The casket lid was locked again, and the descent once again got under way. When the casket was at the bottom of the hole, the assistants shoveled in about three feet of dirt. A cement truck backed up and poured in another three feet—seven tons—of wet cement.

"There was only supposed to be about a foot of cement at the top of the grave," Joseph Burrus insists, "just to make it a little bit harder. And it was like three feet of cement. It was actually way too much, and I don't know if it was an accident or if he changed it at the last minute, but I know from being with them the entire month and listening to what he was saying, there was only supposed to be a very small amount on top, just to give it that extra 'wow factor.'"

The truck pulled away. The cement had filled the hole completely. An assistant was raking the surface, evening it out at ground level, when in an instant, the cement sank about two feet and settled. There was an audible crack, and the sound of plastic and glass shattering. It was obvious what had occurred.

"As soon as we finished and the truck pulled away, the whole thing dropped," Henderson said. "The cement busted the coffin. It buried him alive."

Joseph recalls, "There was a backhoe there, and he had told everybody, 'If something goes wrong, don't come digging right away, because you're going to end up sinking in the grave with the vibration of the truck, and it's gonna end up crushing me more.' And so in a few minutes of their waiting, it just seemed like it was forever. And I already knew something happened.

"So I took off. I went to go walk around the park. I ended up over at the water slide area, and I was just sitting there crying, kind of looking up and asking God, 'Please let everything be OK.' And I was up there for quite a while, and then I heard my name being paged over the intercom. And when I came back down, it was just a chaotic sight. I mean, there were chairs thrown everywhere. It was people crying. There was a clown there that was doing balloon animals, and he was in the corner crying. There were just police everywhere, ambulances everywhere, and they had paged me because they were trying to make us leave before they actually brought him out of the grave.

"They didn't want to pull him out with anybody there. So they made us leave, and we went home and pretty much turned on the TV and saw the news."

––––––––––––

Nearly three decades after that fateful Halloween, Joseph Burrus launched a GoFundMe campaign for a memorial to Amazing Joe at the spot where he died. "The thing was, he was actually already out of the coffin," he says with some pride. "He'd made it out, he was already pretty much on his way up when it collapsed. So he didn't get crushed inside the coffin. He basically suffocated, because of all the weight of the dirt and cement."

Joseph Burrus continues: "One thing that I want to also make clear, he wasn't just a guy who was performing a wild stunt. He was dedicated to magic. What's made it easier to talk about over the years is because he died doing what he wanted to do, and there was no other way he would have wanted to die. And even if in his mind he knew that his trick's not gonna work, he would have still done it, because he had already hyped it up and he had already had a crowd there, and he didn't want to disappoint anybody.

"He had another stunt planned. He was going to jump out of an airplane with his hands tied so he couldn't reach the ripcord. And then he was going to free himself just in time to pull the ripcord."

Trevor Revell

All of Britain celebrated on July 29, 1981, when Charles, Prince of Wales, married the lovely, young Lady Diana Spencer. No one could have predicted the troubles that would follow in that marriage, or what would transpire that day at a Royal Wedding celebration in Portsmouth, when Trevor Revell performed.

Three thousand people crowded the square outside the Portsmouth Guildhall venue as various street performers showed off their acts. One of them was Revell, a thirty-five-year-old magician, stunt artist, and escapologist, whose exciting finale was a straitjacket escape.

Harry Houdini claimed that he came up with the escape after visiting a lunatic asylum in Canada and watching a maniac inmate struggle to break free from his restraints. The story may have been myth, but the straitjacket escape became a key part of Houdini's act.

At first, he'd be buckled and strapped into the jacket and then wriggle his way free while hidden from view behind a curtain. Once he perfected this combination of technique and strength, he let the audience watch the process, a somewhat disturbing display in which he jerked, heaved, pulled, and gyrated like a madman in a padded cell. In years to follow, Houdini added more drama, creating huge scenes and generating news coverage by performing the stunt while suspended from tall buildings, upside down (which actually made it easier for Houdini to get his arms over his head—the key to escape).

Trevor Revell added additional pizzazz—and an element of danger—to his straitjacket escape. Like Houdini, he'd be hoisted upside down, thirty feet in the air, on a rope. But additionally the rope suspending him would be set on fire; Revell would have to free himself from the straitjacket before the flames burned through the rope and he fell to his death.

A way to avoid tragedy, one escapologist suggests, is to "gimmick" the rope—that is, to use one that will not burn through. That would not do for Trevor Revell. As he was buckled and tied into the long-sleeve garment, police handed another rope to some members of the crowd closest to the performer and asked that everyone stand behind it to give the magician room. Suitably strapped in, Revell was then raised upside down, thirty feet into the air. The rope was lit; the fire caught. Flame on.

All eyes looked up as Trevor Revell spun, swung, twisted, and turned to escape his bonds before the the rope burned to ash. He managed to get free in under a minute. Revell was about to signal the crane operator to lower him when, unfortunately, as police explained in a later statement, "the rope burnt through too quickly and he plunged head-first onto a concrete paving slab."

A witness who was a child at the time later wrote on an Internet message board about a scene he would never forget:

He was the father of a girl I went to school with. I was at the front. I saw him hit the ground head first. I heard his skull shatter; I heard his skull crack like a boiled egg being hit with a spoon. I saw the puddle of blood and brain he left behind after they loaded his still twitching body onto a stretcher and into the ambulance.

I thought at the time that this was the most horrific thing I'd ever seen until, as the crowd dispersed, a group of rowdy skinheads who had been standing behind us pushed their way forwards and began jumping and dancing in the pool and blood and brain.

That was, and still is the most horrific thing I've ever seen.

The police report concluded: "Revell later died in Queen Alexandra Hospital."

Interlude

The Bullet Catch

MAGICIANS HAVE BEEN PERFORMING the bullet catch for hundreds of years. Today, its most acclaimed practitioners are the team of Penn & Teller. In their long-running show at the Rio Hotel & Casino in Las Vegas and performances around the world, the pair have caught bullets in their mouths simultaneously, thousands of times. Penn Jillette, the taller, vocal member of the pair, made it clear that the bullet catch is neither an illusion nor a stunt.

"It is," Penn tells us, "a trick. And we tried to follow Houdini's rule, and you may not know Houdini's rule, but it's fairly important to your book. Houdini wouldn't do anything more dangerous than sitting in his living room. And we set up a system of checks and balances that I believe makes our version of the bullet catch as safe as standing onstage.

"I mean, a light could fall on you. There could be a crazy domestic terrorist. There are all sorts of ways to die, but none of them related to the trick that we're doing. And that's really important. But I'll tell you something more important, which is, I not only think that show business should be completely safe but also that people should know it. And this is probably the more radical approach. We've had many, many people—lay people and producers and showbiz people—tell us, 'Put a thing in your lobby that talks about how many people have died doing this trick! Talk about how much danger you're gonna be in!' And I go, 'That's not what art is!' Art is beautiful. Art is a roller coaster ride where your intellect and your emotions collide head-on as fast as possible. When you get in a roller coaster, your viscera tells you you're gonna die. And your mind tells you, 'You know, if they killed everybody on this thing, their insurance rates would be too high.'

"And those two things are colliding at huge speed. What I want during the show is for you to watch the bullet catch and go, 'Oh my fuckin' God! This is the most dangerous thing I've ever seen.' And then say, 'But these guys don't fuck around. This is completely safe—and beautiful.'

"If we were to advertise our Bullet Catch as we can possibly get hurt, then it is an immoral act to come to our show—because you are supporting someone injuring themselves.

"I have my favorite tricks we've done in terms of hipness, in terms of patter, in terms of originality. Obviously the bullet catch isn't on any of those lists. It's one of the rare tricks that we did not try to come up with from scratch. Our version certainly added a lot to it, but it's not original. But for a trick qua trick, for just, *I do not know how the fuck they did that*, I believe it's our best trick.

"By the way, doing a bullet catch that isn't safe is not very skilled. Doing the bullet catch with 99 percent safety is harder than doing it with 73 percent safety, which is harder than doing it with 43 percent safety. In terms of actual skill, we are better magicians if our tricks are safer. That's what Teller always reminds me: 'Nothing more dangerous than sitting in your living room.'"

Chung Ling Soo

One of the most influential stage magicians of the early twentieth century was Chung Ling Soo. This mysterious man from the Orient staged lavish presentations of mostly Western magic tricks, but with a Chinese touch. The performer who never spoke onstage, and only did interviews through an interpreter, was the highest-paid magician in the business.

Chung Ling Soo used ancient secrets to amaze, and nothing was more amazing than his version of the bullet catch, the trick he called "Defying the Boxers" or "Condemned to Death by the Boxers" (as in China's Boxer Rebellion). In this very dramatic piece of stagecraft, which he first performed in 1906, six assistants, dressed in armor as the Chinese rebel Boxers, would point guns at him, as if they were a firing squad. Each gun had two barrels, one with a real bullet, the other a blank. Soo would stand in front of them, a few yards away, holding a plate, like a target. The "Boxers" would fire the guns. The magician would "catch" the bullets and drop them into the plate (he actually had the bullets in his palm all along).

On the evening of March 23, 1918, Chung Ling Soo played to a sold-out house of 1,840 at the Wood Green Empire Theatre in north London. Throughout the evening, he astonished the audience with various illusions. At about 10:45 PM, he arrived at his old standby. According to magic historian and Chung Ling Soo biographer Jim Steinmeyer, his assistant Kametaro announced in broken English: "Ladies and gentlemen, if you would . . . Chung Ling Soo now demonstrates how he was condemned by the Boxers during the rebellion and executed by firing squad. How he defied their bullets. And again, tonight, on our stage just as in Peking many years ago."

Twelve years into performing the bullet catch, Chung Ling Soo was no longer relying on the trick as his pièce de résistance. Now, there were only two "Boxers" onstage. Assistants Dan Crowley and Jack Grossman were handed the rifles. Neither had any knowledge of how the trick worked. (Soo was very protective of his secrets.) Their job was to simply point the guns at Chung Ling Soo and fire. Chung Ling Soo got into place with his plate. He stood defiantly against the firing squad. The shots rang out.

For the first time, Chung Ling Soo dropped the plate. Blood seeped through his silk costume. He uttered, "Oh my God, something's happened! Lower the curtain." The audience was shocked, not so much that the star had been shot point-blank in the chest but that he'd spoken English. It was the first time he'd ever spoken English onstage.

And the last. The magician billed as the Marvelous Chinese Conjurer died the following day. He was fifty-six.

At first, foul play was suspected, because Chung Ling Soo had been involved in a very public feud with another magician, Ching Ling Foo. Foo was an acclaimed performer from Peking who was the first East Asian magician to achieve worldwide fame. Foo accused Soo of ripping off his stage persona and his act. The death was ruled "death by misadventure"—accidental—after a firearms expert testified that a buildup of gunpowder in a rifle led to a real bullet being fired into the magician. The expert testified only after Soo's Chinese widow and assistant, Sue Seen, reluctantly gave away the secrets and mechanics of the trick at the inquest.

That's when the truth came out. Sue Seen was not Chinese. She was Olive "Dot" Path. She wasn't really Chung Ling Soo's wife, because he was still married to someone else. The public was most shocked to learn that Chung Ling Soo was not Chinese either. He was William Ellsworth Campbell Robinson from Westchester County, New York. An American of Scottish descent, he'd performed under such exotic names as Achmed Ben Ali and Nana Sahib, before shaving his facial hair, rubbing on some greasepaint, and wearing his hair in a Chinese-style queue, as Chung Ling Soo.

On November 6, 1982, magician Paul Daniels reenacted Chung Ling Soo's bullet catch on British television. The bullet was fired by Jack Grossman, one of the assistants who fired the final shots at Chung Ling Soo.

More than sixty years earlier, Harry Houdini had intended to perform his own tribute to the late magician, by attempting the bullet catch himself in 1918. He opted out, however, after his elder colleague Harry Kellar begged him not to do it. "There is always the biggest kind of risk that some dog will 'job' you," Kellar wrote in a letter, "and we can't afford to lose Houdini. . . . You owe it to your friends and your family to cut out all stuff that entails risk of your life."

The bullet catch was too dangerous for Houdini! Yet many a less-experienced illusionist has attempted the trick, to tragic results. The misadventures of failed bullet catchers have been chronicled many times in newspapers, on websites, and in books (like *Twelve Have Died* by Ben Robinson with Larry White).

When it comes to dying onstage, it seems that these magicians are giving themselves an unfair advantage—it's just too darn easy to check

out this way—but in the interest of comprehensiveness and inclusive-
ness, we list their fatal blunders:

- French magician **Coulen** claimed that black magic allowed him to
  catch bullets in his bare hand. While attempting the trick in Lorraine in 1597, one of his assistants got angry with him and used the
  pistol to bash in Coulen's brain.
- **Kia Khan Khruse**, a member of the Ramo Samee Juggling Troupe
  from India, was rumored to have been shot to death attempting
  the bullet catch at the Pall Mall Music Hall in Dublin in 1818. This
  would have made him the first recorded shooting victim during a
  bullet catch (as opposed to being beaten to death). Yet, Kia Khan
  Khruse himself laid the rumor to rest in one of his playbills later
  that year: "And again (though it has been said that he was killed
  in performing this Astonishing Trick) he will catch in his hand a
  marked Bullet, added to the powder-loading of a Pistol which anyone present may fire at him for that purpose." The magic world
  is grateful that Khruse did survive, for that year he introduced the
  needle-swallowing trick.
- **Madame DeLinsky**, wife and assistant of a Polish magician, faced
  a firing squad of six soldiers—shills who loaded their rifles with
  blanks. During a performance before a German royal court in 1820,
  one rifleman loaded a real bullet and shot Madame DeLinsky in
  the gut. She died two days later. Adding to the tragedy, she was
  pregnant, her unborn child was lost, and her husband went mad.
- **Giovanni de Grisy** was killed onstage by a spectator in 1826; a real
  bullet got mixed in with the fake ones during the bullet catch. His
  father, the magician Edmund de Grisy, was convicted of "homicide
  through imprudence" and sentenced to six months in prison.
- **Arnold Buck** picked the wrong audience member to load his gun
  during a bullet catch demonstration in 1840. The volunteer loaded
  a blank bullet into the barrel. He also dropped in some nails. It was
  a sharp end to Buck's career, and life.
- In preparation for the bullet catch, **Professor Adam Epstein** used
  his magic wand to ram the ammunition into the barrel of a rifle.

At one show in 1869, the tip of the wand broke off. When the gun was fired, the tip was launched like a sharp projectile through his forehead.

- **Raoul Curran** was about to show off his bullet catch in 1880 when a member of the audience jumped out of his seat and shot him with his own pistol.

- **DeLine Jr.** was killed attempting the bullet catch in 1890. His magician father shot him.

- **Michael Hatal** attempted to catch a bullet with an American flag at an Odd Fellows benefit in lower Manhattan on October 28, 1899. He handed a gun, powder, and container with twenty-five large-caliber cartridges to audience member Frank Benjo and instructed Benjo to load two marked cartridges of his choosing. Hatal wrapped himself in the flag. Benjo fired the double-barreled rifle at close range. Hatal lived long enough to indemnify his accidental executioner, blaming himself for not switching cartridges.

- A German performer named **Edvin Lindberg** reportedly died attempting the bullet catch in 1905.

- **Professor Otto Blumenfeld** (a.k.a. Blumenfeld "Herr" Bosco) attempted the bullet catch at the Basle Music Hall in Basle (now Basel), Switzerland, on January 24, 1906. He invited a volunteer to come onstage and fire a revolver at him at close range. He, too, forgot to switch the cartridge, and died on the spot.

- Weeks after Chung Ling Soo's death, as the *Washington Post* and other papers reported, **H. T. Sartell** had "perverted the trick" to commit suicide by bullet catch onstage in Lynn, Massachusetts.

- The *Post* also mentioned that in 1918 a magician known as **the Black Wizard of the West** "fell at Deadwood, S.D." As the story goes, the Black Wizard made two serious mistakes before attempting the bullet catch for the first time. He didn't rehearse, and he allowed his wife to be his assistant. She was angry with him and switched wax bullets for real ones. She shot the Wizard dead in front of the audience, before turning the .45 caliber pistol on herself.

- **Horace Goldin** capped his performance at London's Wood Green Empire Theatre on August 21, 1939, by imitating Chung Ling Soo's bullet catch on the very same stage. He survived but died in his sleep at home early the next morning, at sixty-five.

- **Theodore Annemann**, best known as a mentalist and, from 1934 to 1941, publisher of the legendary magician's magazine the *Jinx*, performed a theatrical bullet catch outdoors. He'd jerk back, spin around and collapse as if thrown back by the force of the projectile before he'd pull the bullet from his bloody mouth. He was scheduled to perform the routine indoors for the first time in January 1942, but on January 12, two weeks before the performance, he committed suicide. Significantly, Annemann did not shoot himself. According to his biographer, Max Abrams, Annemann's wife found him "on a couch with a bag over his head and a pipe from the gas stove under the bag. No notes or anything to explain." Did the bullet catch kill him? Perhaps. Annemann was known to be a victim of severe stage fright.

- German magician **Ralf Bialla** performed more bullet catches than anyone—over three thousand. In his version, the bullet was fired through three panes of glass, through a funnel he made with his hands (covered in steel gloves), and into his mouth, where he hid a set of steel teeth beneath his dentures. Bialla was seriously wounded nine times, and eventually all those bullets in his face led to circulation problems that caused him to black out. He was recovering from an injury in 1975 when he went for a stroll in the mountains, got dizzy, and fell off a cliff.

- **Doc Tahman Conrad** was a magician, fortune-teller, and bullwhip artist. While performing at an outdoor festival in Canada in the summer of 1974, Doc was shot in the stomach while practicing a version of the bullet catch that he called "the Russian Roulette Trick."

- In 1988, Argentinian magician **Professor Marvo** (Fernande Tejada) was about to perform the bullet catch (with his mouth) for about fifty people in a tavern in Azul. Before his assistant could fire a blank, however, a man named Marco Asprella stood up from the audience, shouted, "Catch this one, professor!" and shot him with a .45 caliber pistol. Asprella went on trial for murder, but got off with a fine and probation after testifying that he truly couldn't understand why the professor couldn't catch the bullet.

- **Nellie Fell** would pretend she'd caught a bullet in her mouth after her sharpshooting partner fired a blank. On September 13, 1991, at a circus in Napier, New Zealand, the gun was loaded with a live bullet. Four hundred spectators watched Nellie get shot in the temple. Many of the adults and children applauded before they realized they'd witnessed an execution. The sharpshooter faced firearms charges.

- African magician Kofi Brugah, known professionally as **Zamba Powers**, died during a show in Adukrom, Ghana, on June 14, 2007. For his "final illusion," he handed a gun to a member of the audience and told the man to fire it at him. Ghana's largest newspaper, the *Daily Graphic*, takes it from there: "Boom! Horror of horrors! There lay Brugah in a pool of blood screaming and pleading to be saved."

Of the versions on that list, Penn Jillette reveals that he and Teller "actually did not like any of the performances of the bullet catch. They all seemed kind of empty," he says.

"And they all seemed to have nothing other than the danger going. They were, by definition, not safe enough, because people died. And also, I didn't think they were beautiful, because they were so foursquare, so clumsy. I mean, I have a great deal of respect for brute art that just slams you through the head. I've seen the Sex Pistols. I love the Clash. I'm a big fan of the Troggs. I understand all of that. But that is not the only note you can hit. And because the bullet catch has such obvious brutality and horror built into it, it seems like putting an intellectual gloss on it is really beautiful. It seems like it kind of needs that. If you're gonna have that much sour, you need to have a little bit of sweet, you know?"

That, Penn Jillette says, is why Penn & Teller "don't ever say we're gonna catch bullets in our mouth. We say we're gonna move the bullet from one side of the stage to the other. And we never refer to the guns. We refer to the guns as 'magic wands.' And I love the idea of reducing the bullet catch to 'We're moving small pieces of signed metal from one side of the stage to the other, using a magic wand' and letting the audience put all the tension on it. It just gives it the backbeat. That's the syncopated way to do it. That's not the foursquare way to do it. That swings."

One more thing, Penn adds. "I say very sincerely, I certainly hope there'll be an addendum to the book at some point with me in it. I intend to die in office. Certainly, I'm not going to retire, so since I spend about two, maybe three hours of my day onstage, it seems like I have probably a ten percent chance of dying onstage. So yeah, I'll probably very likely die doing what I love."

6

Dance

THE *DANSE MACABRE* WAS a medieval literary and pictorial depiction of a procession or dance of figures living and dead, expressing the universal equalizing power of death. There is a danse macabre at the finale of Ingmar Bergman's *The Seventh Seal*. Danse macabre imagery also appears in Walt Disney's 1929 Silly Symphony short *The Skeleton Dance* and at least two Mickey Mouse cartoons. The most macabre, of course, have been played out onstage.

Clara Webster

Filippo Taglioni's ballet *La révolte des femmes* premiered at the Paris Opéra in 1833. The story of an uprising by a community of female slaves against a sultan was adapted, with a new title, for the British audience a year later. *The Revolt of the Harem* premiered at the Theatre Royal in Covent Garden, London, and became an immediate scandal because of two very controversial sections: a bathing scene in the second act that contained female nudity and, in act 3, an even more shocking tableau in which women donned men's soldier uniforms and executed military maneuvers. Revealing the feminine form and assuming the form of a male were equally effective in generating ticket sales.

The bathing scene was ultimately a disappointment to men who were willing to be dragged to the ballet on the chance of seeing some female flesh. The dancers were covered in so many layers of gauzy fabric and crowded in such a way that no nakedness was on display at all. Yet this fantasy of domestic revolt and feminine solidarity captured the imagination of the audience's better half. This was the first ballet to deal with the emancipation of women, and at a time when women were exploited in the workplace and often abused at home, *The Revolt of the Harem* not only was a sensation but also soon represented a cause. The ballet was even credited with inspiring social reform in the United Kingdom, including the 1839 Custody of Infants Act, which permitted mothers to petition for custody of their young children, a right that was not assumed previously.

So when the work was revived at the same Theatre Royal on Drury Lane in 1844, it was already a favorite. This revival would turn out to be as memorable, historic, and traumatic to those in the audience as was the original a decade earlier, only for a very different reason.

The performance in question occurred on the evening of Saturday, December 14, during the controversial bathing scene in act 2. The dancers gathered and sprinkled water on one another, their graceful figures swathed in muslin and illuminated by gas lamps throwing light upward from their placement slightly below the stage.

Clara Webster, in the role of Zelika, a royal slave, entered the scene. She was a British girl and a favorite with London audiences. Not at all like the intense foreign ballerinas who visited the London stage, Clara was short, but described as "extremely airy and delicately proportioned." She had a light complexion and expressive, round face. Her style of dancing was described as "remarkable for its neatness, elegance, and finish."

Clara swept across the stage in her filmy gown, splashing water on the other slave girls, who also moved about gracefully. While men craned to see how much of Clara's body they might yet get to see, she stepped into a bath.

As she did, her muslin dress caught the flame of a gas lamp. A London newspaper reported what happened next:

> Feeling the fire, she sprang and rushed upon the stage. The motion fanned the flame, and almost in an instant the whole of the slight and inflammable material of her dress was a mass of fire. With piercing shrieks she sought for safety among her companions on the stage. For a moment they surrounded her; but the frightful spectacle the unhappy girl presented made them shrink from the contact with her. It was fortunate they did so,

as nothing could have prevented their own dresses catching fire; and the consequences would have been indescribably terrible.

It happened so quickly it could have been a stage illusion. The audience watched in bewilderment, then horror. Many women in the theater screamed. As soon as Clara ran to the wings, a carpenter grabbed her. He threw her to the floor and managed to extinguish the flames, burning himself in the process.

Clara's mother was in the house that evening. She was one of the first at Clara's side. "My child," she said. "If I had but been in the wings, I could have saved you with my cloak."

Clara managed to whisper a reply. "Yes . . . mama . . . you could." Her face, neck, arms, and bosom were burned and blistered. Artificial flowers were burned into her hair. They took Clara Webster to her apartment in Regent's Park, where two doctors were called in.

Back at the Theatre Royal, there was a slight delay before W. H. Payne, the master pantomime clown, stepped onstage. He told the audience that Clara Webster had only been injured slightly, and that the ballet would proceed. The following morning, the stage manager wrote a letter to the newspapers, saying that Clara was out of danger and that there would be a benefit performance for her the following Monday.

The stage manager was overly optimistic. Clara was burned quite severely, and she died from those burns at 2:00 AM on Tuesday, December 17. She was twenty-three.

At the inquest two days after her death, the coroner told the jury why and how Clara Webster's death could have been avoided. Thomas Wakley was a celebrated surgeon, founder of the medical journal the *Lancet*, and a social reformer. With a patch of muslin and a flame, he demonstrated how Clara's and other costumes could easily be made flameproof with a preparation of muriate of ammonia. He also recommended that wire screens be placed over the stage gas lamps to keep the flames in check. The jury agreed that proper safety precautions were not taken. They declared Clara Webster's death to be accidental.

Clara's accident got a lot of press. All the London papers reported her death, as well as the announcement that *The Revolt of the Harem* was closing and would not be presented in public again. Despite that promise, the ballet opened in London four years later at Astley's Royal Amphitheatre, only under a new name. *The Revolt of the Harem* was now *The Battle of the Amazons*. The characters had new names, and there were changes in scenes. But the plot remained the same, and each night the stage was filled with female warriors.

Yoshiyuki Takada

Yoshiyuki Takada specialized in *butoh*, a form of Japanese dance that rejects traditional, Western dance forms and allows the body to express itself in an organic, natural way. *Butoh* performers commonly wear white rice flour body makeup and use slow, hypercontrolled motions. Takada and his five-man *butoh* troupe, Sankai Juku, went a step beyond. They performed their dances high in the sky, hanging off the sides of tall buildings.

The Tokyo-based Sankai Juku boys made their American debut at the Olympic Arts Festival in Los Angeles in 1984. As they did often when they arrived in a new city, the dancers opened their residency with a thirty-minute "dance of life and death" titled *Jomon sho* ("Homage to Prehistory"). The dance was performed on the outside of the Los Angeles Music Center's Dorothy Chandler Pavilion. Their bodies shaved of hair and painted white, with touches of red at their fingertips, the performers were suspended upside down by ropes attached to their ankles. They began in the fetal position and slowly writhed, undulated, and reached out while being lowered to the ground.

"Our main theme is life and death, so we try to realize the situation of death and the state of just being born," Takada told the *Los Angeles Times*. "When we are born, we first realize the situation of death. The mind is nothing, just like the body. That's why we are white and we shave our bodies—to be nothing."

When Sankai Juku arrived in Seattle to launch their second United States tour in September 1985, they were really something! They'd gotten permission to perform their life-and-death dance on the side of the Mutual Life Building, a historic six-story structure on the corner of First and Yesler, in the Pioneer Square neighborhood downtown. Their team spent days building a scaffold atop the Yesler Way side of the building and handing out yellow photocopies advertising the September 10 lunchtime performance.

By noon that day, when Ushio Amagatsu appeared on the building's roof and blew on a conch shell, hundreds of people had gathered below. The crowd went silent at the sight of four men, hairless, nearly naked, and powdered white, inching out over the platform and swinging out over the side. They hung in the fetal position, their feet in the air, backs to the pavement below.

Within a minute or so, Yoshiyuki Takada began to spin slowly, and his rope began to twist. This was not part of the show. His rope was unraveling. He reached up and attempted to grab the rope above the section that was fraying—but it was too late. The rope snapped. Takada plunged eighty feet toward the ground.

People in the crowd screamed, but Takada didn't utter a sound. He remained in the fetal position all the way down, and when he smashed into the sidewalk, the impact sent up a puff of white rice flour. Then there was silence.

A doctor was sitting on the sidewalk only ten feet from where Takada hit. He rushed over and began administering CPR. A woman from the crowd helped, but they couldn't get the dancer to breathe on his own. When the ambulance arrived, the two of them walked away, according to one account, "their hands and faces white with powder."

Yoshiyuki Takada had suffered compound fractures of the left elbow and shoulder and, most crucially, severe head trauma. He was declared dead at Harborview Medical Center twenty-four minutes after the blowing of the conch shell. He was thirty-one.

That night, the sidewalk on Yesler Way was filled with candles, flowers, and messages. One note, written on a napkin, read, "It was the most beautiful thing I had ever seen before he fell and after, I was lost."

After the accident, and before an autopsy was performed, the surviving Sankai Juku dancers performed a ritual cleansing of Takada's body. His parents were notified, and they traveled from Japan to take his body back for burial. It was later determined that Takada's rope wasn't strong enough to hold his weight. All four ropes used in the spectacle were supposed to be tested with sandbags, but because the risk had become so routine, three of them, including Takada's, were not.

7

Classical Musicians & Opera Stars

ONE OF THE EARLIEST RECORDED onstage deaths in classical music was that of Anton Cajetan Adlgasser. Adlgasser was a German; a composer of liturgical music, oratorios, and orchestral and keyboard works; a friend of Wolfgang Amadeus Mozart (they collaborated on an oratorio); and, beginning in 1750, the organist at Salzburg Cathedral in Austria.

Adlgasser's death on December 23, 1777, has been described as "dramatic." He was playing the massive, ornate pipe organ at evening services when he suffered a stroke, fell over, and died at forty-eight.

His temporary replacement at the organ was Michael Haydn, younger brother of composer Joseph Haydn. When Michael Haydn first filled in, his performance was so shaky that panic began to spread through the cathedral. Many people feared that he, too, was having a stroke at the keyboards. It turned out that he was drunk.

It was a stroke of bad luck when Wenzel Pichl dropped dead on January 23, 1805, while performing a violin concerto in the Lobkowitz Palace in Vienna. He, too, suffered a stroke. In 1847, a stroke felled pianist Fanny Mendelssohn Hensel while she was rehearsing an oratorio by her brother, the legendary German composer Felix Mendelssohn. Felix died less than six months later, also from a stroke (strokes also killed both of their parents, as well as their grandfather Moses).

Death is a constant theme in some the greatest works of classical music, in suites, sonatas, symphonies, and, most obviously, its theatrical subgenre, opera. Opera, of course, inspired the modern proverb "It ain't over till the fat lady sings." The expression reminds us to never assume the conclusion to an event until it's played out. The proverb has most often been tied to sporting events (its first recorded usage was in 1976, attributed to a Texas college sports official talking about a close basketball game), but the fat lady in question is clearly the zaftig soprano, most specifically the Valkyrie from *Götterdämmerung*, the last opera of Richard Wagner's cycle *Der Ring des Nibelungen*. Brünnhilde, the big-boned gal with the horned helmet, spear, and shield, sings a twenty-minute aria that leads to the end of the opera, which turns out to be the end of the world.

So we can gather that while "It ain't over til the fat lady sings" leaves open the possibility for a situation to change, once the fat lady has sung, it's over. When a performer dies onstage, classical or otherwise, the fat lady has sung.

Simon Barere

Simon Barere was known as a great if sometimes wild classical pianist who, according to Pulitzer Prize–winning critic Harold C. Schonberg, "sometimes let his remarkable fingers run away with him," rushing through pieces and running roughshod over the score in his singularly brilliant fashion.

That appeared to be the case on April 2, 1951, when the Ukranian-born musician appeared onstage at Carnegie Hall. The concert was a benefit for the American-Scandinavian Foundation and was dedicated to the work of Scandinavian composers. Barere would, for the first time, perform Edvard Grieg's Piano Concerto in A Minor. He'd be accompanied by the Philadelphia Orchestra, conducted by Eugene Ormandy.

"Mr. Ormandy," Barere said to the maestro, in his last words before the concert began, "this is the first time that we are playing together. I hope it won't be the last." Ormandy conducted the opening number, then walked off stage. Following tradition, he returned, on the heels of pianist Barere.

Barere dashed to the piano, settled in, and waited for Ormandy's downbeat. Barere seemed to be in top form through the thunderous introduction. He performed his solo brilliantly—until he began to speed up. "There he goes again," thought more than a few aficionados in the audience, but as the musician barreled toward the passage where the violincellos announce the second theme, *New York Times* music critic Olin Downes realized something was amiss: "After a moment it seemed as if Mr. Barere were bending over to one side, listening with special attention to the instruments as he matched his time with theirs. In another moment, his left hand fell from the keyboard and in another second he fell senseless from the stool to the floor."

Stop the music! The orchestra did. Someone onstage shouted for a doctor, and the unconscious pianist was carried offstage to a dressing room. It was decided that the show would go on. The Metropolitan's Swedish tenor Set Svanholm was rushed onstage to sing a five-song cycle.

Meanwhile, word spread that Barere was backstage, recovering from a heart attack. In reality, Simon Barere was dead before Svanholm finished his third song. Three doctors, including his personal physician, attended to the fallen pianist. They used oxygen tanks and every other device that was available, to no avail. He never regained consciousness.

After intermission, Lithgow Osborne, chairman of the board of trustees for the American-Scandinavian Foundation, stepped onto the stage and asked the audience to rise. He announced that Simon Barere had died and that all the musicians agreed they should skip the final number and end the program.

Simon Barere was fifty-five. Wrote the *Times* critic, "His end was that of a great and modest musician, one of the leading interpreters of his day and it was not inglorious. Others might wish such a thrilling exit from life, while nobly making music. Mr. Barere was indeed at the height of his art when the summons came."

Somewhat less glorious was the fact that Barere's wife, Helen, and son, Boris, were in the audience to witness his death. After the body was taken away, Barere's physician said he'd been treating the musician for high blood pressure for the past four years. Death was attributed to a cerebral hemorrhage.

Barere never got to hear his final recordings. His last studio session for Remington Records took place about a week before his death. With new, long-playing microgroove technology, it was hoped that Barere's first commercial release in fifteen years would prove that he was one of the greatest pianists in the world. Instead, it was released as a memorial album.

Frederick Federici

Frederick Federici was an opera singer whose death was played out not only on the stage but also beneath it. Born Frederick Baker in Italy in 1850, he was a British baritone who gained a reputation in the earliest performances of Gilbert and Sullivan's Savoy Operas. From 1879 to 1887, he was the very model of a modern major Gilbert and Sullivan star, touring the United Kingdom, Europe, and North America with the D'Oyly Carte Opera Company. He played, among other roles, the pirate king in the first performance of *Pirates of Penzance*, the title role in *The Mikado*, and Captain Corcoran in *H.M.S. Pinafore*. In 1887 Federici and his wife moved to Australia to join J. C. Williamson's theater company, which owned the rights to produce Gilbert and Sullivan operas and other works Down Under.

On Saturday night, March 3, 1888, Federici was at the grand Princess Theatre in Melbourne, starring as the demon Mephistopheles on opening night of Charles Gounod's opera *Faust*. The 1,488-seat house was filled to capacity. Federici put on an energetic performance that showed no signs of lagging until the fourth and final act, when the conductor noticed his voice was wavering a bit.

The maestro wrote it off to fatigue until Federici missed one of his cues, coming in a bar and a half behind the orchestra and rushing ahead to catch up. Federici continued to struggle and had to brace himself to complete his, and the opera's, final solo. He made it to his position over a trap door for the spectacular finale in which Mephistopheles carries Faust down into the smoke and fires of hell.

Jack Leumane, singing the role of Faust, knelt beside him as Federici sang the final words, "It might be." A hidden choir sang a celestial chorus, and as an overhead limelight bathed them in red, the mechanical trap began to move. The twelve-by-thirty-inch platform descended, slowly, evenly, and on a slight angle so the men appeared to be sinking directly into the stage.

Federici kept a hand on Leumane's shoulder for balance, but at that first movement of the trap, he swayed. His hand slipped off and he fell forward. Just as his shoulders cleared the floor of the stage on this dramatic descent into the underworld, Federici grabbed onto the boards. It was as if the demon had changed his mind and wanted to remain with the living. The trap continued its slow drop. Federici lost his grip and then his balance, and he tumbled off the trap, down into the darkness, taking Leumane with him.

The men dropped three feet and landed in a heap on the cellar floor. Leumane got up. Federici did not. Lights were brought over and four attendants worked to revive him from what they assumed was a fainting spell. When Federici didn't regain consciousness, they carried him to a greenroom and laid him on a mattress and pillows. Someone commented that he appeared to be dead, but a messenger was sent to fetch Federici's doctor.

When Dr. Willmott arrived, he knew what was wrong. He'd been treating Federici for heart disease and had been concerned that the five weeks of rehearsals and demands of the role might be too much for him. Federici had known as well that any performance might be his last, but he kept his condition a secret from the rest of the company. He had a small pocket sewn into each of his costumes to hold nitroglycerin pills to treat the symptoms.

The doctor detected a slight heartbeat, so in hopes of increasing it, he took out a galvanic battery to stimulate the heart with jolts of electricity. The charges were increasing when the patient died. Frederick Federici was thirty-seven, still dressed in his crimson costume and pointy shoes.

As all this commotion went on below, the rest of the cast of *Faust* was onstage, taking their bows before a rapturous cheering audience. None had any idea that Federici was dead in the greenroom. When they were told what had happened in the final moments of the opera, they were confused. How could he have died before the curtain call? They insisted they'd seen Federici onstage, taking the bows with them.

So began Frederick Federici's second act, in the afterlife. Many sightings of Federici's ghost have been reported at the Princess Theatre over the years. He's been seen in full evening dress, sitting in the dress circle late at night during dress rehearsals, and as a shimmering light moving about the theater. For many years, a third-row seat in the dress circle was kept vacant in his honor on every opening night.

Another footnote comes from the unnamed journalist who reported on the "Shocking Occurrence at the Princess's Theatre," "an astonishing and melancholy incident," for the following Monday's edition of the *Melbourne Argus*. He also wrote of other "fatal theatre events" that the Federici tragedy brought to mind:

> When the "Mystery of the Passion" was exhibited before John II of Sweden, the man who played the part of the centurion was so carried away by the reality of the scene that he drove his spear right into the body of the representative of the Redeemer, who fell dead upon the spot, crushing the person representing the Virgin Mary, who was kneeling at the foot of the cross. The King, infuriated by the spectacle, rushed upon the centurion and slew him with the sword, but the populace, siding with the victim of the Royal anger, fell upon the King and killed him.

Our research was unable to confirm that John II died in such a manner, but it seemed to be a story worth repeating.

Leonard Warren

The first time an opera singer died onstage at the Metropolitan Opera House in New York City, the audience cheered! Most everyone on the evening of February 10, 1897, believed that the popular buffo (a male opera singer in a comedic role) Armand Castelmary was pulling off the performance of his life in Friedrich von Flotow's romantic comic opera *Martha*. Dropping to his knees, clutching his hair, thudding to the boards as the curtain fell, no one realized the old ham's heart had stopped at sixty-two.

There was no such confusion at the Met when Leonard Warren sang his last on the night of March 4, 1960. It was an evening that promised to be among the most memorable in the Metropolitan Opera's entire history. A performance of Giuseppe Verdi's *La forza del destino* featured the return to the company of the prima donna soprano Renata Tebaldi, along with a superstar lineup of three of America's greatest male opera singers: the bass Jerome Hines, tenor Richard Tucker, and, most celebrated of all, baritone Leonard Warren. A full house was already buzzing before the golden damask curtain was raised, and the audience erupted in applause and cheers after each of the arias and ensembles in the first act.

Warren was singing the role of Don Carlo. He entered in the second act, joining with Tucker in the duet "Solenne in quest'ora." Witnesses said it was perfection, and it ended in a wash of bravos. Tucker stepped away, leaving Warren onstage alone to sing the recitative that begins "Morir! Tremenda cosa!" ("To die! What a tremendous thing!") and the aria whose opening words are "Urna fatale del mio destino," which translate to "Fatal urn of my destiny." Warren was never in better form as he flowed smoothly across long legato phrases and flew and spun through cadenzas leading to climactic high notes. When he was done, he simply stood quietly and waited until the applause and shouts faded.

The scene continued as Roald Reitan, playing the surgeon, strode onstage to announce that Don Alvaro, Don Carlo's fighting comrade, had been saved. Warren replied in song: "Oh gioia, oh gioia!" or "Oh joy, oh joy."

With a portrait of his character's sister in his hand, Warren turned to exit stage left. He stood at the right side of the stage next to a table set in an encampment near a battlefield. Then, the picture slipped from his hand, and Warren fell forward, as if he'd tripped. His face hit the floor. It was 9:55 PM (or 10:05 PM—more on that later).

Conductor Thomas Schippers stood with his arms outstretched, waiting for his cue to bring in the orchestra. Warren wasn't moving. For a moment, no one was quite sure what had happened. Reitan moved quickly to the tenor, knelt by his side, and raised his head. Warren groaned something that sounded like "Help." Then he went limp.

The audience only saw Reiten look desperately toward the conductor. Someone yelled, "Bring down the curtain!" As the curtain dropped, Tucker, Warren's longtime friend, rushed over, calling, "Lennie! Lennie!" Lennie didn't reply.

The Met's doctor, Adrian Zorgniotti, was in the house. He rushed onstage, did a quick examination of Warren, and called for oxygen. While a supply was fetched from the Met's first-aid room, fellow baritone Osie Hawkins and two other staffers applied mouth-to-mouth resuscitation. A call was made for an ambulance and a police emergency truck with additional oxygen. Someone else put in a call to a replacement baritone, Mario Sereni, to get over to the opera house as quickly as possible.

All this activity took place onstage, behind the curtain. In front, the Met's general manager Rudolph Bing walked out onto the stage and promised the audience that the performance would continue. A few minutes later, another staffer came on to announce an intermission until Sereni arrived.

Leonard Warren remained where he had fallen. His wife, Agathe, was by his side; she'd attended the performance and realized immediately that he hadn't tripped. Msgr. Edwin Broderick of St. Patrick's Cathedral, who'd also been in the audience, was now backstage to administer the last rites of the Roman Catholic Church (Warren was a convert).

Mrs. Warren was escorted off the stage and into a backstage office before Leonard Warren was pronounced dead at 10:28 PM. At 10:30, the house warning bells rang, and those audience members who'd left their seats—most hadn't—filed back in to the auditorium. Bing stepped out onstage once more. The news was written on his face.

Let's hold it there for a moment. There's always been controversy surrounding the details of Leonard Warren's death. The *New York Times*, the supposed newspaper of record, reported that he collapsed at 9:55 PM and that Bing announced, "This is one of the saddest nights in the history of the Metropolitan. May I ask you all to rise in memory of one of our greatest performers who died in the middle of one of his greatest performances. I am sure you will agree with me that it would not be possible to continue with the performance."

The *New York Herald Tribune*, however, reported that Warren face-planted onto the stage at 10:05 PM and that after his death, Bing announced the following to the audience: "It is one of the saddest days. I ask you to stand in tribute to one of our greatest performers: he died as I am sure he would have wanted to die. He died in the middle of a performance. I'm sure you will agree that under these circumstances we cannot possibly continue."

Which paper got it right? *Herald Tribune* reporter Sanche de Gramont (a Frenchman who'd later change his name to Ted Morgan) has the upper hand in this one. When the call came in that Leonard Warren had collapsed onstage, he ran from the paper's rewrite desk at 230 West Forty-First Street to the Met, which occupied the entire west-side block of Broadway between Thirty-Ninth and Fortieth Streets. He arrived in time to witness Bing's 10:30 announcement and got the story written and cleared in time to make the late city edition at 11:30. His work would win him a Pulitzer Prize for local reporting.

The *New York Times* article, which hit the streets the next morning, carried the byline of respected music critic Howard Taubman. Taubman was seated in the audience with his wife, Nora, when the curtain rose. He would have had a ringside seat to the entire chain of events—if he hadn't left the opera after the first act to write his review. When all hell broke loose, Howard Taubman was back at the *Times*, leaving schoolteacher Nora, a woman with no journalism experience beyond her long marriage to the critic, to observe, scribble notes, and phone her husband to give him her version of what he'd missed.

Leonard Warren had died of a cerebral vascular hemorrhage. The *Times* quoted Dr. Zorgniotti as saying, "Mr. Warren never knew what hit him." He was forty-eight—though the *Herald Tribune* reported he was forty-nine.

Leonard Warren's surprise exit marked the first and only time the Metropolitan Opera had canceled a show midperformance due to a death in the original opera house that opened on Broadway in 1883. The first death onstage at the new Metropolitan Opera House in Lincoln Center occurred on January 5, 1996, opening night for the Met's production of *The Makropulos Case*. Tenor Richard Versalle suffered a heart attack and fell from a ten-foot ladder onto his back after singing the line, "Too bad you can only live so long." He was sixty-three.

William Bennett

William Bennett lived for the oboe. He studied the woodwind instrument at Yale University and the Juilliard School and joined the San Francisco Symphony Orchestra upon graduation in 1979. He was made the symphony's principal oboist in 1987. When he wasn't playing with the San Francisco Symphony, he was performing with the Berkeley Symphony across the bay or teaching the oboe at the San Francisco Conservatory of Music.

A genial, youthful man, quick with a joke and often cracking up his fellow musicians with his caricature sketches, Bill Bennett—everyone called him Bill—was regarded as one of the best oboists in the world. The critic from the *San Francisco Chronicle* hailed the lively, unpredictable twists he'd add to the most worn-out warhorse and called the musician "an artist of extraordinary skill and imagination" with "a distinctive tone that was both full-bodied and lyrical, and a ferocious technical ability."

In 1992, Bill Bennett played the world premiere of composer John Harbison's Oboe Concerto, which had been commissioned for him by the San Francisco Symphony. He toured with the music throughout the United States and Europe and, with the orchestra, recorded the concerto for Decca Records. Bennett told a *Chronicle* writer that he hoped Harbison's concerto would "be a piece that young players would hear and say, 'That's a reason for learning this instrument,' the way the Strauss concerto was for me."

Bennett was referring to Richard Strauss's Oboe Concerto—written by the German composer in 1945 and inspired by one of the US soldiers who commandeered his home at the end of World War II—which is considered the finest oboe concerto of the twentieth century. Despite the esteem in which Bennett held the piece, it would take another twenty years before he'd get a chance to perform the difficult work with the San Francisco Symphony. The opportunity was almost denied when, in 2004, he received a devastating diagnosis of tonsil cancer. Bennett left the symphony for radiation and chemotherapy treatments. Nine months later, in the summer of 2005, he was back, and he finally got to play the Strauss Oboe Concerto with the symphony in February 2013.

The *Chronicle* critic who reviewed the performance in Davies Symphony Hall wrote that the oboist "sounded as virtuosic and forthright as ever. He sailed through the technical challenges of the opening movement, and brought limpid purity of tone to the slow movement." With reviews like that, the crowd that filled the hall on Saturday night, February 23, looked forward to Bennett's star turn with an excitement that only true fans of classical music can know.

Bill Bennett walked to his place, stood before the orchestra, and began to play. As he produced the bright, powerful sound, he began to sway. He seemed to be getting lost in the music, but it was soon clear that Bennett was unsteady. He lost his balance and began to fall—but as he did, he fell in a way that no one who saw would ever forget. As his legs gave way, Bennett raised his arm and held his treasured oboe over his head, just long enough for a violinist to swoop in and grab the instrument before he hit the floor.

There is always bound to be at least one doctor in the house at a symphony performance, and on this night, a doctor was in the front row. He rushed to the stage and attended to the musician until paramedics arrived. At the hospital, Bennett was diagnosed with a cerebral hemorrhage. He never regained consciousness but hung on until Thursday, the last day of the month. William Bennett, oboist, was fifty-six.

Reporting on Bennett's death, a blogger for WQXR, New York's classical music radio station, noted that "oboe playing is known to put pressure on the cardiovascular system, as the performer must push a great deal of air through a small double reed. But while the profession is littered with stories of dizzy spells or fainting, evidence of any deeper medical effects is spotty and inconclusive."

Interlude

The Deadliest Occupation in Show Business

Israel Yinon

The death of internationally renowned orchestra conductor Israel Yinon in January 2015 sent shockwaves through the music world. It was seen by many as inexplicable. How could such an energetic, seemingly healthy maestro die suddenly at the relatively young age of fifty-nine—in the middle of a performance?

Yinon, who happened to be an Israeli but who lived in Berlin, was known for his intensity and youthfulness. With his Peppermint Patty mop of hair, he was an enthusiastic performer, often wearing the ill-fitting jacket of a classic film comedian. He was sought the world over as a guest conductor, with a selection of material that elevated his status to that of a noble cause.

Yinon made it his specialty and mission to revive works of forgotten German composers who were banned under Adolf Hitler. Thanks to Yinon, modern audiences got to hear compositions by composers like Erwin Schulhoff, who died in a Nazi concentration camp, and Pavel Haas and Viktor Ullmann, who went to the Auschwitz gas chambers.

On Thursday evening, January 29, 2015, the globe-trotting orchestra leader was at the Lucerne University of Applied Sciences and Arts in

Switzerland, conducting the Youth Philharmonic Orchestra of Central Switzerland. The group was performing *An Alpine Symphony* by Richard Strauss. Yinon was just arriving at the point where the music reaches the mountain summit when he suddenly collapsed. People in the first row saw him tumble off the conductor's platform and hit the floor headfirst. The sound of music was replaced by the piercing screams of musicians and audience members alike.

Serious head injury now compounded whatever ailment caused Israel Yinon to drop. An audience member climbed over to try and help him, as the musicians, who included Yinon's girlfriend, left the stage. The rest of the audience was asked to leave the hall. Israel Yinon was pronounced dead in the ambulance on the way to the hospital.

The Swiss media would later point out that the title of his last concert was somewhat ironic: *The Healing Alps.*

Israel Yinon's untimely passing led almost immediately to questions about what could have killed him. One would think that the art of conducting an orchestra—standing on a raised podium, waving around a ten- to twenty-four-inch stick, setting the tempo, bringing in various instruments, and gesturing, signaling, and communicating with the musicians to shape the phrasing of a symphony—would provide hours of aerobic activity and mental stimulation and be one of the least hazardous occupations in the world.

One would be wrong. Conductors' deaths onstage have prompted health studies, warnings from experts, and, according to leading music and cultural affairs commentator Norman Lebrecht, macabre speculation among maestros "as to whether they were more likely to die in fast or slow passages." Lebrecht made the observation in April 2001, in a column in London's *Daily Telegraph* titled "Why Conducting Is a Health Hazard." He ran through the details surrounding the onstage deaths of conductors he'd counted. Most were in their fifties or sixties. Two were smokers. One was a heavy drinker. One had a genetic predisposition to heart disease. "Their peripatetic, late-night concert lives did not facilitate a low-cholesterol diet," he wrote. "There are ticks in every negative box of their health profiles." The modern conductor, who spends time waiting in airports, flying between engagements, maintaining long-distance relationships with various orchestras, and arranging recording contracts and sessions, is certainly in the high-risk group.

Lebrecht's quick study was prompted by the literal fall six days earlier of the towering, fiery, larger-than-life conductor Giuseppe Sinopoli. Sinopoli had returned to conduct at the Deutsche Opera in Berlin on April 20, 2001. It was the first time he'd set foot in the place since he stormed out in 1990, after a fight with its general director, Götz Friedrich.

After nine years of a bitter cold war, Friedrich flew to Rome to make peace, and Sinopoli agreed to conduct Verdi's *Aida* in Berlin, in the spirit of renewed friendship. After Friedrich died of cancer in December 2000, it was decided that the premiere performance would go on, only now in Friedrich's memory. With his bushy hair, beard, and rimless glasses, Sinopoli was instantly recognizable as he made his entrance, and Berlin's cultural elite greeted him with a warm ovation. It was during the third act, around 10:00 PM, that Sinopoli dropped. In the words of a financier in the second row, "He just went down like a tree." Sinopoli was pronounced dead of a heart attack at fifty-four.

Two nights later, Swiss conductor Marcello Viotti stepped in to conduct *Aida*. He dedicated his performance to the memory of Giuseppe Sinopoli. On February 9, 2005, Viotti would suffer a stroke while rehearsing with the Munich Radio Orchestra. He remained in a coma until he died a week later, on February 16. He was fifty.

Early in his career, Viotti had been assistant to conductor Giuseppe Patanè. Patanè collapsed without warning at the podium of the Bavarian State Opera in Munich on May 29, 1989, while American baritone Thomas Hampson was singing *Il barbiere di Siviglia* ("The Barber of Seville"). He was dead of a heart attack at fifty-seven. (Hampson witnessed Sinopoli's fall from the second row.)

Lebrecht counted at least nine conductors who died at work. We found more, which points to the conclusion that orchestra conducting may be the most dangerous occupation in show business:

- **Narcisse Girard** collapsed on January 17, 1860, while conducting the Orchestra de la Société des Concerts du Conservatoire at the Paris Opéra. He was sixty-two.

- **Felix Josef von Mottl** collapsed at the podium of Munich's Royal Opera House on June 21, 1911, while conducting the one hundredth performance of Wagner's *Tristan und Isolde*. He suffered a heart attack at the very moment his mistress Zdenka Fassbender, portraying Isolde, belted out the words "Death-doomed head, death-doomed heart." Mottl married her on his deathbed two days later. He passed away on July 2, at fifty-four.

- **Albert Stoessel**, a maestro from St. Louis, suffered a heart attack on the afternoon of May 12, 1943, while conducting fifteen members of the New York Philharmonic and Metropolitan Opera baritone Hugh Thompson in the American Academy of Arts and Letters auditorium in Manhattan. There was a doctor in the house, but by the time he reached Stoessel, he was already dead. He was forty-eight.

- **Gaetano Merola**, founder of the San Francisco Opera, was in failing health and had turned over many of his duties as director by August 30, 1953, when he dropped dead while conducting an excerpt from Puccini's *Madame Butterfly* at a free outdoor concert at the city's Sigmund Stern Grove amphitheater. He was seventy-two.

- Good Friday 1956 turned out to be a particularly bad Friday for **Fritz Lehmann**. The fifty-one-year-old German was conducting Bach's *St. Matthew Passion* in Munich on March 30 when he collapsed from a heart attack during the intermission.

- **Eduard van Beinum**, chief conductor at the Royal Concertgebouw in Amsterdam, was rehearsing the first two movements of Johannes Brahms's Symphony No. 1 on April 13, 1959, when he told the musicians he needed a break. Before he could leave the podium, van Beinum slid from the conductor's seat to the floor, dead of a massive heart attack at fifty-eight.

- **Jesús Arámbarri Gárate** conducted the Banda Sinfónica de Madrid outdoors in the Parque del Buen Retiro on July 11, 1960. In the second half of the concert, he had a heart attack during the overture to Daniel Auber's *Fra Diavolo*. He, too, was fifty-eight.

- **Dimitri Mitropoulos**, the Greek conductor who was Leonard Bernstein's predecessor at the New York Philharmonic (and—described as "quietly known to be homosexual"—once Bernstein's lover) died in Milan, Italy, on November 2, 1960. He was sixty-four. Mitropoulos suffered a heart attack while rehearsing Gustav Mahler's Third Symphony. Norman Lebrecht writes that the second bassoonist drew a cross in his score at the eighty-sixth bar and noted, "*In questa misura e morto il Maestro Mitropoulos.*" ("Maestro Mitropoulos made it to here and died.")
- A heart attack killed **Franz Konwitschny**, conductor of the Leipzig Gewandhaus Orchestra, on July 28, 1962, during a recording session in Belgrade, Yugoslavia. The sixty-year-old maestro was such a boozer that his nickname was "Kon-whisky."
- The curse of Wagner's *Tristan und Isolde* (divorce, deaths, wars, and bad reviews) struck again on July 20, 1968, during the same act, in the same opera house, and at the same podium where Felix von Mottl fell. **Joseph Keilberth** tumbled to the floor moments after conducting Tristan's line "Let me die, never to awake." He was fifty-nine.
- **Franco Capuana**, younger brother of mezzo-soprano Maria Capuana, was in the middle of Gioachino Rossini's *Mosè in Egitto* at the Teatro di San Carlo in Naples, when he died on the podium on December 10, 1969. He made it to seventy-five.
- **Benjamin S. Chancy**, music director of the New York City school system, conducted the All-City High School Orchestra and Choral Concert at Philharmonic Hall on May 5, 1971. He was about to walk onstage just before 9:00 PM to conduct excerpts from *Swan Lake* when a heart attack knocked him to the floor. Dr. Paul Beck, a family friend and gynecologist, rushed from the audience but failed to revive him. Chancy was sixty-two.
- **Fausto Cleva** spent twenty years as an assistant conductor at the Metropolitan Opera before making his official conducting debut in February 1942. His heart gave out in Athens on August 6, 1971, while conducting Christoph Gluck's *Orfeo ed Euridice*. He was sixty-nine.

- Polish conductor **Paul Kletzki** was in Liverpool, England, for a concert with the Liverpool Philharmonic Orchestra on the evening of March 5, 1973. While rehearsing the orchestra that afternoon, the former conductor of the Dallas Symphony dropped from a heart attack. He died that night in a hospital at age seventy-two.

- High school band conductor **Carl Barnett** died of a heart attack on April 23, 1974, while conducting at Will Rogers High School in Tulsa, Oklahoma. Carl was fifty-nine. He gets a mention because he died during Johann Sebastian Bach's *Come, Sweet Death*.

- Latvian conductor **Arvīds Jansons** collapsed while conducting the Hallé Orchestra in Manchester, England, on November 21, 1984. He was dead of a heart attack at seventy. (Arvīds Jansons's son, **Mariss Jansons**, a renowned conductor in his own right, suffered a massive heart attack at fifty-three, while leading the Oslo Philharmonic in the Oslo Concert House on April 25, 1996. He survived.)

- Dominican orchestra conductor **Billo Frómeta** suffered a stroke at the podium in Caracas, Venezuela, on April 27, 1988. He was rehearsing with the Venezuela Symphony Orchestra for a tribute concert in his honor the following day. He died on May 5, at seventy-two.

- **Jean-Marc Cochereau** was rehearsing the Orléans Symphony in Northern France on January 10, 2011, when he buckled and collapsed during the first movement of Ludwig van Beethoven's *Eroica* Symphony. His death from cardiac arrest occurred moments before he was to lead the orchestra through the "Funeral March." Cochereau was sixty-one.

- **Vincent C. LaGuardia Jr.** died of a heart attack on March 9, 2012, while conducting the Arapahoe Philharmonic's second-to-last concert of the season at Mission Hills Church in Littleton, Colorado. He was two-thirds of the way through the first number, J. S. Bach's Toccata and Fugue in D Minor, when he suddenly leaned forward and slammed face-first to the floor. Tracy LaGuardia, his wife of twenty-five years, was playing lead violin. "It happened so fast," she told the *Denver Post*. "He always said that's the way he wanted to go."

- Swiss maestro **Carl Robert Helg** took a break from orchestra and choir rehearsal at the Badisches Staatstheater in Karlsruhe, Germany, on July 23, 2011. He climbed up to a lighting catwalk, ostensibly to get a better view of the positioning of his choir on the stage. Then he fell to the stage, landing hard in front of the entire company. He was pronounced dead at a hospital. Police speculated it may have been suicide. Helg's contract was to expire at the end of the season, and insiders said that he'd suffered from severe depression.

Surely, that last scenario fits in with the health risks associated with what appears to be not only the most dangerous but the deadliest occupation in show business.

8

Rock 'n' Roll 'n' Hip-Hop

ROCK 'N' ROLL DOES NOT FEAR the Reaper. As band names like Grateful Dead, Dead Kennedys, the Dead Milkmen, Dead Boys, Slayer, Suicidal Tendencies, Suicide, the Killers, the Strokes, and of course, Death, attest, the specter rides with rock 'n' roll stars, and its constant shadow only makes them seem all the more edgy. Death and rock 'n' roll go together like rum and coke, coke and heroin, heroin and Kurt Cobain, and Kurt Cobain and guns, and the history of rock 'n' roli is littered with the debris of drug overdoses, plane crashes, beatings, shootings, car wrecks, and suicides. Deaths onstage, though? Ahhh, that's another level of immortality altogether.

"Dimebag" Darrell Abbott

From Sam Cooke, rubbed out in December 1964 by mobbed-up music moguls who wanted ownership of his songs (talk to his family), to John Lennon, shot dead in December 1980 by a programmed assassin (read Fenton Bresler's book), to Kurt Cobain, murdered in April 1994 (see Nick Broomfield's documentary), to Marvin Gaye, shot point blank on April Fool's Day 1984 by his cross-dressing preacher dad (that's simply a fact), many a rock 'n' roll star has fallen to gun violence. The majority were not onstage at the time.

Darrell Abbott just happened to be. Born in Ennis, Texas, south of Dallas, in 1966, Darrell Abbott was twelve when he learned to play a guitar and fifteen when he formed the heavy metal band Pantera with his big brother drummer, Vinnie Paul. "Diamond" Darrell was regarded as the Texas Van Halen, the hottest metal guitarist in the Dallas–Fort Worth region, even before the group's groove metal sound broke nationally in 1990. Pantera was at its peak in 1994 when he took on the moniker "Dimebag" Darrell. After Pantera broke up for all the usual rock 'n' roll reasons in 2003, Darrell and Vinnie formed a new group called Damageplan.

Damageplan's first album, *New Found Power,* was released in February 2004. The band flew to Japan for four nights of shows in Nagoya, Osaka, and Tokyo, before embarking on a grueling year of concert promotion across the United States. Whereas Pantera in its prime played arenas, the *Devastation Across the Nation* tour made stops at smaller venues and clubs.

On December 8, 2004, thirty-two dates in and two dates from the end of a tour leg that began in September, and on the twenty-fourth anniversary of the murder of John Lennon, the band arrived at the Alrosa Villa club in Columbus, Ohio. Pantera had played the club in its early days. The venue could hold 600 people; about 250 were in the club, and four warm-up bands had performed by the time Damageplan took the stage at about 10:15 PM. "We were all in a good mood and we had a full house that night and went up on the deck, and right before we went on Dime was warming up his hand and putting his lip gloss on," Vinnie Paul told *Loudwire.* "The last thing I ever said to him was 'Van Halen?' And he gives me five and says, 'Van fuckin' Halen!' That was our code word for letting it all hang out and having a good time. And that's the last thing he ever said to me, man. It's insane."

The band was a few bars into its opening song when a six-foot-five-inch former US marine named Nathan Gale emerged from behind the seven-and-a-half-foot-high wall of amps and ran across the stage with a Beretta 9 mm handgun. He stopped directly in front of Dimebag Darrell and fired three shots into the guitarist's head and one through his hand. Darrell fell forward, face-first toward the crowd.

His right leg twisted under his body; his guitar screeched feedback. Members of the crew charged the shooter, who kept firing. Nathan Gale killed three other people and injured seven others before grabbing Vinnie Paul's drum tech, John "Kat" Brooks, in a headlock and taking him hostage.

While most audience members fled, a few dragged Darrell's body off the stage and a nurse attempted CPR. Gale was backing through the club, holding a gun to Brooks's head, when police officer James Niggemeyer arrived, alone, less than three minutes after a 911 call. From twenty feet away, he took aim and blasted Gale dead with a single shot to the face from a 12-gauge shotgun. Niggemeyer later told MTV News, "I knew from that distance I could shoot the suspect, as long as I aimed high enough and wouldn't hurt the hostage. At that point, almost immediately, I fired."

Gale had thirty-five rounds of ammunition remaining when he was killed. After some witnesses said he shouted, "You broke up Pantera!" before he began shooting, he was initially written off as a disappointed fan. A police investigation, however, determined that the thirty-five-year-old Gale was a schizophrenic who believed members of Pantera were stealing his thoughts.

Dimebag Darrell Abbott was thirty-eight. The song he was playing when he died was titled "Breathing New Life."

———————————

After the death of Dimebag Darrell, the mantle of Dallas–Fort Worth heavy metal guitar hero was passed to Mike Scaccia. Brooklyn born, Scaccia formed the thrash/speed/death metal band Rigor Mortis with a pair of high school pals in 1983. Rigor Mortis became the center of the metroplex heavy metal scene and broke nationally when Capitol Records released the band's debut album five years later. Scaccia left Rigor Mortis in 1991 to work with Al Jourgensen's industrial metal band Ministry and its offshoots, Revolting Cocks and Buck Satan and the 666 Shooters. When Rigor Mortis reunited in 2003, Scaccia was again part of the lineup and divided his time between the quartet and Jourgensen's projects.

On December 22, 2012, Scaccia was onstage with Rigor Mortis at the Rail Club, Fort Worth's heavy metal mecca. It was a fiftieth birthday party for singer Bruce Corbitt, and Scaccia had the place rocking with lightning riffs and slashing chords from his Les Paul guitar. Shortly after midnight, December 23, the band was charging through its sixth number when Scaccia suddenly collapsed.

The music stopped. An ambulance was called, and Scaccia was taken to Texas Health Harris Methodist Hospital Fort Worth, where he was pronounced dead at age forty-seven.

It was originally reported that Scaccia had suffered a seizure, possibly caused by the strobe lighting at the venue, but the club owner was quick to absolve his place of any blame. He posted on his Facebook page that the strobe lights had been turned off during the first song, at the request of drummer Harden Harrison.

Rigor Mortis vocalist Corbitt used Facebook to second the story:

> Please everyone . . . I know there has been so many rumors and reasons that Mike passed away. This stuff about strobe lights is totally false. I wanted to wait for the official cause of death to be released. But I already knew when it happened. Here is the official word . . . RIP Mike Scaccia.
> SUDDEN CARDIAC DEATH Due to: ATHEROSCLEROTIC AND HYPERTENSIVE HEART DISEASE.

The Tarrant County medical examiner confirmed that death was caused by a heart attack brought on by heart disease.

Edmond Turner

Edmond Turner was one of those diehard rock 'n' rollers who was able to make the music his life without ever achieving anything close to financial success. A guitarist and composer who friends and fans compared favorably to Jimi Hendrix, he arrived in Nashville from Chicago and was a fixture on the Music City club scene since the 1980s, in bands like the Movement and Blacks on Blondes.

Edmond Turner stood out, and not only because he was a big man, and an African American in the country music capital. "Edmond was a very large man, large enough that many times white men felt intimidated by him and fights would ensue," Michael Custer, a renowned Nashville rock guitar slinger who played bass in Blacks on Blondes, recalls in a conversation with the authors. "He was a gentle giant, but he was also very brash. There was a word he used: *galoot*. Edmond was a bit of a galoot. People loved him or hated him. Always, I would say, loved and hated him with equal ferocity."

Custer is among those who loved Edmond Turner: "He really was a great guitarist. He didn't like picks, so he played straight with his fingers. I used to like to play with Edmond because he wasn't afraid of the jam. I would push him musically. I'd take a song in another direction, and he'd follow. It's hard to describe, but I was able to communicate with him. It's not easy to find someone like that, and I really haven't found it since."

By 2010, "Big Edmond" Turner had a reputation, according to Steve Haruch of the *Nashville Scene* weekly, as "a hard-living rocker, an infamous mooch and a loyal friend." Some friends of Edmond were offended by the "mooch" label, but the mention only makes Custer smile. "You can be offended by the truth. Let's just say there wasn't a couch Edmond didn't appreciate. And if you gave him drug money, he'd come back with at least a roach." Turner had also lost almost all of his belongings in a fire the previous year.

On Saturday night, September 25, 2010, the Blacks on Blondes trio, including Chris Wall on drums, had a gig at the La Hacienda Mexican restaurant in the suburb of Franklin. "We played a pretty good mix of Edmond's material and cover songs," Custer remembers. "We did some Zeppelin, some Thin Lizzy; we did some Jimi Hendrix. When we covered a song, if you were listening, you knew we owned it. But I preferred to play Edmond's originals. The power went out during our first set. They finally got it back on, and we got back onstage."

Big Edmond had friends at tables in the audience. He stopped on the way to the stage to thank his pal David for giving him a place to live after the fire. He noticed David's friend Troy and lifted him off the floor in a bear hug. Then he strapped on his Stratocaster and got back to the music with Blacks on Blondes.

"We were on our fourth or fifth song when Edmond invited this girl onstage," Custer says. "Yes, she was a blonde." Kalli Nolen would be guest vocalist on Prince's "Raspberry Beret":

> *She wore a rasp-berry beret*
> *The kind you find in a secondhand store . . .*

Somewhere in the middle of the song, Turner hit an A chord and stopped playing. Kalli turned to look at him, thinking she'd made a mistake. "Oh, no. You did fine, little sister," Turner assured her.

Those would be his last words. Edmond Turner suddenly stumbled backward, toward the amps, and slammed into the drum kit before falling back against the wall and onto the stage floor.

"He got caught on the A chord," says Custer. "I turned around and looked at him and kicked his feet and said, 'Hey man, get up.' And then I saw his face. He was smiling. His eyes were open. He wasn't there, but he was smiling. He was gone."

Another big man, Turner's musician buddy Dale Allen, had to pry Turner's fingers from neck of his Strat so he could start administering CPR. All the while, the sound of Turner's last chord continued to resonate from his amp, squealing with Hendrixian feedback.

"That A chord was still playing. It was that chord," says Custer. "We had to turn the sound down on the amp."

By the time the ambulance arrived, it was definitely too late. "Turner suffered a massive heart attack doing what he loved most," *Nashville Scene* reported. "Turner was fifty years old."

"He played his heart out," Dale Allen said. "He truthfully did."

Edmond Turner's body was cremated, and his friends scattered his ashes along Nashville's Music Row.

Michael Custer would switch from bass to a Les Paul guitar and, with Chris Wall, carry on with a new band, Creature on a Rock. But the memory of Edmond Turner's last gig at La Hacienda has never faded.

"He died doing what he loved the most, with people he loved doing it with, in the middle of doing it," Custer recalls. "And I know when

I'm in the middle of a groove and there's a crowd out there getting into it, that is my heaven. I feel Edmond experienced that heaven in his death, and I can't think of a better way to go. I don't want to die in pain, laying in a bed somewhere. If there's such a thing as a Viking death, in battle, onstage, that was a Viking death. And I think Edmond would like the idea of having a Viking death.

"He lived rock 'n' roll, and he died rock 'n' roll. I'm honored I got to play with him on his last song."

Colonel Bruce Hampton

It was another very special event at the celebrated Fox Theatre in Atlanta. The lavish Moorish palace was the place where, in 1976, the southern rock band Lynyrd Skynyrd recorded its album *One More from the Road*—the one that included the definitive version of the anthem "Free Bird"—and where, on April 14, 2016, Prince gave his last concert.

The show on May 1, 2017, would have none of the tragic implications of those historic occasions. (The Skynyrd album was the band's last before the 1977 plane crash that took the lives of two band members.) This would be a party, a birthday party for Colonel Bruce Hampton.

Colonel Bruce Hampton was a guitarist and spiritual godfather—no, make that *granddaddy*, because that's what they called him—of the American jam-band community. He was described by the *New York Times* as "the 1970s rock star who wasn't: a comic, bearish, Dadaist spieler with a deep Georgia accent, a Dali in the body of a Southern wrestler." That was a pretty apt appraisal of the man born Gustav Berglund III.

Hampton first came to attention in Atlanta in the late 1960s with the Hampton Grease Band, an eclectic, avant-garde bunch that toured with the Grateful Dead and the Allman Brothers Band. He went on to form or work with many other groups, including the Aquarium Rescue Unit, the Fiji Mariners, and the Codetalkers. In the early 1990s, he helped launch the H.O.R.D.E. Festival music tours and was credited with helping inspire improvisational jam bands, including Widespread Panic, Blues Traveler, Dave Matthews Band, and Phish.

Members of those bands and their fans convened at the Fox Theatre that Monday evening for an all-star concert celebrating Hampton's seventieth birthday the day before. *Hampton 70: A Celebration of Colonel Bruce Hampton* featured more than thirty music heavyweights, including Jimmy Herring, Chuck Leavell, Warren Haynes, Derek Trucks, Susan Tedeschi, Oliver Wood, John Popper, Jon Fishman, Mike Woods, and Peter Buck. Hollywood heavyweight Billy Bob Thornton would also bring his musical chops. He'd given Hampton a role in his 1996 film *Sling Blade*. (Hampton played the tour manager.)

The show kept throwing on more surprises and highlights, with four hours of music and unannounced guest appearances. At the end, many of Hampton's acolytes joined him for an encore jam on the song "Turn On Your Love Light."

Hampton growled out the first part of the song, and then, as various stars soloed, he paced the stage theatrically and teased the audience by pretending to make his exit, only to return, to their delight, James Brown–like.

The guitar heroes traded solos. Then it was Brandon "Taz" Niederauer's turn. He was a fourteen-year-old blues guitar prodigy, and he was whipping out a searing guitar solo when Hampton walked back onstage. The colonel was blown away—as was everyone else in the place—by Taz's skill, and he dropped to his knees, and then to the stage floor, in front of the young axman. The theater resounded with cheers. It appeared that the showman was really hamming it up.

Taz, though, could tell something wasn't right. The old man, sprawled with one arm over a speaker, wasn't moving. Taz continued to play while shooting glances to the adults crammed onstage, looking for help. John Popper of Blues Traveler was unaware. He stood behind Hampton and wailed on his harmonica. The fans danced wildly. Everybody grooved, and the jam went on for several minutes, waiting for the birthday boy to get up.

When he didn't, somebody checked and realized Colonel Bruce was having some kind of medical emergency. The music came to a clanging halt. The fans stopped dancing and looked to each other in confusion. What happened?

Billy Bob Thornton made the announcement: "We're going to take care of business backstage here. Thank you so much. We love you so much. Thanks for honoring Bruce Hampton on his seventieth."

The stage was cleared. The curtains were drawn. An ambulance arrived to take Colonel Bruce away to Emory University Hospital, where he was pronounced dead. A statement issued by former Allman Brothers guitarist Haynes confirmed that "after collapsing on stage surrounded by his friends, family, fans and the people he loved, Col. Bruce Hampton has passed away."

Former bandmate Jeff Mosier posted a tearful video on Facebook in which he said, "Bruce looked like he was jokingly worshipping that young guitar player. And he got down on his knees and I was getting ready to do the same thing. . . . I've dreaded this day for years, but could have never imagined a more joyful departure."

Leavell, who played keyboards with the Allman Brothers Band and toured with the Rolling Stones, observed that Colonel Bruce Hampton died doing what he loved: "A poetic exit. I'm sure if he had written the script himself, that would've been the last page of the last chapter."

Nick Menza

What better place for a wild, extreme, heavy metal drummer to beat his last skin than in a cozy jazz club? The club was the Baked Potato, a cool little spot in Studio City, California, just down the street from Universal Studios. The jazz promised to be a little less cool and a lot more explosive on May 21, 2016, when a trio of heavy metal legends took over the Baked Potato's small stage.

OHM was a progressive jazz rock fusion group led by guitarist Chris Poland, who twenty years earlier was headbanging with thrash metal band Megadeth. Bassist Robertino Pagliari had held the bottom for metalists Divine Rite. Between them, wielding sticks behind an extravagant orange drum kit that took up most of the stage, was the heaviest metal legend of the group. Nick Menza had joined Megadeth in 1989, two years after Poland's departure. He pounded the beats on Megadeth's most successful albums, including *Rust in Peace* and *Countdown to*

Extinction, and was with the band for eight years, until he was sidelined by a benign tumor on his knee and ultimately given the boot.

Promotion of his subsequent solo album, *Life After Deth*, hit a speed bump in 2003 when guitarist Ty Longley set out on tour with the reformed Great White—and was killed in the Station nightclub fire in Rhode Island. A year later, Menza's bassist Jason Levin died of heart failure.

Menza had his own close calls. In 2007, he almost lost an arm in a gruesome run-in with a rusty power saw. He recovered and auctioned off the bloody saw blade and X-ray to a lucky fan. When he joined OHM in 2015, he was the sixth sticksman to occupy the throne, replacing David Eagle, who died that August after a heart attack and open heart surgery. (Menza was the *seventh* drummer if you count Gar Samuelson, who was to be the third piece in the original lineup when he died of liver failure at forty-one.) With enough death and mayhem in his past to fill a book, Menza decided to do just that: he was planning to fly to Cape Cod, Massachusetts, after the Baked Potato gig to finish a comic book version of his autobiography, *Menza-Life* (ultimately released as *Megalife*).

While some fans thought it strange that the power drummer wound up playing in a tasteful jazz club, the music of OHM was not a far cry from the jazz that Menza's German-born father Don Menza played in his years blowing tenor sax in the *Tonight Show* band. Though the Baked Potato had been a jamming room for many *Tonight Show* musicians before the show was moved back to New York City in 2014, it also made room for outfits like OHM that played a fiery, precise, Jeff Beckian jazz rock, full of blazing solos and tricky time signatures.

On the night of May 21, Chris Poland recalled, Nick Menza played with an intensity "like I'd never heard before. It's not the volume intensity; it's just how intense he was playing it," he said on the podcast *As the Story Grows*. "He had a fire under his butt. It was the best I've ever heard him play drums.

"We get to the end of the first song, and I look at him like, 'What is going on with you?' He just laughed. We get to the end of the second song, and I'm sweaty already. Normally I'm not sweating until the fourth song. I got sweat dripping off my nose, and he's still laughing. We get to the end of the third song, which I think was 'Peanut Buddha,' and . . . my guitar, where the right arm is hitting the body, is all wet. I'm drying myself off, and he goes, 'Dude, are you OK?' I go, 'No, I'm good.'

"He tightened his high hat, and he sat his hands down on his lap, and then he just leaned over into the monitor. I thought he was fucking with me. He's still there, and I said, 'Hey, man, let's go.' I thought, 'Of course he's messing with me.' I said, 'Nick, come on, man.' I look over, and his eyes are open. That's when I knew that something had happened. I couldn't believe it."

The problem looked at first to be a seizure. Two patrons rushed to the stage and began CPR until EMS arrived. The paramedics worked on the drummer for more than twenty-five minutes. They gave him shots of adrenaline, three shocks, and nonstop chest compressions.

None did any good. Nick Menza was gone at the Baked Potato and pronounced dead on arrival at the hospital. He was fifty-one. The Los Angeles County Coroner would rule that Menza died of natural causes: a heart attack as a result of hypertensive and atherosclerotic cardiovascular disease. In the days to follow, his manager Robert Bolger said that friends and family took some comfort knowing that on several occasions Nick Menza said that when he died he wanted to do so onstage.

Goodbye to Gravity

After the Station fire, you might think rock 'n' rollers and the nightclub owners who book them would have learned their lesson. The Station was a nightclub in West Warwick, Rhode Island. On February 20, 2003, 452 people entered through the front door for a show by Jack Russell's Great White, a quintet fronted by the former lead singer of the 1980s hair band Great White. Four hundred and fifty-two heads is not a turnout a former MTV star would usually crow about, but the number included fifty-eight more heads and bodies than the fire regulations allowed. The joint was packed.

The band was only moments into the show when its tour manager lit the pyrotechnics: three gerbs, thick cylindrical tubes that set off a fifteen-second spray of sparks. The sparks shot out, high over the heads of the band members, toward the walls and ceilings. As soon as the spray subsided, it was clear there were flames on the ceiling and the walls on either side of the stage, burning through the polyurethane foam acoustical padding. Within minutes, the club was engulfed in fire and thick, choking black smoke.

Almost everyone ran toward the same front door they'd entered. In the words of firefighter Fred Bricker of the Coventry Fire Department, "You could see people laying at the door, stacked up like a cord of wood, arms hanging over the pile."

A hundred people died, including Ty Longley, the thirty-one-year-old guitarist for Jack Russell's Great White. As the fire spread, Longley reportedly had run from the stage and used his guitar to smash out windows, allowing at least three other people to escape. He was the only band casualty. (Despite the black cloud that still hovers over the Great White brand, Jack Russell continued to tour into 2019 with a new lineup of Jack Russell's Great White.)

———————

In the wake of the worldwide outrage over the Station nightclub fire, it would seem obvious that no one in his right mind would ever use flames or spark-shooting pyrotechnics in a crowded, indoor, low-ceiling venue. Not quite. In the years following the Station nightclub fire, there have been a number of similar tragedies that have claimed the lives of hundreds of music fans. One of the horrors stands out, for reasons that will become obvious.

The free concert at the Club Colectiv in Bucharest, Romania, on October 30, 2015, was a homecoming and celebration. The metalcore band Goodbye to Gravity was back home after conquering Europe, celebrating the release that very day of its second album.

The five heavy metalists had first joined forces in 2010, when singer Andrei Gălut, winner of Prima TV's *Megastar* competition series (Romania's version of *American Idol*), pulled together a backing band by plucking members of the popular Bucharest metal group Thunderstorm. The self-titled album *Goodbye to Gravity*, their first, was well received by hardcore metal fans. In its review, the German website Metal proclaimed that "every note played and every note sung . . . clearly demonstrates why Goodbye to Gravity can effortlessly play in the upper league." Tours across Europe followed, and there were music festivals in Germany, Portugal, and Italy.

In 2015, the band got down to recording its second album. *Mantras of War* was released on October 30, and that was the reason four hundred fans jammed into the Club Colectiv, a venue in the basement of a building that was a factory during the Communist era.

The band took the stage and led off with the first song from the new album. It was a blast of fast tempos, precision riffing, and growling, razor-gargling vocals. Lights flashed and pyrotechnic gerbs attached to metal trusses at the sides of the stage spewed a vomit of sparks toward the crowd and ceiling.

That burst of hazardous theatricality went off without a hitch. At about 11:00 PM, when Goodbye to Gravity was in the middle of its set, the firework candles belched out another spray of hot sparks. This time, some sparks caught on the polystyrene foam soundproofing wrapped around a pillar that supported the club's ceiling.

Delia Tugui, a Spanish teacher who was in the audience, described on her Facebook page what happened after the sparks turned to flames: "The lead singer made a quick joke: 'This wasn't part of the program.' The next second, he realized it wasn't a joke and asked for a fire extinguisher. In 30 seconds . . . the fire spread all over the ceiling."

The flames whipped through the club, and toxic smoke filled the space. The fans stampeded toward the exit—the one door, the only exit. It was too narrow for everyone to fit through at once. People climbed on top of each other, over each other, in an attempt to escape.

Sixty-four people died inside the Club Colectiv that night. Another 173 were injured. It was another terrible rock 'n' roll tragedy, but one with an important distinction that separated it from others, including the Station nightclub fire. Here, the victims included multiple members of the band, who died onstage.

Guitarists Vlad Telea and Mihai Alexandru fell dead where they played. Bassist Alex Pascu and drummer Bogdan Enache (known to fans as Bogdan Lavinius) were carried offstage but died in the hospital.

Goodbye to Gravity's sole survivor was its lead singer, Andrei Gălut. He did not escape unscathed—far from it. He was seriously injured, with burns over forty-five percent of his body, and internal damage from inhaling the toxic smoke. He'd spend more than a year of treatment in hospitals and clinics in the Netherlands and Germany.

When he finally made it home in February 2017, Gălut announced that he wanted to resume his career and rebuild Goodbye to Gravity. Close to two years later, he was still struggling to recover.

There is one footnote to the story, a detail that may have been overlooked. The first song on the album that was released on that fateful day, and the song that opened Goodbye to Gravity's final show that evening, was entitled "The Day We Die."

It was water not fire on December 22, 2018, when three of four members of the Indonesian pop group Seventeen died in the middle of a show. The band was playing an outdoor concert before a large crowd at the Tanjung Lesung beach resort in Java when their stage was swept away by a giant, unexpected tsunami. As was the case with Goodbye to Gravity, the band's lead singer survived.

Jax the Axehandler

Dianna Theadora Kenny, professor of psychology and music at the University of Sydney, conducted a study in 2015 on the connection between musical genre and the life expectancy of musicians. She found that the leading cause of death among rap and hip-hop artists is homicide. (Cancer and heart ailments are the main causes of death among blues, jazz, country, gospel, R&B, folk, pop, and world electronic musicians—and even rock musicians. Punk and heavy metal? Accidents. Go figure.)

Despite Professor Kenny's conclusions, the chances of a rap artist dying *onstage*, be it by violence or natural causes, are far less than for artists of other musical genres. In fact, a rapper stepping onto a stage in a smoke-filled warehouse without metal detectors at the door and an audience full of warring gang members has less of a chance of going belly up than he would if he stepped up onto a podium in an orchestra pit.

That makes the case of Jax the Axehandler, of Atlanta's indie hip-hop crew Binkis Recs, all the more intriguing. "Binkis Recs was created due to the lack of creative and honest hip-hop music"—so claimed the mission statement from the trio of rappers consisting of Killa Kalm, Flux da Wondabat, and Jax. The group emerged during the city's indie-rap renaissance of the late 1990s and helped launch the career of DJ Drama, who provided their backup beats before breaking out nationally with his *Gangsta Grillz* mixtape series and album. In the decade to follow, Binkis Recs were considered legends on Atlanta's underground hip-hop scene, acclaimed for their thick beats, flash rhymes, and old-school authenticity.

The magic was on display on Monday night, November 3, 2008, at Lenny's Bar, a strip-mall dive known as "the CBGB of Atlanta." A few minutes after midnight, November 4, Jax was onstage, spitting out the lyrics of his signature rap:

> *I grew up in Queens, been saggin' my jeans!*
> *People always wanna know just what Binkis means.*
> *"Before Ignorant Niggas Killed Intelligent Songs."*
> *But hold on, it won't be that for long . . .*

Jax raised a hand. "Hold up, hold up, hold—" Midlyric, he dropped more than the mic, collapsing in a saggy-jeaned heap to the floor. Folks at Lenny's got him to a hospital as quickly as they could that Tuesday morning, but Jax was dead.

What killed him? An assassin's bullet shot from a rival crew? Was he caught in an early morning robbery? A drive-by? Was it simply a case of senseless rap violence? The Fulton County Medical Examiner made the announcement the following day: Jax, born Christopher Charles Thurston, died of "natural causes due to hypertension." He was thirty-two.

Nick Lowe

It's long been accepted that the first rock 'n' roll star to die onstage via electrocution was Les Harvey, lead guitarist for the Scottish rock band Stone the Crows. The date was May 3, 1972. There were twelve hundred people in the Top Rank ballroom in damp Swansea, Wales. Harvey was onstage, tuning his black Gibson Les Paul, when he grabbed a microphone and was zapped into membership in the "27 Club"—the least famous among the group of pop stars who died at age twenty-seven but the only one, so far, to have died onstage. Whether he was standing in a puddle from the rains outside or had damp hands because he'd just quaffed a beer when he handled the improperly grounded mic is still subject to debate.

The actual "honors," however, go to British musician and producer Nick Lowe, who was shocked to death onstage in London three years earlier, on July 6, 1969. That was the night his band Brinsley Schwarz opened for Yes at the Marquee Club in Soho, the night after the Rolling Stones had played a free concert in Hyde Park in memory of their recently fired guitarist Brian Jones, who'd drowned in his swimming pool two days earlier.

"Anyway, the P.A. had been in the shop, and they'd somehow connected up the plugs the wrong way," Lowe told *Musician* magazine editor Vic Garbarini years later. He continued:

> We finished the number "Chest Fever," and the place went wild. I went up to the mike to say something, and I had one hand on the guitar and one hand on the mike, and I got this violent electric shock, but it was one of those where you can't let go! And I was literally flung about eight feet across the stage and went crashing into the back of those amps. I remember lying on the stage, unable to let go, shaking like a doll . . . but my mind was very clear, and it was like this person was talking to me, saying, "God, you've got a nasty electric shock here, Basher. . . . I'm afraid you're going to die any second now." . . .
>
> Meanwhile, there were people screaming and fainting and leaping up and down. The thing is, they couldn't turn the power off because those huge stacks of Marshalls were blocking the way to the power point. I was lying with the mike across my

chest and the bass in my hand, jerking like a puppet, and no one would grab them or touch me because of the current. So [keyboard player] Bob Andrews ran up and tried to kick the thing out of my hand, to break the circuit. But in doing so, he kicked me really hard in the ribs . . . which doctors later told me got my heart going again!

Lowe was taken to Middlesex Hospital with severely burned hands but "was so grooving on being alive" that he sneaked out and walked to the pub across the street from the Marquee, where his bandmates were "hideously drunk."

"I walked in and they freaked, 'cause they really thought I'd died," he said. In fact, Nick Lowe had died at twenty and been brought back to life. The boys all went back to the Marquee to play the second set.

9

Country & Gospel Music

ON JULY 11, 1975, FRAGILE country music star Barbara Jean starred at a political rally for independent presidential candidate Hal Phillip Walker on the steps of the Parthenon, the full-scale replica of the Athens temple in Nashville's Centennial Park. Dressed in a flowing white chiffon gown, Barbara Jean had just sung her classic hit "My Idaho Home," and while the crowd cheered, rhinestone legend Haven Hamilton strode onstage holding aloft a bouquet of flowers. At the moment he joined Barbara Jean at the microphone, a loner identified as Kenny Frasier, standing in the audience about ten feet from the stage, opened a violin case, removed a revolver, pointed it toward the stage, and fired four shots.

The first bullet slammed into Barbara Jean's chest and knocked her onto her back, killing her. Hamilton was hit in the left shoulder but survived.

The killing of "Nashville's sweetheart" was the climactic scene in Robert Altman's film *Nashville*. Ronee Blakley scored an Oscar nomination for her role as Barbara Jean (inspired by Loretta Lynn, although originally based on Lynn Anderson, the role was to be played by Susan Anspach). Henry Gibson played the Roy Acuff stand-in, Haven Hamilton.

Yes, it was all just playacting, but the film and its shocking finale brought together many constants of country music: poverty, family values, mental illness, sexism, patriotism, right-wing politics, guns, Nudie suits—and tragedy. Untimely deaths, hours after performing or on the way to a show, are benchmarks in country music history, and primary in the legacies of the first two performers inducted into the Country Music Hall of Fame when it was created in 1961.

Tuberculosis derailed Jimmie Rodgers's career as a brakeman for the New Orleans and Northeastern Railroad and helped push him full-time into the music business in 1924. The Singing Brakeman became country music's premier yodeler and its first superstar—though he never did kick that TB. When he arrived in New York City on May 17, 1933, to record at RCA Victor Studios, the disease had him so weak that he was forced to sit down to sing and rest on a cot between takes. He died on May 26, thirty-six hours after his final session, hacking out a lung hemorrhage in his room at the Taft Hotel. He was thirty-five.

Country's greatest star, Hank Williams, was known for his reckless lifestyle, alcoholism, and pill-popping long before he died in the backseat of his baby blue 1952 Cadillac convertible on New Year's Day 1953, while a seventeen-year-old college kid was driving him to his next gig at the Palace Theatre in Canton, Ohio. Chloral hydrate, alcohol, and two shots of vitamin B12 that contained a quarter-grain of morphine were in his system when his heart gave out. He made it to twenty-nine.

Patsy Cline died in a plane crash. Ira Louvin went in a car wreck. Western swing star and convicted wife killer Spade Cooley was on furlough from a prison hospital when he died backstage after fiddling for a crowd of deputy sheriffs. *Grand Ole Opry* and *Hee Haw* star Stringbean and his wife were murdered by a pair of halfwit cousins who believed rumors the banjo-playing comedian had millions stashed away in his cabin. (Twenty-three years later, $20,000 in cash was found stuffed behind a chimney brick.) Conway Twitty's gut busted on his tour bus, rolling through the Ozarks. Mindy McCready shot herself and her dog, but not in that order.

Yet a death onstage to rival Barbara Jean's? There was but one.

Onie Wheeler

The six-foot circle of wood that makes up center stage of the Grand Ole Opry House is sacred wood, removed from the historic Ryman Auditorium when the weekly *Grand Ole Opry* country music concert show moved from 116 Fifth Avenue North in Nashville to the Opryland amusement park in the suburbs in 1974. This sacred circle is ground zero not only of the tradition that was founded in 1925 but also of the genre itself.

Virtually every star of country music, from Hank Williams to Patsy Cline, George Jones to Brad Paisley, has stood at the microphone at the center of the Circle. Only one country music star died there.

His name was Onie Wheeler, and he was born on a farm in Senath, Missouri, on November 10, 1920. His daddy grew cotton. Onie learned to play guitar and harmonica when he was just a boy, but he didn't perform until he joined the US Army. He enlisted at age eighteen and spent five years in uniform. Onie was stationed at Schofield Barracks on Oahu, in the line of fire when Pearl Harbor was attacked, and fought in the Guadalcanal campaign. He also won several talent contests, playing and singing. When he injured the index finger on his left hand, he just tuned the guitar to an open C so he could make chords by barring all the strings with one finger.

After the war, Onie returned to Missouri and got his first taste of the music business when he got his own show on KWOC radio in Poplar Bluff. That's where he met Little Jean, a teenage gal who had her own radio show. Onie married Little Jean when she was seventeen, and they'd have two children. Onie's radio career would take him to KBTM in Jonesboro, Arkansas, and stations in Michigan and Kentucky.

He formed his own band in 1950; Onie Wheeler and the Lonesome Ozark Cowboys were all Missouri boys. A. J. Nelson played lead guitar and sang baritone. His brother Doyle Nelson played rhythm guitar and sang high tenor. Ernie Thompson was on drums. The quartet traveled to Nashville in 1953 to record four sides for Okeh/Columbia Records. None of the songs was a hit, but Lefty Frizzell took one of Onie's compositions, "Run 'Em Off," and took it to the Top Ten. Onie's career as a songwriter was underway.

Two years later, Onie was recording solo for Columbia. During this period, he moved into country boogie, music that was distinguished by his deep voice, distinctive harmonica, and rhythmic bass. For a time, he toured with young Elvis Presley; Onie got top billing. He and Elvis became fast friends, and any time Onie showed up at Graceland, the big gates would swing open to let him in.

"Onie's Bop," his rocking single from 1956, was so close in spirit to Elvis's early recordings that it was natural when Onie signed to Elvis's first label, Sun Records in Memphis, in 1959. Onie toured with the other members of the Million Dollar Quartet—Johnny Cash, Jerry Lee Lewis, and Carl Perkins. He turned out some impressive rockabilly but didn't reach the heights of the others.

For a time, Onie moved his family to Venice, California, where he wrote songs that were covered by stars like George Jones, Flatt and Scruggs, and Little Jimmie Dickens. He returned to Nashville, and in 1964 joined Roy Acuff and His Smoky Mountain Boys as harmonica player. He recorded for a number of labels and was in demand as a session player with his harmonica. He finally had his first and only hit record in 1973. "John's Been Shucking My Corn" made it to number 53 on the *Billboard* country chart.

By then, Onie was best known among *Grand Ole Opry* fans as the first performer to use his mouth to produce the train whistle sounds during "Wabash Cannonball." "*Whooooooooot!*" "All aboard!" It sounded like the real thing, from deep in his throat, and always got a cheer.

In the late 1970s and into the '80s, Onie Wheeler owned a guitar repair shop in Nashville. He continued to perform with Roy Acuff at the Grand Ole Opry, and everything was going well, until 1984.

That February, he had surgery for a stomach aneurysm and spent weeks recovering. During this time, he wrote and recorded some gospel numbers with A. J. and Doyle Nelson, the brothers who'd played with him from the start. When Onie was well enough to rejoin Roy Acuff at the Opry, he wasn't allowed to imitate the train whistle, because it required too many stomach muscles. Roy did allow Onie to come up and play the harmonica.

So Onie Wheeler was looking forward to Friday, May 25. Memorial Day weekend always means big business at Opryland, but the holiday that kicked off on that Friday was even more special for Onie. He'd perform as usual that evening with Roy Acuff, but after the show, he'd return to the stage with the Nelson brothers to sing with a cavalcade of Opry performers in the taping of a gospel television special.

They'd rehearsed that Thursday at Onie's daughter's house. Karen Wheeler was a country music star herself. She'd gotten her first contract with Columbia Records when she was fifteen. Usually, she'd come to the Opry to watch Daddy perform, but Friday was her daughter's birthday, and she had to attend to the party.

After Roy Acuff's Opry show had ended, about fifteen hundred people remained in the forty-four-hundred-seat theater for Rev. Jimmie Snow's *Grand Ole Gospel Time*. The taping got under way close to midnight. Sometime around then, Onie Wheeler was standing at the microphone, in that circle, on the holy wood from the Ryman, the Nelson brothers beside him, singing his gospel tune "Mother Rang the Dinner Bell and Sang."

Suddenly, Onie stopped, stricken. He fell forward onto the stage and landed on his face, flat down dead, dead of a heart attack, dead center in the Circle. Rev. Jimmie Snow called for the Opry curtain to be drawn. A nurse who was in the audience jumped onto the stage and attempted CPR, but there was nothing to do.

So what did the Grand Ole Opry performers do? They stood along the perimeter of the Circle and joined hands to form a prayer circle. They prayed in a prayer circle around the Opry Circle over Onie Wheeler. When the ambulance came to take Onie to Memorial Hospital, Rev. Jimmie led the crowd in prayer.

Back at home, Karen Wheeler's phone rang around 12:30 AM. Karen tells us, "We were gonna have some friends over, and I got a call from Mama, and she said, 'Your dad has collapsed onstage.'" Karen and her mother arrived together at the hospital in Madison. No one told them that the doctors had set Onie Wheeler's official time of death at 12:59 AM on May 26. No one told them that Onie was dead at sixty-two.

"We got inside the hospital," says Karen, "and they came up to me and said, 'Are you Mrs. Wheeler?' and Mama said, 'No, *I'm* Mrs. Wheeler.' And the nurse started giving us his things. Mama said, 'What are you giving us his things for?' We thought everything was OK. I said, 'Where is A. J. and Doyle Nelson?' She said, 'In that waiting room.'

"And we walked in the waiting room, and A. J. said, 'He didn't make it.' I just crumbled, and Mama was just a mess."

———————

Back in Opryland, longtime announcer Grant Turner was clearly shaken. "This is the first time this has happened," he told the reporter from the *Tennessean* on Saturday night. "I can't recall ever having a death on the Opry stage before."

Among the stars who spoke of Onie Wheeler was Boxcar Willie, an Opry member who was backstage when his colleague fell. "A deejay friend of mine was waiting to interview him when he came offstage. That's how I had first gotten to know him, when I was a disc jockey," said the man born Lecil Travis Martin, who'd hit it big singing in the guise of a classic train-hopping hobo. "I used to play his records. A lot. Onie was a great showman. He could make that harmonica talk. He'll be missed here at the Opry by everybody."

The most lavish praise came from Onie's boss, Roy Acuff, "the King of Country Music," and the model for Henry Gibson's Haven Hamilton in the movie *Nashville*. "Onie Wheeler was a man of very fine morals. Excellent. I don't know of anyone else at the Opry finer," he said. "He was a real gentleman. Onie was an individual. He had such a fine singing voice, wrote such good songs and was such a good player. That's why I hired him. I've recorded several of his songs myself."

———————

"It haunted A. J. Nelson," Karen Wheeler reveals. "He said, 'I started with Onie, and it'll end with Onie.' He never picked up a guitar again."

A couple of months after Onie's funeral, Roy Acuff convinced Karen to come onstage at the Opry and blow that train whistle the way her daddy taught her. "I couldn't hardly do it," she says. "But I blew the train whistle because Daddy had asked me to blow it. I was mad at Roy Acuff for making me do that, but later he said, 'I know you're mad at me, but I had to find some way to get you on that stage, because your daddy died there and it's not right that you avoid the Opry.' And I couldn't go by the Grand Ole Opry without hating it, because I remember that my dad died onstage in that very building."

In 2017, thirty-three years after the death of her father in the Circle onstage at the Grand Ole Opry, Karen Wheeler pulled out a cassette tape she'd been holding for decades but had never played. "I've got a tape of him that night and his last breath. It took me thirty-three years to listen to that, but I listened to it. He was trying to sing the words as he was falling and tried to mumble out the words, but he was gone. He was gone when he started falling. I cried because it had his last breath on it.

"I admire that he was doing something that he loved," she says, "but death is death."

Shawn Jones

Shawn Jones believed in miracles. He saw his own life as proof they existed and spread that word across the country. In the end, though, he didn't have a prayer.

The handsome thirty-two-year-old pastor of New Thing Empowerment Church in Auburn, Alabama, was known throughout the South as leader of the black gospel quartet Shawn Jones & the Believers. Deep into the old-fashioned, foot-stomping, hand-raised-to-heaven, make-me-wanna-shout school, Jones was a little bit Rev. Al Green and a little bit Sam Cooke (in fact, one of his popular songs, "You Saved Me," was simply a rewrite of Cooke's secular "You Send Me").

On the evening of Saturday, November 18, 2017, Jones & the Believers were raising the roof at the Event Center in Pensacola, Florida. The auditorium-sized room was popular for banquets, weddings, and school reunions. The stage at one end, three steps up from the dance floor, was the perfect platform for Jones to get the audience up, singing and clapping along.

Looking smart in his shiny brown suit and designer glasses, he started strong with the hand-clapping "Me, My God and I." The three dudes who completed his quartet moved in step behind him, the five-piece band chugged along, and Jones growled, howled, and praised, bringing the crowd to its feet and their hands in the air as the song built to a close:

> *Everybody that's saved, let me hear ya holler one time!*
> *Hallelujah! God is good . . .*

Then he led into "Return No More," a song about the afterlife and his desire to leave this world for one in which he "won't have to deal with heart attacks and strokes, and sugar diabetes, high blood pressure." Sexy, soulful, and stirring, Jones stood at the edge of the stage, removed his glasses and wiped the sweat from his face. Less than fifteen minutes into the show, he'd transported his audience out of the big, echoey hall into something intimate, hot, and holy.

"They were doing a fantastic job. It was a nice show," the center's manager Kenneth Woodson told the *Christian Post*. "This fellow was blowing. It had a little jazzy feel to it and this was my first time hearing him, but I was very impressed. I said, 'Wow, this is gonna be nice. I can't wait to hear some more music from this guy and his band.' They were tight."

Shawn Jones was nothing if not a showman. He kicked right into "Worthy Is He," a guaranteed showstopper in which he'd testify, half-sing and half-preach—with more than a little risque humor. "You got folks coming out the closet, you got men loving men, you got women loving women, so I might as well come out of the closet tonight!" he preached. "*I'm in love with a man! I'm in love with a man!* Every night, my wife sleep between two men! And I tell you, if I had to kick some-body out the bed, sure wouldn't be my man!"

There were shouts and whoops and more than a few shrieks of shock. "Ain't no use in you all you lookin' at me funny tonight, because the clothes you got on, my man bought 'em! The car you drove tonight, my man paid for it! Ain't nobody but Jesus! Ain't nobody but Jesus!"

The Lord giveth. Shawn Jones took off his designer glasses once more and wiped his dripping face with a silk handkerchief. He took a sip of water, and collapsed.

The Lord taketh away. "I guess the young man got hot," Woodson said. "He took some water and he drank some more water, sat down and was speaking and he passed out. Everyone went into shock. It was a shock because he is a young man. They contained themselves well and they were praying for him in their own little spirit. They took him to the back and were trying to revive him but then, of course, the sorrow was in the building. There were several medical people in the building and they tried to revive him. They tried to do what they could for him before the EMT got there."

The entire gospel community was shocked when it was reported that Shawn Jones had died of a heart failure caused by a blood clot. Those closest to him shouldn't have been surprised at all. He'd been having heart trouble for more than a year. His most recent hospitalization was a month earlier, and, despite doctors' warnings, he was back performing two days later.

The most startling warning was recorded before an audience in the summer of 2016, when Jones testified during a song at a revival in Alexander City, Alabama. As the band kept the beat, he told the crowd that he'd recently suffered a "light stroke" onstage in Baltimore but refused medical treatment for three days. He'd believed the attack was from the devil and that he could fight the devil by thinking about the song he was singing.

That song was "Worthy Is He," the same one he was performing when he collapsed and died. *The Lord works in mysterious ways.*

Interlude

The Long Goodbyes

Jackie Wilson

Cherry Hill, New Jersey, is in the southern part of the state, a suburb of Philadelphia, Pennsylvania, across the Delaware River. In the movie *Harold & Kumar Go to White Castle*, the White Castle hamburger restaurant Harold and Kumar eventually descend upon is located in Cherry Hill. In reality, Cherry Hill has no White Castle, but for years it was home to a swank Las Vegas-style nightclub called the Latin Casino.

Opened in 1960 on Route 70 after a dozen years in downtown Philly, the Latin Casino wasn't particularly Latin, and it didn't feature gambling, but it did offer top performers and big stars, from Liberace to Frank Sinatra, the Four Seasons to James Brown. The place could accommodate upward of two thousand people for dinner and a show at long banquet tables in its curved, "plush cavern" showroom. Between New York and Miami Beach, there was nothing like the Latin Casino. South Jersey's "Showplace of the Stars" was one of the classiest joints on the East Coast, and only the Copacabana in New York City could boast more zing.

On Monday, September 29, 1975, rock 'n' roll rolled into the Latin Casino for a weeklong engagement. *Dick Clark's Good Ol' Rock and Roll Revue* was a package of oldies acts, including Jackie Wilson, Cornell Gunter's Coasters, and Dion DiMucci, formerly of Dion and the

Belmonts, accompanied by old film footage from the glory days of Clark's *American Bandstand*.

This was a homecoming of sorts for Dick Clark. His career as a rock 'n' roll star-maker and world's oldest teenager took off in Philadelphia, when, in 1956, the ambitious radio deejay took over as host of *Bandstand*, the local afternoon rock 'n' roll dance show, on WFIL-TV, and remained with the show when it went national on ABC a year later as *American Bandstand*.

Clark had cooked up the multimedia oldies show in 1973 for a run in Las Vegas, after that summer's release of the movies *Let the Good Times Roll* and *American Graffiti* launched an oldies boom. As his gang of yesterstars arrived at the Latin Casino, 1950s nostalgia was already showing its age. Fewer than 250 people turned out for the first of two shows that opening night.

Dick Clark was emcee and presented his clips. Cornell Gunter, who'd replaced lead tenor Leon Hughes in the Coasters in 1957, got everyone going with comic flamboyance in the Little Richard vein, leading one of several competing yakety-yakking Coasters lineups working the decade. Dion sang his hits "Runaround Sue," "Ruby Baby," and his post-doo-wop stab at social relevance, "Abraham, Martin and John."

And then the headliner burst onto the stage. Jackie Wilson was the showstopper, a soulful R&B singer with a four-octave operatic range and dramatic stage moves that rivaled James Brown's and inspired Michael Jackson's. The critic for the *Philadelphia Inquirer* noted that his performance in that evening's early show was fast-paced and physical as it built to the finale: his 1958 hit "Lonely Teardrops":

> *My heart is crying, crying*
> *Lonely teardrops.*
> *My pillow's never dry of lonely teardrops!*

They called Jackie Wilson the Black Elvis and they called him Mr. Excitement, and even at forty-one, eight years after his last Top Ten single, he worked what there was of a crowd into something approaching a frenzy with his amazing footwork and dips—sliding, gliding, dropping into splits, and rearing back to plead, "Just say you will! *Say you wi-hill!*"

The crowd was on its feet, and Jackie was at the point where his voice would ring a cappella through the big old showroom. "*My heart is crying, crying!*" This time, he repeated the words:

My heart . . . my heart . . .

Jackie Wilson balled up both fists and drew them to his chest. Then he extended his arms out to the sides and fell backwards, landing flat on his back, his head smacking the hard stage floor. Promoter Walt Cohen was in the audience and he heard the crack of the skull. Reporter Chuck Darrow also heard "a sickening thump" but told *South Jersey Magazine*, "I'll never know whether it was the microphone or Wilson's skull hitting the floor." Regardless, Darrow admitted almost forty years after the fact that the sound "haunts me to this day."

The band played on. They, like most everyone in the audience, figured this was part of the act. Dick Clark was backstage, and he had seen Wilson perform enough times to know that it wasn't.

"I'd never seen him do that before," Clark recalled in Tony Douglas's biography *Jackie Wilson: Lonely Teardrops*. "It looked like it was part of the act but he never got up. The irony of it is that just before Jackie was singing, 'My heart is crying, crying,' and doing the splits."

After a minute or so, it was evident Jackie Wilson wasn't getting up again. One of the band members called out. Clark ran onto the stage, stopped the music, and called for the maroon curtain to drop. A few seconds later, he walked out in front of the curtain in tears and said, "Is there a doctor in the house?"

The show was over. The other stars of the revue moved in to Wilson's side. "I ran out on stage, and he was biting down on his tongue," Dion told *Atlantic City Weekly*. "His body froze up." Cornell Gunter was the first to point out that Jackie Wilson wasn't breathing. He attempted mouth-to-mouth resuscitation, but it didn't seem to help.

"None of us knew CPR," Clark said. "This is probably some of my guilt coming forward." A nurse stepped up from the audience, and paramedics ultimately showed up. Dick Clark asked the audience to pray for Jackie Wilson.

"The audience was asked to exit the premises," said Darrow, who'd been scheduled to interview Clark for the *Temple University News* after the show. "I definitely remember one guy in the audience screaming he wanted his money back."

The evening's second show was canceled, but someone told a reporter for the *Philadelphia Inquirer* that the revue would resume the following evening, possibly with local hero Chubby Checker taking Jackie Wilson's headlining spot. Ultimately, R&B singer Chuck Jackson filled in.

Jackie Wilson was rushed to Cherry Hill Hospital, where doctors said he'd suffered a "severe heart attack." They managed to stabilize his vital functions, but the lack of oxygen to his brain, possibly exacerbated by a stroke resulting from that hit to the head, caused him to slip into a coma.

For a time, friends and fans had hope that Jackie Wilson would recover. In early 1976, he emerged briefly from the coma. He wasn't able to speak, but he was aware of his surroundings and even managed to take a few unsteady steps before falling back into the purgatory of a semi-coma and total dependency.

––––––––––

Later that year, the rhythm and blues vocal group the Spinners and their manager organized a benefit concert for Jackie Wilson on the same stage at the Latin Casino where Wilson had fallen. One of the Spinners' lead vocalists, Philippé Wynne, was, like Wilson, born in Detroit and was greatly influenced by Wilson's singing and performing style. The group and its management put up $10,000 to cover travel, hotel, and other expenses and vowed that every penny of the proceeds, minus 5 percent for the taxman, would go to Wilson's family. (Money for the taxman was something Jackie Wilson did not set aside. At the time of his collapse, he owed the IRS hundreds of thousands of dollars.)

Twelve ringside tables, each seating ten, were set aside for $1,000 each. The rest of the tickets were twenty dollars. No dinner would be served. The all-star line-up would also include Al Green, Harold Melvin & the Blue Notes, Sister Sledge, Stephanie Mills, B. T. Express, and comedian Irwin C. Watson. *Soul Train*'s Don Cornelius and Dick Clark would serve as emcees.

The Latin Casino was sold out for the benefit on October 3, 1976. Record industry execs scooped up the ringside tickets. Al Green at first declined to sing, but then performed an a cappella version of "Let's Stay Together" and donated $10,000 to the Jackie Wilson Fund. Dick Clark once again hauled out a film clip from his collection, this one of Jackie Wilson singing "Lonely Teardrops" on *American Bandstand*. The Spinners, including Philippé Wynne, put on an exciting show that included a medley of their hits. Later, the Spinners management announced that $60,000 had been raised for Jackie Wilson's medical expenses.

Legalized gambling and big Vegas entertainment an hour away in Atlantic City took business and headliners from the Latin Casino and led its owners to close the nitery in 1978. Totie Fields headlined the last show on June 28. Like the Latin Casino, the comedienne had suffered serious health problems in the past couple of years—in her case, breast cancer, two heart attacks, complications from eye surgery, and the amputation of her left leg.

She entered the stage on a wheelchair. "Jesus Christ, they had to cut off my goddamn leg to get me to lose weight!" she crowed. "If they could just whack my other leg and both of my arms I think I could reach my goal weight!" Totie Fields died thirty-five days later, the morning she was to have opened a two-week gig at the Sahara in Las Vegas. She was forty-eight.

Meanwhile, several million dollars were poured into converting the Latin Casino into Emerald City, which *Billboard* called "one of the nation's most spectacular discotheques." Within three years, the owners filed for bankruptcy. After the building burned to the ground a few years later, it was gutted. The corporate headquarters of Subaru of America rose on its spot.

The Jackie Wilson whom rock 'n' roll and R&B fans knew and loved died that Monday evening in 1975, never to sing, dance, or split again. The mortal Jackie Wilson lived on, in various stages of a coma and in need of constant attention. In 1977, he was moved to the Medford Leas Retirement Center in Medford, New Jersey, about twenty-five minutes east of the old Latin Casino, while a court battle raged over his finances.

On April 14, 1978, a Camden County Court judge awarded guardianship to Wilson's estranged wife, Harlean Wilson (they'd married in 1967). The judge ruled against Tony Wilson, a son by a previous marriage, and Joyce McRae, who was described as a fan who moved to New Jersey to be near her "friend."

On January 8, 1984, Wilson was admitted to Memorial Hospital of Burlington County in nearby Mount Holly. That's where he died thirteen days later, on Saturday, January 21, 1984, from complications of pneumonia. He was forty-nine.

Philippé Wynne left the Spinners and in 1977 went solo with his new manager, Alan Thicke. In 1979, he joined up with George Clinton's Parliament-Funkadelic crew and was a featured vocalist on the funk classic "(Not Just) Knee Deep," which went to number 1 on *Billboard*'s Black Singles and R&B charts.

In 1984, Wynne was on the road to promote his new self-titled LP, released on the Sugar Hill label. On July 13, nearly six months after the death of Jackie Wilson, he was in Oakland, California, playing Ivey's nightclub, a popular showplace in Jack London Square, the waterfront entertainment district. It may have been Friday the Thirteenth, but it was a lucky night for the two hundred patrons of Ivey's, for if ever the spirit of Jackie Wilson was alive, it was onstage that night. Philippé Wynne put on a show that was high on energy and full of hits; it had everyone on their feet. The crowd brought him back for two encores. Wynne left the stage that third time to another standing ovation.

Now, it was forty-five minutes before midnight and he was back for a third encore. What more could he give? The band kicked into the Spinners' 1974 hit "Love Don't Love Nobody." Like "Lonely Teardrops," the song summed up the pain of a man who loved and lost. It was a song that could have been sung in church, and it was a perfect final encore. It would wring every last drop of sweat from Philippé Wynne and the audience alike.

The band eased out the song in a slow burn and built from there. Gradually, Philippé Wynne's soulful voice rose from regret to the shouts of the gospel singer he once was. Women in the crowd raised their palms toward the ceiling. Men cheered him on.

Wynne removed the microphone from the stand and stepped off the stage and began to walk through the audience, like a preacher, roaring, testifying, that love . . . don't love . . . nobody!

> *Sign of pain is on my face, well . . .*
> *My heartbeat stops—*

Yes, he did. Just as his hero Jackie Wilson had sung, "*My heart is crying, crying—my heart, my heart—*" before falling backwards to the floor, Philippé Wynne sang, "*Sign of pain is on my face! Well, my heartbeat stops!*" Then, standing amid the crowd, he suddenly dropped the microphone, and he himself dropped to the floor. The music stopped. The women who were screaming in ecstasy were now screaming in alarm. Two police officers and a nurse who happened to be in the club made their way through the audience to administer aid. As the singer was taken from the club to Providence Hospital, many women cried.

Philippé Wynne's heartbeat had indeed stopped. Like his hero, Jackie Wilson, he'd suffered a severe heart attack. Unlike Jackie Wilson, he did not hang on. Wynne was pronounced dead a little over an hour after he fell, at 12:27 AM on Saturday morning, July 14. He was forty-three.

Jackie Wilson was buried in an unmarked grave at Westlawn Cemetery near Detroit. In 1987, a fundraiser by a Detroit radio station collected enough money to re-inter him next to his mother in a mausoleum. The fact that Jackie Wilson did not die onstage but hung on for many years before finding a need for a grave may seem unique in recent pop music history. Yet he wasn't the only one.

Curtis Mayfield

Curtis Mayfield was another R&B and soul music legend. With the Impressions in the 1960s, he brought social consciousness and activism to the charts with songs like "People Get Ready," "Keep On Pushing," and "It's All Right." As a solo artist in the 1970s, he was a funk music pioneer who turned a soundtrack for a blaxploitation flick called *Superfly* into a commentary on violence, crime, and drug abuse in America's urban ghettos—and a very soulful and funky commentary, at that.

Curtis Mayfield may have been the embodiment of soul. He'd reached his commercial height with the *Superfly* soundtrack in 1972 but remained a vital artist into the next decade. In 1990, he and his band toured Europe and returned that summer to the States, where, on July 7, they headlined the SummerStage in New York City's Central Park.

On August 13, Mayfield was back in New York City, in East Flatbush, Brooklyn, for a free outdoor concert at Wingate Field. The show was sponsored by State Senator Marty Markowitz, a glad-hander who was known as "Senator Impresario" because most of his constituents knew him for the free concert series he promoted. He was referred to by the *New York Times* as "the only politician in the city who deliberately seeks to entertain" and by the *Daily News* as a moonlighting "non-profit concert promoter" who brought headlining acts from Manhattan to the eastern side of the New York City bridges.

The stage, sound system, and lighting rigs were set up that Monday afternoon. The ten thousand people who streamed into the park brought along their own chairs and blankets. As they settled in, there was some concern about the weather. Official policy called for an outdoor event to be canceled in case of heavy thunder, lightning, or high winds—anything more than a "light rain." People who were there will tell you that winds were whipping around the park that day, but in these cases, most everyone seems to err on the side of the show going on.

Shortly after the sun went down, at 7:30, Harold Melvin & the Blue Notes, who'd opened for the Spinners, with Philippé Wynne, at the Latin Casino Jackie Wilson tribute in 1976 (and whose former lead singer, Teddy Pendergrass, had been paralyzed from the chest down in a car accident in 1982), began their opening set. An hour later, Curtis Mayfield was introduced. He was carrying his guitar as he walked up the steps to the stage and surveyed the thousands of cheering fans before him when, Marty Markowitz told United Press International, "an overwhelming wind hit us and blew the speakers off the stage and the lighting trusses down."

The lighting towers, weighing several hundred pounds, crashed to the stage. At least seven people were injured, including three crew members and a twelve-year-old girl. No one was hurt as badly as Curtis Mayfield.

The scaffolding and the tower of lights smashed on top of him, onto his head and back from behind. One moment he was holding his guitar. The next, he was flat on his face with a broken neck. He was admitted to Kings County Hospital in critical condition and placed in intensive care.

The next morning, Markowitz told local reporters the accident was "a terrible tragedy" caused by "a freakish gust of wind like a mini-tornado" that no one could have foreseen. The next show at Wingate Field took place on schedule the following week, and everyone in the crowd was asked to sign a giant get-well card.

Eight days after the accident, the *New York Times* published a letter to the editor from the vice president of Local 4 of the International Alliance of Theatrical Stage Employees, criticizing Markowitz for using prison inmates rather than skilled union professionals to set up the stage. "Rigging and setting up an outdoor show with electric lights and sound on tall steel towers requires skill and experience," the union veep wrote.

Eleven days after the accident, Curtis Mayfield was transferred from Brooklyn to Shepherd Spinal Center in Atlanta, near his home. He was paralyzed from the neck down, but there was hope his spinal injuries would heal.

He made his first public appearance six months after the accident. On February 12, 1991, he arrived in Miami to donate a $100,000 check to set up the Curtis Mayfield Research Fund at the Miami Project to Cure Paralysis.

The hope soon faded. Curtis Mayfield would remain paralyzed for the rest of his life. He'd never be able to play guitar or walk again, but he wasn't wheeled into a convalescent home. He continued to compose and sing.

In 1996, he directed the recording of one last album. He recorded his vocals, one line at a time, while lying on his back. It was the only way he could draw enough air into his lungs to get the words out. The lines were edited together to assemble each of the thirteen tracks on the album. *New World Order* didn't crack the Top 100, but it received three Grammy nominations. Reviewer Leo Stanley of the AllMusic website called the album "a touching, moving comeback." He wrote, "The songs are hit-and-miss, but the main strength of the record is that it illustrates that Mayfield can make music that is still vital."

Curtis Mayfield died of complications of type 2 diabetes, related to the accident, on December 26, 1999. He was forty-eight when he was paralyzed, fifty-seven when he took his last breath.

It took Jackie Wilson more than eight years to die; Curtis Mayfield held on for more than nine.

10

Jazz

JAZZ IS DEAD. CRITICS AND musicians alike have been making the claim for decades. Ever since the 1940s, when bebop moved jazz away from its dance-music roots, students of the genre have treated it more like a museum piece than a form of popular music, while jazz innovators have taken their sounds further beyond mainstream patience or comprehension. Jazz lives, if only in a shrinking corner of the music world.

Jazz musicians, though? They often keep playing until they're dead. Their careers don't depend on pop success, only the proximity to a bar or club. Jazzmen and jazzwomen die when their hearts give out, when their livers go, or if they're younger, with a needle in his arm like Freddie Webster, in a hotel suite of a perforated ulcer like Charlie Parker, in a fall or push out a hotel window like Chet Baker, handcuffed to a hospital bed like Billie Holiday, or, like Lee Morgan, shot through the heart while making his way to the bandstand.

More than a few have died on the stage.

Lil Hardin

Without Lil Hardin, there might not be a jazz scene today. There most definitely wouldn't have been a Louis Armstrong, at least not the Louis "Satchmo" Armstrong who became the greatest and most influential jazz virtuoso of all time.

"I was a Southern Doodle Dandy, born on the Fourth of July, 1900," Armstrong once told the *New York Times*. "My mother Mary Ann—we called her Mayann—was living in a two-room shack in James Alley, in the Back O' Town colored section of New Orleans. It was in a tough block, all them hustlers and their pimps and gamblers with their knives, between Gravier and Perdido Streets." Recent research places Louis Armstrong's first bleats thirteen months later, but the Fourth of July at the turn of the century was the birthday he celebrated, and it fit right in with the image and myth of the man who was the defining figure of America's one true original art form.

Louis Armstrong did grow up dirt poor and was taught bugle and cornet (that compact brother of the trumpet) while in the Colored Waifs Home for Boys, to which he'd been sentenced for shooting a gun on New Year's Eve, 1913. He played in the home's brass band, and when he was released after eighteen months, his formal education ended and his jazz life began. He played his cornet in every honky-tonk and joint that would take him. Joe "King" Oliver, the great cornet player, noticed him, befriended him, tutored him, and gave him a new horn.

Louis married a twenty-one-year-old prostitute named Daisy Parker in 1918. The marriage didn't last, he lamented, because Daisy "wouldn't give up her line of work." That same year, King Oliver quit the Kid Ory band, the hottest and best jazz combo in the city, and headed to Chicago. Louis was hired in his place. With his reputation spreading as one hot cornet player, Louis got the call in 1922 to join King Oliver in Chicago. He became second cornetist in Oliver's Creole Jazz Band.

That's where Louis met Lil. Lil Hardin was the Creole Jazz Band's pianist and featured performer. She recalled Oliver telling her that "Little Louis" was about to come on board.

"Little Louis! He weighed 226 pounds," Lil scoffed, according to UPI. "He was wearing a second-hand suit that didn't fit, he had a hat that was too small sitting on top of his head and I didn't like his hairdo—he had bangs sticking straight out, which was the style in New Orleans."

"He was a greenhorn trumpeter from New Orleans," she recalled, "but he had nice white teeth and a nice big smile."

Lil was a sophisticated, classically trained musician who studied at Fisk University in Nashville and the Chicago Music College. She taught Louis musical arrangements, wrote songs with him, and saw something in him that he didn't see in himself. The collaborations led to friendship, and in 1924, marriage—with vows that came with an ultimatum.

"The big moment was when King Oliver was talking privately to Lil and said, 'You know, as long as Little Louis stays with me, he'll never pass me. I'll always be the King. He's a better cornet player than me, but I'll always be the King.'" Ricky Riccardi, archivist for the Louis Armstrong House Museum in Queens, New York, knows the story. "Lil heard that and realized that all this time Oliver was holding Louis back. So she said to Louis: 'I didn't marry no second cornet player. Either you're leaving King Oliver or I'm leaving you.'" Louis did indeed quit the band. He landed in New York City, playing with pianist and bandleader Fletcher Henderson.

"Lil stayed back in Chicago. She left King Oliver and actually formed her own band," Riccardi tells us. "But in New York, Louis was not being properly featured. He was only getting short solos. Henderson wouldn't let him sing. Louis made some outstanding records, but his name wasn't on any of them. Nobody knew who he was. So Lil was not happy."

Lil called Louis back to Chicago in the fall of 1925. She assembled a small group and arranged him a headlining gig at the Dreamland Cafe. Lil not only negotiated Louis a salary of seventy-five dollars a week—twenty dollars more than Henderson was paying—but also got the manager to slap a sign on the marquee that read, COME HEAR THE WORLD'S GREATEST CORNETIST—LOUIS ARMSTRONG.

"He said I was crazy," Lil told the *Chicago Sun-Times*. "He didn't think he was as great as he was. He didn't want to be a star. Louis wanted to play with the band and have fun with the fellows."

With Lil's guidance, Louis "Satchmo" Armstrong continued his rise in the jazz world. "In November 1925, she helped him get his own band together: Louis Armstrong's Hot Five," says Riccardi. "She played the piano, and he was allowed to make records under his name for the first time. And they've become the most influential jazz recordings of all time. For that reason, I've always said that Lil deserves almost all the credit for making Louis into what he became. She really is the architect of his career. If you take Lil out of the equation, maybe he doesn't make those records. And who knows what happens to the course of jazz history."

As Louis gained confidence, he bristled under her control. The couple separated in 1931, though they didn't make the divorce official for another seven years. Louis would remarry, twice. Lil never did.

Louis became an international star whose celebrity crossed all boundaries. Lil, who composed more than 150 songs, was a dynamic performer herself. Billed as Mrs. Louis Armstrong, she led an "all-girl orchestra" and recorded both as a solo artist and accompanist before drifting from music in the late 1940s. She became a clothing designer, restaurateur, and teacher and performed only occasionally.

Louis Armstrong died on July 6, 1971, officially at the age of seventy-one. While the world mourned the loss of the Jazz King, Lil Hardin attended the funeral in Queens, New York. Lucille, Louis's fourth wife, invited Lil to stay with her and to ride in the family limousine. "Lucille thought that Louis would've struck her with a bolt of lightning if she had not done that," Riccardi says. "Even Lucille knew that there was some kind of bond there between Louis and Lil, right to the end."

Seven weeks and three days after Satchmo's death, Chicago's Reach Out Program sponsored a noontime back-to-school concert at Civic Center Plaza. The highlight of the afternoon would be a tribute to Louis Armstrong by the Red Saunders Band (with which Lil Hardin Armstrong had often played) and a performance by Lil herself.

Two thousand people gathered in the shadow of the five-story cubist Picasso statue. Miss Lil, as she had come to be addressed, complained of chills as she sat through a choral group and several speeches.

Art Hodes, once described by jazz historian Rudi Blesh as "the most Negroid of all living white pianists," performed a "Salute to Louis," and Red Saunders came onstage to introduce Lil Hardin Armstrong. He told the story of how she encouraged and guided Louis from his place as second cornet to King Oliver to becoming the greatest performer in jazz history.

Miss Lil had the crowd laughing and swinging as she played and sang her rollicking blues jazz, often tinkling the keys with one hand while snapping her fingers with the other. Her last number was "St. Louis Blues," the W. C. Handy standard that was one of Louis's favorites. When Bessie Smith recorded one of the best-known versions in 1925, Louis Armstrong was backing her on cornet.

Miss Lil's hands danced across the eighty-eights. Then, suddenly, they stopped. There was a moment of silence, and she slid, almost elegantly, off the piano stool and onto the stage floor. She had suffered a massive heart attack.

Mouth-to-mouth resuscitation was attempted and failed. Lil Hardin Armstrong was pronounced dead at Wesley Memorial Hospital, but all agreed she was already dead when she hit the stage.

"It's an old show biz thing. And you know, there's something with Lil going at a Louis Armstrong tribute concert, it's almost romantic," Ricky Riccardi says. "If you put that in a movie, someone would say, 'Ah, that's too cliché.' But that generation, they were serious about that. I interviewed five surviving members of Louis's band in the last twenty-five years of his life. And they always said that he would say his ideal way to die was to die onstage. He mentioned his drummer, Big Sid Catlett, who died after telling a joke in Chicago. He'd told a joke backstage (at the Civic Opera House in 1951) and boom, just had a heart attack right there. And Louis thought that was like the best way to go.

"I do think some people get into show business or entertainment because they want to be rich and famous and all that. But back then, for some of these people, this was it. And if they couldn't do what they loved, then life wasn't worth living. So there is something kind of romantic about this whole notion of dying while doing what you love."

Miss Lil Hardin Armstrong was sixty-eight.

Sylvia Syms

"When you perform, it's a one-to-one love affair with the people out there. That's how it has to be." That's how Sylvia Syms once described her art, and that quote defined her jazz singing style: intimate and storytelling-like, in the deep contralto that made her the apotheosis of the *saloon singer*, the term Frank Sinatra often used to describe himself.

Sinatra didn't resent her authenticity; he worshipped at the smoky altar of Sylvia Blagman Syms, the moonfaced chubette he called "Buddha." He also called her "the world's greatest saloon singer." She called him "Francis Albert." They were friends since they met in the 1940s at a Billie Holiday show. Sylvia had made her singing debut in 1941 at Kelly's Stable, one of the many hot jazz clubs on West Fifty-Second Street in Manhattan, when West Fifty-Second was America's Swing Street. She'd arrived there years earlier, when she was only fifteen, underage, and standing in the coat-check room to hear the music and befriending Billie Holiday and other jazz greats like Lester Young and Mildred Bailey.

Sylvia called Billie "Eleanor," her given name. When Billie burned her hair off with a curling iron, Sylvia had the solution. She knew a coat-check girl who sold flowers, so she ran down the street and came back with a gardenia to cover Billie's burn spot. Billie liked the look. The gardenia in her hair became her trademark.

Mae West "discovered" Sylvia Syms when she saw Sylvia sing at the Cinderella Club in the Village in 1949. In a Cinderella kind of story, Mae West gave her the role of Flo the shoplifter in a revival of her Broadway hit *Diamond Lil*. Sylvia then set off on a companion career in Broadway musicals.

She recorded dozens of albums. One record sold more than a million copies: her 1956 single "I Could Have Danced All Night." But it was in the clubs, with a spotlight, a microphone, and a trio behind her, that Sylvia Syms could enthrall an audience, drawing them in as she worked with a song and made it her own.

"This may be my last time on the pike," she told the *New York Times* on April 27, 1992. It was three days before she opened a five-week engagement at the Oak Room, the dark-paneled cabaret mecca in the old Algonquin Hotel on West Forty-Fourth Street. The extended run was a surprise. By now, Sylvia Syms was a jazz treasure, seventy-four years old, living on one lung and dealing with a variety of other health issues, including emphysema. Sylvia Syms shows were rare by then.

This show was called *Syms Celebrates Sinatra*, a tribute to her friend of close to fifty years. Sinatra had conducted (a thirty-four-piece orchestra) and coproduced her album *Syms by Sinatra* ten years earlier. She considered it one of her best.

When she performed two shows on Saturday night, May 9, Sylvia Syms was almost midway through the engagement. Her publicist Keith Sherman said she'd been "complaining of allergies" that day, but her manager Jack Globenfelt told the Associated Press that she seemed fine: "She was very up and bubbly between shows. She was very excited."

It was around 1:00 AM Sunday as Sylvia neared the end of the second show. Her breathing was labored, her voice rough. The years had definitely taken a toll—but that was all part of the appeal. Like her friend Francis Albert, she was putting all of her life's wisdom and experience into each song, turning them into stories.

She'd just completed a medley and, as the standing ovation continued, was about to go into her finale, "This Will Be My Shining Hour." In appreciation, she spoke the words of a Frank Loesser song:

> *My heart is so full of you, so full of you*
> *There is no room for anything more there.*

She took a moment to talk to the audience, stopping at the table of Cy Coleman, the composer who cowrote Sinatra standards like "Witchcraft" and "The Best Is Yet to Come." Sylvia had sung Cy's songs years before he hit it big on Broadway. She put her hand down on his table, to introduce him.

"It was at the very end of the second show, and she was getting a standing ovation," said Steve LaSpina, her bass player. "She put her right hand up, and the next thing we knew she fell back and hit the ground." Sylvia Syms had suffered a heart attack. She was taken to St. Clare's Hospital, but she was gone. They pronounced her dead on arrival.

"Sylvia lived alone," Arthur Pomposello, the Oak Room's talent coordinator, told a reporter for the Associated Press. "This is probably the best way she could have gone and probably the way she wanted to go."

Warne Marsh

Then there's the story of that night at Donte's and the jazzman who dropped from out of nowhere.

Donte's jazz club opened as a piano bar on Lankershim Boulevard in North Hollywood on June 22, 1966. Hampton Hawes was featured on piano, with Red Mitchell on bass and Donald Bailey on drums. By winter, the piano bar was replaced by a bandstand, and Donte's was on its way to becoming the hippest, hottest jazz club in Los Angeles. Donte's hosted big-name jazz stars like Chet Baker, Al Cohn, Zoot Sims, Art Pepper, Joe Pass, and Pete Jolly. Stan Kenton, Buddy Rich, Woody Herman, and Count Basie brought in their big bands. Doc Severinsen, Tommy Newsom, and the Tonight Show Band would set up after their regular gig with Johnny Carson in Burbank. Comedians like Redd Foxx and Mort Sahl liked to try out new material in the room. Celebs including Clint Eastwood, Frank Sinatra, and Pearl Bailey mixed with the locals.

Donte's held on for more than twenty years. By the final weeks of 1987, the club was just holding on; the place was worn out. The IRS had shuttered it more than once. The owner, old Carey Leverette, had to thank local musicians like Ross Tompkins, who kept up a regular weekly jam with his Thursday Night Band. Tompkins had a regular gig as pianist for the Tonight Show Band, so he never hassled the owner about late or bounced paychecks.

December 17, 1987, was a Thursday night, and the Thursday Night Band was on the bandstand. Led by Tompkins, with Buddy Clark on bass and drummer Larence Marable, the quartet usually included *Tonight Show* trumpet player Conte Candoli. Candoli couldn't make it on this night, so a call went out in the afternoon to a tenor sax player named Warne Marsh.

The name Warne Marsh, often misspelled on marquees as "Warner" or "Wayne," may not have been a household one, but among jazz enthusiasts it was highly respected. Warne Marsh was lauded as one of the best improvisers in jazz history. *Downbeat*, the jazz bible, described him as "a tenor saxophonist of immense resourcefulness and great technical command . . . a truly innovative and original musician and a master of the particular jazz art of instant composition."

Marsh first got attention in the late 1940s as a student of and player with reclusive, blind avant-garde pianist Lennie Tristano, bringing improvisation to new directions and heights. "When I arrived in New York in 1947, I met Charlie Parker, Lester Young and Lennie Tristano all at once—and that really changed my whole musical outlook," Marsh told *Downbeat*. "It was Lennie who obliged me to study Lester and Bird and told me that an improviser had to know music just like a composer, because an improviser is a composer-plus."

Marsh was a founding member of Supersax, a band conceived in 1972 to play harmonized arrangements of Charlie "Bird" Parker's saxophone solos with a saxophone section.

He was a cult figure, though his recordings were scattered. Marsh was a daily marijuana smoker, and liked his amphetamines, cocaine, and occasionally heroin. The afternoon he got the call to fill in for Conte Candoli, he'd been taking a nap after getting high and doing lines with other musicians at a music store in Hollywood.

There wasn't much of a crowd at Donte's when the Thursday Night Band took their places on the stage. Warne Marsh called the tune to open the second set, a favorite of his called "Out of Nowhere." He performed his solo as expertly as ever, and when he was finished, stepped back and sat on his stool. Then he stepped off and staggered. Gene Lesner, an amateur sax player and Donte's regular, was in the room. In Safford Chamberlain's book *An Unsung Cat: The Life and Music of Warne Marsh*, Lesner related that Marsh then "gently laid his horn on the floor, and lay down on his side.

The first to notice was Marable. Larence kind of leaned forward and stood up. He said something like, "What the fuck you doing, Warne? What's going on?" Tompkins looked around with his usual quizzical look on his face. It was so slick, so smooth, the way he went down. Everyone of course knew that he'd had that heart attack.

The drummer called out: "For Christ's sake, somebody call an ambulance!" The lights went on. Warne Marsh wasn't moving. There was a small puddle of vomit by his mouth.

It seemed a long wait for the ambulance, though it probably arrived within about ten minutes. By then, Warne Marsh was already dead. Someone covered his body with a coat. The paramedics tried some CPR and drove him to St. Joseph Medical Center in Burbank, where doctors pronounced him dead early Friday morning. He was sixty.

The band never got paid at all that night. Old man Carey Leverette said they didn't deserve to, because they didn't finish the set. Four months later, he announced he'd sold Donte's to a Japanese businessman. Two days after that, the sale of the club closed escrow. The next day, Leverette was found dead in his cluttered office. He was sixty-three.

"I thought he wouldn't last a month after he sold it," Ross Tompkins told the reporter from the *Los Angeles Times*. "That place was his whole life."

Tiny double bassist Jane Little, the holder of a Guinness World Record for the longest tenure with a single orchestra, tumbled to the stage near the end of what already was planned to be the final number of her career. *Photo by Dustin Chambers, courtesy of the Atlanta Symphony Orchestra*

ACTOR BLOWS OUT BRAINS.

Comedian Commits Suicide in Full View of Audience While Responding to Encores.

Emil Hasda, the leading comedian in a German company playing at Nimptsch, Silesia, committed suicide recently in full view of the audience.

The company was on a tour from Berlin and was making a great success. Of all the players Hasda was the public favorite.

ACTOR DROPS DEAD, AUDIENCE THINKS ITS PART OF THE PLOT

'Golden Boy' Halted at Santa Barbara as Greenwald Succumbs

Santa Barbara, Cal., April 2 (U.P.) —The audience thought it was part of the plot when Joseph Greenwald, a well known Broadway character actor, collapsed last night as he said "all my life."

But Mr. Greenwald's collapse was genuine. He had died of a heart attack.

LEFT: A more concise headline has never been written. *Coffeyville (KS) Daily Journal, May 10, 1904, via Newspapers.com*

RIGHT: Everyone agreed that the death of Joe Greenwald made for a sensational headline, but few would agree on his final words. *Binghamton (NY) Press, April 2, 1938, via Newspapers.com*

Broadway star David Burns, best known for his role opposite Carol Channing in Broadway's *Hello, Dolly!*, died of a heart attack out of town, onstage in Philadelphia during a tryout run of the musical *70, Girls, 70*.
Courtesy of Wikimedia Commons

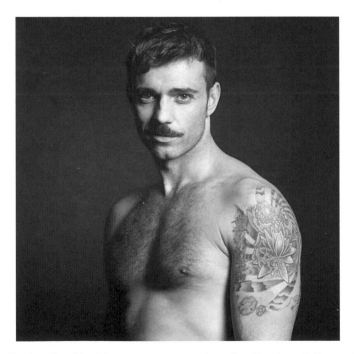

Aerial artist Pedro Aunión Monroy was opening for the band Green Day at the Mad Cool music festival when he fell a hundred feet to his death. *Courtesy of Monica Aunión Monroy*

The last photo of dialect comedian Harry Einstein, a.k.a. Parkyakarkus. After his hilarious routine at the Friars Club testimonial dinner for Lucille Ball and Desi Arnaz, he plotzed into Milton Berle's lap. *Los Angeles Herald-Express, courtesy of Wikimedia Commons*

Comedian Al Kelly (left), the king of double-talk, flummoxes fellow Friar and king of jokes Joey Adams on a 1953 quiz show. When Al collapsed during an ovation from a star-studded crowd at the Friars Club, he was carried out and pronounced dead atop the Round the World Bar. *Publicity still*

Comedian Dick Shawn's habit of lying motionless onstage before and during intermission of his one-man show led to confusion when he dropped from an apparent heart attack. *Publicity still*

When comic magician Tommy Cooper collapsed and died on live television, audiences in the theater and at home laughed. *Video still*

LEFT: When lecherous British comedy star Sid James suffered a fatal heart attack onstage, someone asked, "Is there a doctor in the house?" The audience laughed. So did the doctor. *Publicity still*

RIGHT: Mentalist Washington Irving Bishop often fell into a death-like cataleptic state during his performances. After he was stricken onstage at the Lambs Club in Manhattan in 1889, doctors removed his brain before he could recover.

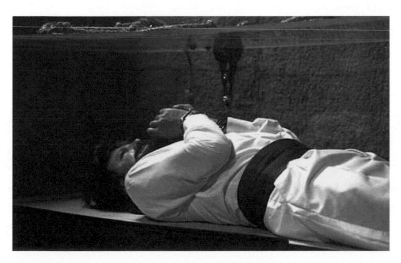

"Amazing Joe" Burrus in the plastic-and-glass coffin in which he would perform his final stunt. Seven tons of wet cement made sure of it. *Courtesy of Joseph Burrus*

Mysterious Chinese magician Chung Ling Soo, celebrated for his ability to catch bullets, was not really Chinese, and, as he proved in his final performance, couldn't really catch bullets. *Courtesy of Mike Caveney's Egyptian Hall Museum*

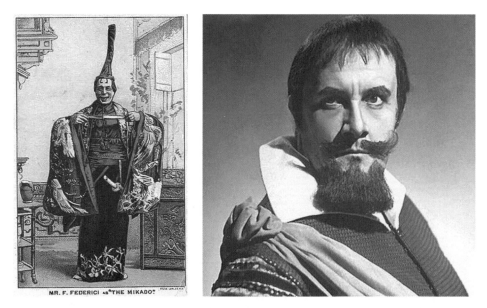

MR. F. FEDERICI as "THE MIKADO"

LEFT: Frederick Federici, famed for his roles in Gilbert and Sullivan comic operas, was playing the demon Mephistopheles in *Faust* when he suffered a fatal heart attack while descending beneath the stage to "hell." *Burrow-Giles Lithographic Co., courtesy of Wikimedia Commons*

RIGHT: The death of baritone Leonard Warren onstage at the Metropolitan Opera House led to a journalism scandal, and also a Pulitzer Prize. *Publicity still*

Conductor Israel Yinon tumbled headfirst from the podium while conducting a concert titled *The Healing Alps*, one of many conductors to die by the baton. *Photo by Etan J. Tal, courtesy of the photographer, via Wikimedia Commons, https://commons.wikimedia.org/wiki/File:IsraelYinon2003.jpg*

LEFT: Heavy metal guitar hero "Dimebag" Darrell Abbott was shot to death onstage during a show in Columbus, Ohio, on the twenty-fourth anniversary of the assassination of John Lennon. *Photo by April Ashford-Forsythe, courtesy of the photographer, via Wikimedia Commons, https://commons.wikimedia.org/wiki/File:Dimebag.jpg*

RIGHT: A nightclub security camera recorded a six-foot-five, schizophrenic ex-marine as he ran across the stage of the Alrosa Villa club and shot "Dimebag" Darrell Abbott, killing the heavy metal guitar god and three others. *Video still, Columbus Division of Police, Columbus, OH*

After Edmond Turner suffered a massive heart attack while playing Prince's "Raspberry Beret" onstage in a Mexican restaurant, they had to peel his fingers from the neck of this Stratocaster guitar. *Photo by Kriss Famous, courtesy of the photographer*

When jam band godfather Colonel Bruce Hampton collapsed onstage during the encore of his all-star seventieth birthday celebration, the other musicians played on. They assumed it was part of his act. *Video still*

Sparks flew as Romanian metal band Goodbye to Gravity opened their last show with the song "The Day We Die." When another pyrotechnic display later in their set ignited a fire, four out of five band members did die.
Video still, Arhiva Mea

LEFT: Pub rocker Nick Lowe was electrocuted to death onstage in 1968 but brought back to life—a life made very comfortable after his song "(What's So Funny 'Bout) Peace, Love & Understanding" was featured on the soundtrack album for the movie *The Bodyguard*, the bestselling soundtrack of all time.
Photo by Juan Gonzalez Andres, courtesy of the photographer, via Wikimedia Commons, https://commons.wikimedia.org/wiki/File:Nick_Lowe1.jpg

RIGHT: Country star Onie Wheeler (right) with A. J. and Doyle Nelson, just moments before Wheeler fell down dead of a heart attack in the sacred circle at the Grand Ole Opry. *Courtesy of Karen Wheeler*

It took several years and a radio station campaign for R&B star Jackie Wilson to get a marked grave, but when he did, he was hailed not only as Mr. Excitement but also as The Complete Entertainer. *Photo by John Shetler, courtesy of the photographer*

Soul artist and social activist Curtis Mayfield died nine years after he was paralyzed in an onstage accident. *Courtesy of Netherlands Institute for Sound and Vision, via Wikimedia Commons, https://commons.wikimedia.org/wiki/File:Curtis_Mayfield.png*

Lil Plays Blues and Dies

UPI Telephotos

Lil Hardin Armstrong, 73, second wife of the late Louis (Satchmo) Armstrong, was playing "The St. Louis Blues" (photo left) at a tribute to Satch in Chicago yesterday. Then, suddenly she collapsed (center) into the arms of her son, Ted Sanders. They tried to revive Lil (right), but she was dead of a heart attack on arrival at hospital.

Seven weeks after the death of Louis Armstrong, his ex-wife and mentor Lil Hardin died while performing at a tribute concert in honor of the jazz great. *Courtesy of the Louis Armstrong House Museum*

LEFT: Frank Sinatra said Sylvia Syms was the world's greatest saloon singer. She fell over and died during her tribute to Ol' Blue Eyes. *Publicity still*

RIGHT: Jazz saxophone legend Warne Marsh was performing at a club in North Hollywood when, from out of nowhere, he died, after soloing on the song, "Out of Nowhere." *Photo by Rob Bogaerts/Anefo, courtesy of the Dutch National Archives, via Wikimedia Commons*

Like other dangdut pop singers in Indonesia, Irma Bule worked with a snake, usually a boa constrictor or python. When she performed with a deadly king cobra named Rianti, she was bitten but kept singing and dancing for another forty-five minutes—until the venom reached her heart. *Video still*

In concert, the final moment of life for Mango, Italy's favorite singing star. Midsong, he uttered the word "*Scusa*" ("Sorry"), then collapsed across the keyboard of his electric piano. His death led to two funerals. *Video still*

Congolese singer and fashion plate Papa Wemba was best known for his work with Peter Gabriel—and his conviction for smuggling people into France by claiming they were in his band. *Courtesy of Radio Okapi, via Wikimedia Commons, https://commons.wikimedia.org/wiki/File:Papa_Wemba.jpg*

Nutritionist J. I. Rodale (left) died of a heart attack during a taping of *The Dick Cavett Show*. The show never aired. *Video still, courtesy of Daphne Productions*

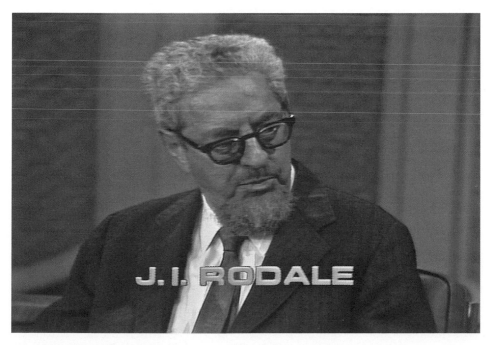

An image of J. I. Rodale in his final moments has never before been released. *Video still, courtesy of Daphne Productions*

WWF wrestler Owen Hart signed autographs at Andrews Air Force Base eight days before he was killed in a spectacular entrance to the ring—dropping from the rafters. *Photo by Telfair H. Brown PA1, courtesy of Wikimedia Commons*

LEFT: Kid Canfield, the notorious reformed gambler, was the first documented case of death by "mic fright." *Newspaper ad, via Newspapers.com*

RIGHT: Radio announcer and *Jack Armstrong, the All-American Boy* actor Carlton KaDell's publicized arrest in a gay vice sting in 1949 may have inspired him to create the series *Case Dismissed*. *Publicity still*

Hostess Deborah Gail Stone, crushed between the moving walls of the America Sings attraction, was the first, and thus far only, performer to die on the job at Disneyland. *Courtesy of Wikimedia Commons*

Tiny Tim suffered a heart attack and collapsed after performing his signature song, "Tiptoe Through the Tulips." *Photos by Mike Carano, courtesy of the photographer*

The wind and faulty wire rigging were blamed for Karl Wallenda's fatal plunge, but photographer Gary Williams, who shot this sequence, says, "A doctor friend called me two weeks after the fall to tell me that my photos show the face of a man having a heart attack."

11

International Pop Music

TENS OF THOUSANDS OF PEOPLE filled the streets in Turkey for the funeral of Zeki Müren, who died on live television on September 24, 1996, after receiving a lifetime achievement award. Müren was sixty-four. His name may be not be familiar to Americans, but there were few more famous artists in Turkey in the second half of the twentieth century. For four decades, he was the country's most popular entertainer, a powerful vocalist, songwriter, composer, poet, actor, and master of Turkish classical music. He was also screamingly, mincingly, flamboyantly, stereotypically over-the-top: a showman who lived his life openly and pushed gender boundaries in an overwhelmingly conservative country. He was, and remains, the country's first and most cherished gay icon. A man who began his career in the same era as Liberace is now celebrated as "Turkey's David Bowie." Zeki Müren was one of many international pop stars whose deaths led to outpourings of grief and publicity, sometimes beyond the borders of their native lands.

Irma Bule

When Britney Spears performed at the 2001 *MTV Video Music Awards* with a Burmese python draped across her shoulders, she created a scandalous, iconic pop moment that would define her image for years to come. Britney's act, though, was nothing compared to the dangdut pop performers of Indonesia. Dangdut is a bouncy music genre with Indian and Arab influences (not unlike some of the styles Britney and her successors appropriate). The dangdut singers are young, sexy, and scantily clad; almost all the time they perform with snakes.

A snake attracts crowds and helps keep grabby male audience members at bay. A snake can be the difference between making twenty dollars and twenty-five dollars a show, and that's a big difference, for although there are a few successful dangdut superstars, most of the performers are poor young women in backwater regions, doing their best to support their families. Some even say that the entire dangdut scene is simply exploitation of poverty-stricken women doing whatever they can to survive.

Irma Bule was a dangdut performer in the Karawang region of West Java. Twenty-six and the mother of three, she worked often with boa constrictors and, like Britney, pythons. Sometimes, she'd wrap a snake around her neck; sometimes she'd wrap a snake around one of her backing musicians. Almost all the time, she duct-taped the snake's mouth shut.

Irma was not a national star, but all that changed on April 4, 2016, when she performed in a village in Karawang. That performance, captured on videotape, spread her name and reputation around the world. It involved a king cobra whose mouth was not duct-taped shut.

The snake had a name: Rianti. Rianti was around Irma's neck for her opening number, as she sang and danced to organ music. For the next number, Irma knelt on one knee and let the snake crawl down her side and behind her leg.

"The accident happened in the middle of the second song when Irma stepped on the snake's tail," Fernando Octavion Auzura, who was in the audience, told local website Merdeka.com. "The snake then bit Irma on the thigh."

At first, Irma didn't seem affected by the bite. The snake was placed in a bag, and she kept on dancing. When the snake's handler offered antivenom, she refused the medication. She joked to friends backstage that she didn't feel any pain.

Irma must have believed the cobra's venom glands had been removed. They had not. She sang and danced for another forty-five minutes before the venom that was pumped into her thigh had moved through her organs toward her heart. Suddenly, Irma began vomiting. She went into seizures on the stage. She collapsed and fell unconscious. She was taken to a hospital, where she was later confirmed dead.

It's not known why Irma was performing with a king cobra. A king cobra is one of the deadliest animals in the world. It can kill an elephant—or twenty people—with a single bite.

Mango

He was born Giuseppe Mango, but friends called him "Pino Mango." As "Mango," he was one of Italy's biggest music stars of the 1980s. With his fusion of pop and world music, and an incredible vocal range, he was Italy's own Billy Joel, Peter Gabriel, and Sting, wrapped into one compact package. His fame and artistry carried over through the 1990s and into the new millennium, as he continued to expand his musical horizons and extend the boundaries of Italian pop music.

On Sunday night, December 7, 2014, the beloved star was performing a benefit concert in the town of Policoro in southern Italy. At a high point in the show, the band had left the stage, leaving Mango sitting alone onstage at the keyboard of an electric piano.

It was time for a special solo version of his biggest hit. "Oro" was from *Odissea*, his 1986 breakout album, so of course many in the crowd sang along with Mango:

> . . . *un diamante per un sì, oro . . .*

Mango let the audience sing the next words: "*Oro, oro . . .*" He sang, "*per averti così—*" then stopped singing and playing. The audience carried on: "*. . . distesa pura ma tu ci stai . . .*" Mango gamely picked up the song. He managed to play four notes before stopping again, hands on the keyboard, head bowed. After the audience crooned the next line, "*Perché accetti e ci stai?*" a cappella, he stopped them, raising a hand and mumbling:

> *Scusa.*

"Sorry." Mango's right hand hit the keys with a *plink*. He looked to his right, gestured for help, then slumped at the keyboard. A stagehand rushed onstage, and as he tried to stop Mango from falling off his seat, Mango's arm hit the piano keys.

An ominous electric bass note tolled the end. Several other stagehands helped move the star to the floor, and a uniformed emergency worker joined them. Mango was dead of a heart attack at sixty.

This tragedy turned out to be only the first for the Mango family. At the wake on Tuesday, Mango's older brother, the grief-stricken, seventy-five-year-old Giovanni, collapsed and also died. Two other brothers, Armando and Michele, had to be hospitalized after they found out Giovanni was dead.

Giovanni's death was attributed to a heart attack, though some speculated his was a true case of broken heart syndrome.

"'Broken heart syndrome' usually affects women, and is similar to a heart attack although the symptoms aren't as severe," Antonio Rebuzzi, a professor of cardiology at Rome's Catholic University told Ansa, Italy's wire service. "It's not unusual for a shock like a death to provoke a cardiological illness like a heart attack or malignant arrhythmia."

Thousands gathered outside the main church in the small town of Lagonegro for Mango's funeral on Wednesday, December 10. They applauded as his casket was brought inside. Later that afternoon, there was a funeral for his brother Giovanni.

Papa Wemba

Music fans in the Western world might know Papa Wemba from his work with Peter Gabriel. The Congolese singer and musician toured with the prog rock star on his 1993 *Secret World Live* tour, and recorded three albums for Gabriel's record label, Real World Records. In Africa, meanwhile, the man born Jules Shungu Wembadio Pene Kikumba was a music superstar, flamboyant fashion icon, and envoy to the world. He was known as "the King of Rumba Rock," a style originally called Congolese rumba, and later *soukous* (derived from the French *secouer*, "to shake"), that blended traditional African and Caribbean rhythms with rock and soul.

Papa Wemba's greatest gift was his voice, a haunting high-pitched tenor that he inherited from his mother, a professional "wailing woman" at funerals. Singing in his native Lingala and in French, Papa Wemba toured the world with his band, Viva la Musica, for almost thirty years—until the early morning of April 24, 2016.

Papa Wemba and the band were three songs into their set at the FEMUA urban music festival in Abidjan, Ivory Coast, when he shook for the last time. His death was captured on the festival's video feed. The band was deep into a groove; Papa Wemba rocked at a microphone center stage, in front of the drum riser. Five female dancers shook and moved in front of him. The entire group was rocking when, suddenly, Papa Wemba fell backwards onto the stage. His final vision was of those ample, shaking booties.

The band kept playing as various musicians, stagehands, and the dancers slowly realized what had happened and went to his aid. They lifted Papa Wemba to a sitting position, and took turns fanning his face with his large stylish pink hat and other objects as if the effect of a breeze would somehow stimulate his heart, which had stopped. This part of Africa had apparently not been exposed to the wonders of CPR. Papa Wemba's eyes remained closed behind his glasses, his face slack, his body slumped. He was dead at sixty-six.

———————

The passing of the cultural hero led to public mourning throughout the continent. Baudouin Banza Mukalay, the Democratic Republic of Congo's culture minister, called the death a "great loss for the country and all of Africa" and praised Papa Wemba as "a role model for Congolese youth."

Peter Gabriel posted a tribute on his website:

> Music flowed out of him effortlessly and he could thrill people with one of the most beautiful and emotional voices I have ever heard. His music was full of gentle rhythms and joy, but the passion came from the power of his singing, which always carried a sadness, especially in his high voice, which I found really moving.

Gabriel also added a puzzling footnote: "His run-in with the French and Belgian immigration authorities for smuggling people into Europe was a real low-point in his career, but we only ever saw him act kindly and always assumed that his motivation had been honourable."

Run-in with immigration authorities? Smuggling people? *Say what?* For those who weren't keeping up with their Papa Wemba news, the run-in to which Gabriel referred was his 2004 trial in Paris for trafficking in visas—also known as human smuggling. It seems that Papa Wemba was running an elaborate illegal immigration scheme for people who wanted to leave the Democratic Republic of Congo and settle in Europe. He disguised them as members of his band.

When Papa Wemba traveled to Europe on tour, he'd earn a little extra pocket money by charging people $3,500 for a seat on his plane. French officials grew somewhat suspicious on December 31, 2001, when ninety Congolese people showed up at Charles de Gaulle Airport, claiming to be musicians involved in a Papa Wemba show at the Bercy Stadium in Paris. Not one of them arrived with a musical instrument. None would take a return flight to Congo.

Papa Wemba was arrested at his home near Paris; he claimed he was acting as a humanitarian, saving many young people from Congo's savage war. He spent three and a half months in Fleury-Mérogis Prison in Paris (where he'd once performed for inmates) before he was convicted and handed a suspended sentence. After the verdict, Congolese fans outside the court danced with joy and carried their hero away on their shoulders.

Interlude

Open Mic Night

Kipp Rusty Walker

When he was a student at Bartlett High School, Kipp Rusty Walker may have been the best teenage skateboarder in Anchorage, Alaska. Had he lived in a city like Los Angeles, Philadelphia, or Tampa, his skills might have led to opportunities, but Anchorage, the isolated gateway to the magnificent wilderness, with its long dark winters and heavy snows, wasn't exactly the launching pad for skateboarding stars. In another city, some-where in the Lower 48—that's what locals call the area between Canada and Mexico—he might have been seen as more than just another with-drawn rebel in a place that was a magnet for them.

His classmates at Bartlett High remembered Kipp as a very cool char-acter, handsome in an Ashton Kutcher kind of way, but also very shy. Kipp wasn't much for conversation, but thanks in part to his skateboard, he did have friends. Once you got him to open up, they said, he had interesting ideas on interesting subjects. They also told the *Anchorage Daily News* that Kipp had "emotional issues." His parents did what they could to get him help, but when he made his break to the "outside"— what locals call the world beyond Alaska—he took those issues with him.

In the summer of 2010, after graduation from Bartlett High, Kipp and some of his skateboarding buddies made their way twenty-five hundred miles southeast to Bend, Oregon. For a kid who grew up in a city on the rugged terrain in the shadow of majestic mountains, the city nicknamed "the Aspen of Oregon" was a polished, sophisticated version of Anchorage, full of interesting people with interesting ideas. The resort city 162 miles southeast of Portland was also a gateway to outdoor activities—only these were year-round, including whitewater rafting and fishing on the Deschutes River and skiing on Mt. Bachelor in the Cascade Mountain Range overlooking the city.

Bend also had its Portlandia side, with many cultural activities and a downtown arts district. With their flannel shirts, wool caps, and skateboards as means of transportation, young drifters like Kipp and his friends fit right in.

In the winter of 2011, the issues that had worried Kipp's parents and school counselors began to spring up more openly. Among the interesting ideas Kipp began speaking of was the inevitability of death and, with it, the futility of life. He talked about making his mark on the world by ending his own life, and doing it in a public place.

"It was almost like he wanted to prove a point, like there's no point in being scared of death because it's going to happen to us anyway," one friend told a reporter for Oregon's NewsChannel 21. When Kipp told him of his plans on March 20, the first day of spring, that friend got in touch with Kipp's parents back in Anchorage. They got their son admitted to the psychiatric unit at St. Charles Medical Center in Bend. When Kipp was released a few days later, he still had a public exit on his mind. There was nothing his parents could do. There was nothing his friend could do.

"I actually told him," the friend said, "I was like, 'Dude, this is going to mess a lot of people up.'"

This is going to mess a lot of people up. Those words may have resonated; for a couple of weeks after his release from St. Charles, Kipp found new interests. He began teaching himself piano. He got a particular tune stuck in his head and kept working on it until he managed to play it.

The second week of April, he told his friends he was going to perform the song in public. There was a place downtown, on Bond Street at the corner of Arizona Avenue, where he could make it happen. The Strictly Organic Coffee Company was a coffeehouse, known for roasting its own fair-trade beans and for its breakfast burritos, lunch wraps, and salads. Strictly Organic also offered entertainment in the evenings, featuring local and traveling-through folk and blues singers, and every Thursday from 6:00 to 8:00 PM held Open Mic Night. Singer-songwriters, musicians, poets, comedians—anyone could get up on the small stage and show off their talents.

In the late afternoon of April 11, 2011, Kipp and his Anchorage pal A. J. Pryzbyla arrived at Strictly Organic, and Kipp signed up for a spot on the open mic stage. The folks who worked at the place didn't recognize him. He wasn't a regular customer, and this was his first time at Open Mic Night.

This is going to mess a lot of people up.

Kipp got his chance around 6:30 PM. He walked onto the small stage, sat at the electric piano and announced the name of the song he was about to play: "Sorry for All the Mess."

Staff included, about fifteen people witnessed Kipp's show. The coffeehouse workers went about their work, and others paid polite attention as Kipp leaned over the keyboard and concentrated. He played for a good five minutes or more before coming to the end of "Sorry for All the Mess."

There was a bit of applause as Kipp hesitated. It looked as if he was thinking about what to do next, whether to do something next. *This is going to mess a lot of people up.*

Kipp Rusty Walker stood and faced the audience. He revealed a knife with a six-inch double-edged blade and plunged it into his chest. He pulled it out and did it again—and again, punching the knife at heart level.

The audience applauded. Some cheered. Obviously, they were being treated to some sort of theatrical piece or performance art. Only when Kipp dropped to the stage, in a rapidly expanding pool of his own blood, did the cheers turn to gasps and screams. People rushed forward to try to save him. They administered first aid until the paramedics from the Bend Fire Department showed up to take Kipp back to St. Charles Medical Center, this time to the emergency room. It was too late. He was a week away from turning twenty.

12

Television

B<small>ROADCASTERS</small> <small>LONG</small> <small>AGO</small> <small>ADOPTED</small> <small>A</small> system, known widely as the "seven-second delay," to prevent profanity, nudity, or any other offensive material from being heard or seen on live television, which might cause viewers to burn up the phone lines with complaints and threaten a station or network's license to broadcast. Occasionally, reality does slip through, and the shocking images are hard to erase.

Many cite the shooting of Lee Harvey Oswald, the alleged assassin of President John F. Kennedy (yes, we'll let the doubts and conspiracy theories linger) as the TV generation's first onscreen killing. Oswald wasn't a performer per se, but a major player in a reality drama that began on Friday, November 22, 1963, at 12:30 PM CST in Dallas, Texas. Two days later, at 11:21 AM CST, Oswald the suspect was shot in the stomach, fatally, by a mobbed-up strip club owner named Jacob Leon Rubenstein, a.k.a. Jack Ruby, as Oswald was being led by detectives past cameras in the basement of Dallas Police Headquarters.

Unlike the shooting of JFK, the shooting of Lee Harvey Oswald was broadcast live to the nation, and a new era had begun.

J. I. Rodale

I am so healthy that I expect to live on and on!

Nutritionist J. I. Rodale uttered versions of that statement more than once. He used those exact words on June 8, 1971, when he died on the set of *The Dick Cavett Show*.

Many people recall watching Cavett's talk show on the night that one of his guests dropped dead mid-interview, a vision providing not only a traumatic, indelible memory but also a living, dying example of the inevitable results of hubris. The man was a health nut! He'd boasted that he was going to live to be a hundred! And then he dropped dead on live television!

Dick Cavett once wrote in the *New York Times* that he's approached "about twenty times a year" by "people who are so sure that they saw it that they could pass a polygraph test." The only problem? "Well, you see, that show never aired."

Videotape of the most infamous incident of a person dying on a television talk show does exist, but for close to five decades, it has never been made public. It has not shown up on YouTube, *Faces of Death* movies, or any historical documentaries. The footage is owned by Cavett's Daphne Productions and has been locked away ever since in the company's storage facility. Cavett himself has one of the few copies, and he tells us he can rarely bring himself to watch.

"About two years ago, my friend Marshall Brickman and I took a mild drink in his New York apartment before loading the disc," he says. "We felt the need of something a bit stronger after watching it. The first hour of the ninety minutes is a perfectly good, airable show, with many laughs. The final half hour is hell."

Cavett's description was confirmed in late 2018, when we, the authors, were granted a private viewing of the lost episode. The screening revealed that many published accounts of what occurred on the Cavett set that day have not been totally accurate, but although the facts may be at odds with the legend, they are no less impressive or ironic.

Jerome Irving Rodale (né Cohen) had spent more than two decades pro-moting controversial, nontraditional health and medical advice in his monthly magazines *Organic Farming and Gardening* and *Prevention*. He'd remained on the fringe of accepted science and mainstream America until the 1960s, when the counterculture and the "back to the garden" move-ment led to interest in organic foods and alternative therapies.

This interest led to an in-depth profile of Rodale in the *New York Times Magazine* on June 6, 1971. For "Guru of the Organic Food Cult," editor Wade Greene visited Rodale at his sprawling home on the sixty-three-acre Rodale Experiment Organic Farm in Pennsylvania. The article portrayed Rodale as a very funny (his first publishing ventures were humor magazines), semiretired eccentric whose greatest passion was the theater (he'd written thirty-three plays and "seldom misses a Wednesday matinee in New York") and who was derided by critics as a "crack-pot," although, at seventy-two, he remained "a walking testimonial to his health theories." The article continued:

> J.I., who, I suspect, is practicing comedy at times as well as writ-ing it . . . certainly does go for some exceedingly unconventional things. . . . He thinks and has written at length that wheat is terrible for people, can make them overly aggressive or daffy, and that sugar is worse. "I'm going to live to be 100," says the author of *Natural Health, Sugar and the Criminal Mind*, "unless I'm run down by a sugar-crazed taxi driver."

The *New York Times* piece was followed two days later by Rodale's appearance on *The Dick Cavett Show*. The late-night program on the ABC network was one of several series with that name that would be hosted by the erudite, witty former comedian over the next half-century. This version premiered on December 29, 1969, and survived five years as an offbeat, intellectual alternative to *The Tonight Show Starring Johnny Carson*. The ninety-minute format was similar to Carson's, with a studio audience and opening monologue followed by a comedy segment and interviews with entertainers and newsmakers of the day. Unlike today's heavily produced late night shows that exist mainly to promote products, Cavett's show provided a forum for conversation about ideas.

The set of *The Dick Cavett Show* at ABC studios on Manhattan's Upper West Side was the same one used for ABC's *Wide World of Sports* broadcast on weekends. Significantly, there was no host desk or couch on which guests could slide over. Everyone, including the host, sat in leather swivel chairs on an orange shag carpet.

Along with J. I. Rodale, the guests on the show recorded on Tuesday, June 8, 1971, included humorist Marshall Efron (who appeared in a cooking segment tied to the imminent White House nuptials of Richard Nixon's daughter Tricia), prominent paleozoologist Elwyn Simons (who brought along some cute monkeys), and *New York Post* columnist Pete Hamill.

After the introduction, with music by drummer Bobby Rosengarden and the orchestra, Cavett's monologue focused on current events, including the final episode of *The Ed Sullivan Show* two nights earlier, and a strike by New York City municipal workers who, as a protest, left dozens of city drawbridges in the raised position.

"It's a wonderful city to live in, if we're attacked by Mongol hordes," Cavett observed, to some laughter. ". . . What else should I mention? Oh, there's one other thing. So, Sophia Loren—can you verify this?— has adopted a baby girl in the paper today. That's the truth. Now, she already has a baby, right? So she now has two babies at once, which the Italian government has hailed as maximum use of natural resources."

J. I. Rodale appeared after the Efron and Simons segments. Cavett introduced him as "an unusual man with a lot of opinions, which the United States Department of Agriculture, to mention one, doesn't necessarily agree with." Rodale walked on as Rosengarden's band played "Doin' What Comes Naturally."

Cavett recalls, quite accurately, that Rodale was "a slight man, and looked like Leon Trotsky with the little goatee." Rodale began the interview by correcting Cavett's pronunciation of his name.

"The accent, second syllable."

"Rodale," Cavett repeated. "Have a chair."

"It's, uh, accented on the first syllable. *Ro*-dale."

"First syllable."

"Don't call me Raw Deal."

And so began three segments and twenty-five minutes of entertaining and informative conversation.

"Organic gardening is using natural fertilizers, like manure," Rodale explained. "I should say, *animal* manure. *Manure* is an all-comprehensive term."

"Oh, is it?"

"Yes, technically even a leaf is manure."

"Huh," Cavett replied, thoughtfully. ". . . You started this years ago. They talk about this, people who believe in it, as a movement that's time has come."

"It started thirty years ago."

"And people thought you were a crackpot then, and now a lot of people practice this."

"'Crackpot' is mild," Rodale said. "They called me 'manure worshipers'—"

That got a laugh. So did Rodale's admission that he was dragging out his explanations, "so you'll call me back again. We don't want to cover too much ground."

"Oh, you don't have to worry," Cavett assured him. "I want to cover ground, because I know that you have acres and acres of it."

"I have acres and acres of ground, but it's organic ground!"

Cavett threw to a commercial break. He recalls, "Rodale was so good and so amusing that I had made a mental note to have him back."

In the next segment, Rodale extolled the wonders not only of organic foods but also of bone meal supplements. The conversation went on from there:

> DICK CAVETT: How old are you? Do you mind my asking?
> J. I. RODALE: I will be seventy-three in August. Now, I am so healthy that I uh, expect to live on and on. I have no aches or pains. I'm full of energy. If you want me to do a—not a flip, but—
> DICK CAVETT: No.
> J. I. RODALE: —kicking my heels up! Not this time, the next time. (AUDIENCE laughter)
> DICK CAVETT: All right.
> J. I. RODALE: I want to get to know you first.

DICK CAVETT: Oh, you don't kick your heels up for just anybody?

J. I. RODALE: For strangers, no. . . . Now, after a few years on bone meal, my bones were so strong, that one night I fell down a whole flight of steps—

DICK CAVETT: Just to test them?

J. I. RODALE: I laughed all the way. I laughed all the way down, 'cause I knew. I knew, that I had been taking bone meal and that nothing could happen to me. And nothing did. And I enjoyed the ride.

The audience laughed, and they laughed and applauded when Rodale talked about the dangers of sugar and wheat, and the importance of protein.

In the third segment, Rodale pulled out props: asparagus spears. He convinced Cavett to take a bite.

"It's all washed," Rodale promised. "All the earthworms are out."

Legend has it that Cavett took a bite of asparagus that had been boiled in urine. That was not the case. Though grown in manure, the vegetable was raw.

"You see, when you eat a piece of raw asparagus, you are getting all the enzymes," Rodale explained. While the audience laughed at Cavett's tentative chewing, he added: "You have just tasted the enzymes. Now, when you cook something, all the enzymes are destroyed."

There was a raised eyebrow from the host when Rodale suggested that eating cooked food could lead to cancer. "In cancerous tissues, the results are always a lack of enzymes."

Cavett upped the raised-eyebrow ante when he asked about the claim in the *Times* article that each day Rodale sat under a machine that sent short-wave beams through his body.

"The whole body runs on electricity," Rodale posited. ". . . But as you get older, some of the electricity drains out. And I know that when I reached the age of about seventy, I got a little tired here and there. So by taking these electric treatments, it gives me more electrical energy."

After he whipped out and cracked open a large, hard-boiled goose egg, it was time for another break. When *The Dick Cavett Show* returned, Rodale was in mid-conversation with the host, explaining that when he ate cooked asparagus "it gave a flavor to the urine that you could smell. Many of you know that. But when I ate *raw* asparagus, there was no such smell. You see, I'm always clinical this way, I'm willing to undress in public if it'll help you."

That may have given birth to the mash-up of memories that erroneously had Cavett chomping urine-boiled asparagus. In real time, it was a cue to bring out Pete Hamill.

When Hamill made his entrance, every inch the suave 1970s reporter with his Broadway Joe sideburns, electric blue sports jacket, and rectangular glasses, Rodale moved to the swivel chair to his right. Hamill got down to business, talking about New York politics that led workers to open drawbridges in protest.

It was three and a half minutes into the conversation. Hamill was talking about Governor Nelson Rockefeller when he was interrupted.

"The basis of his power and the basis of his continuing allegiance is in the Republican party, which in this state is basically a party of big business and homeowners," Hamill stated. "So that two people that run the state legislature here are a fisherman—"

At this point, J. I. Rodale let out a rude, gurgling snore.

". . . uh, fish salesman from—"

Audience members laughed. Hamill stopped short.

Rodale was now on camera, head tilted back. He continued to snore.

Various retellings of this story have Cavett inquiring, "Are we boring you, Mr. Rodale?" and Hamill leaning in and whispering, "This is bad." In reality, the two men stopped and looked at Rodale with immediate concern. And though there were titters from the crowd, there was alarm on the orange shag carpet.

"You all right?" Cavett asked the snoring, unconscious man. He turned to Hamill. "I don't know, I don't know." Then he looked past him. "Mr. Rodale?"

Rodale responded with a snore. A wave of laughter rolled across the studio audience. Not from Cavett. "I think we better do it."

"Do you have a commercial?" Hamill muttered.

"Mr. Rodale, are you all right?"

Rodale responded with a slurping snore, which continued under Cavett's stream-of-consciousness statements. "Maybe we should get a doctor. I don't know . . . Does he have a relative with him? No?"

J. I. Rodale's death-rattle snore ceased. He remained stretched out on the leather swivel chair, head back, mouth open.

"Check— Get a doctor," Cavett called out. "Do you have, do you have a doc— Does anyone know, is there a doctor here? Is there a doctor here?"

Cavett later said he paused deliberately and chose his words when asking about a doctor. Had he said, *Is there a doctor in the house?* he would have gotten a laugh. By this point, however, the seriousness was clear. The audience was silent.

"Is there a doctor here?" one of the studio crew repeated, loudly.

Someone called out, "*Get an ambulance!*"

"Yeah, can you?" Cavett replied. "What do we have for emergency?"

A crew member: "An ambulance is on the way."

"Who is?"

"An ambulance was called."

"Does he have epilepsy or anything?" Cavett asked. "Get the ox— Can you get the oxygen unit?"

"Yes."

"Get the oxygen unit."

Another stagehand: "Call the fire department!"

"Jesus," Dick Cavett muttered.

The video segment ends with the crew sending someone to the firehouse across the street, while Cavett asks who knows how to use the oxygen unit kept in the studio for emergencies. The stage lights are dimmed. The picture fades to black.

Meanwhile, the drama continued. Two doctors, an internist, and an orthopedic surgeon rushed from their seats to the stage. They loosened Rodale's tie and pants, laid him flat on the floor, and administered CPR and mouth-to-mouth resuscitation.

"Naturally, it was assumed that this was somehow part of the show, and then the assurance that it wasn't drifted like a wave, backwards through the audience. People began to cry," Cavett recalls. "As often happens, a vivid and inappropriately amusing image remains: a short cameraman struggling to remain on his toes in order to look down into his tilted camera to focus on Rodale, lying on the floor."

Dick Cavett also reveals a more unsettling memory. "The studio had oxygen equipment, but it didn't work. I try not to think about that."

Pete Hamill took out his reporter's notebook and calmly and professionally took notes for the next day's column. The ambulance attendants arrived to take Rodale to Roosevelt Hospital, though in Cavett's words "he was the ghastly pale of a plumber's candle.

"Poor Rodale was DOA at the hospital," he tells us. "Someone said that he had spent most of his life with a damaged heart and was not supposed to live beyond his youth. An apparent tribute to his health practices?"

J. I. Rodale would not live to be a hundred, after all. He would not live on and on; he would not make it to seventy-three. The snores were his death rattle. Most agree he was dead in the chair.

Death was attributed to a heart attack. A unique theory as to what triggered it came from Marshall Efron, the humorist from the Nixon wedding–themed cooking segment. He watched the Rodale tragedy unfold in a monitor in the greenroom and told the *Realist* a few days later that the "health nut" should never have entered a television studio, because overhead steel beams and the insulated stage floor would sap the electricity that he'd zapped into his body every day. Even worse, "TV cameras and microphones were already draining his body electricity. No wonder he expired. I told that to people and they asked me, 'Do you believe that?' Of course, it doesn't make any difference what I believe; *he* believed it."

––––––––––––

"Who would the gods have die on a talk show but a health expert?" Cavett asked more than once in the decades to follow. Time and again, he's explained that although he described the incident in his opening monologue on the show that aired the following evening, and Hamill wrote about it in his newspaper column, the only ones who witnessed the death of J. I. Rodale were those in the studio. (A repeat episode from the previous April Fool's Day, featuring Jack Benny, Phil Silvers, Jane Asher, and Fats Domino, aired instead that night.)

"That was a live death on camera—we weren't live, obviously," Cavett says. "The show didn't air. I must have described it so brilliantly."

The day after J. I. Rodale died, with the incident "on the news and in the papers," Cavett made a phone call. "I called Johnny Carson to ask how in hell you do the next night's show. He said, 'It's no damn fun, Richard. You walk out and calmly relate the story of what happened. Then, mercifully, there's a commercial break and after that, to your surprise, you feel sort of cleansed and are able to go on and do a show. Before long it's fun and games again.'

"He was right, and I thanked him. It was the first conversation between us that had contained no humor. And then the wonderful, sadness-relieving Carson irreverence: 'Oh, one other pointer, Richard. When telling the story, try not to get more than, say, two big laughs'— followed by a quick hang-up."

Christine Chubbuck

Of all the on-camera deaths in television news, few if any were as big a shock to the system, or as mysterious, as that of Christine Chubbuck, host of *Suncoast Digest*, the morning talk show on Channel 40, WXLT-TV in Sarasota, Florida.

On the morning of July 15, 1974, the attractive, twenty-nine-year-old brunette had a change-up for the crew. She wanted to add a news report near the top of the 9:30 AM broadcast, something that hadn't been done before.

The big story that Monday morning was out of Washington, DC, where seven hostages who'd been held in a basement cell block by armed convicts escaped after an elevator key was smuggled in a box of sanitary napkins. Chubbuck, though, wanted to run a taped package on a shooting at a local restaurant the previous day.

The show went on as usual until eight minutes in, when Chubbuck introduced the news package. The tape jammed. The package didn't run.

Ever the pro, Christine Chubbuck turned to the camera, very non-chalantly, and said, "In keeping with Channel 40's policy of bringing you the latest in blood and guts, and in living color, you are going to see another first," and, looking straight into the camera, stated, "an attempted suicide."

She then pulled out a .38 caliber revolver from a bag of puppets she kept under the anchor desk and shot herself behind the right ear. Smoke puffed from the gun and her hair flew up around her face, which contorted as she fell forward violently against the desk, before slipping out of camera range.

The screen faded quickly to black. Viewers responded. Some called the station, others police, not sure if this was a bad joke, a performance—or an actual suicide on camera.

It was after the anchorwoman was taken to Sarasota Memorial Hospital that news director Mike Simmons got a closer look at the papers she was reading at the desk. The papers included a follow-up story written by Chubbuck: "TV 40 news personality Christine Chubbuck shot herself in a live broadcast this morning on a Channel 40 talk program. She was rushed to Sarasota Memorial Hospital, where she remains in critical condition."

Christine Chubbuck was indeed in very critical condition. She'd suffered irreparable brain damage, and she died on Tuesday. The station's master tape was seized by police as evidence and reportedly was destroyed.

The suicide received minimal coverage on network news, the facts recited much as Chubbuck had written. It has since been cited as an inspiration for Paddy Chayefsky's Oscar-winning screenplay for *Network*, the 1976 film about the "as mad as hell" news anchorman, but whether the suicide was in fact a protest against the "if it bleeds it leads" philosophy of local television news was never clear. (Chubbuck's family members said she was extremely depressed in the weeks leading up to her death and had been under psychiatric care.)

Three years after the suicide, news director Simmons told the Associated Press, "There hasn't really been any changes, not as far as the station goes. That incident didn't happen because of our editorial policy.

We had just been through a particularly violent week, with a kidnaping-and-hostage situation, a shootout between some cops and someone else, and these had bumped a couple of her feature stories. But the crux of the situation was that she was a twenty-nine-year-old-girl who wanted to be married and who wasn't." *Suncoast Digest* was still on the air, and there had been two successor anchorwomen, both young and single.

In the decades that followed the suicide, video of the shooting never surfaced. Two separate films about the death of Christine Chubbuck premiered at the 2016 Sundance Film Festival. In June of that year, it was reported that Mollie Nelson, widow of WXLT-TV's former owner, did have a copy of the suicide tape. She said she gave the video to a "very large law firm" for safekeeping and had no plans to show it.

Owen Hart

Deaths of athletes on the playing field, in the arena, in the ring, or on the pitch are far too numerous to list, and athletes in many sports, like bull-fighters or boxers, can't be counted among performers who die unexpectedly onstage, because death is in the cards every time they step up to compete. Even professional wrestlers, who straddle that fine line of show business with their comic book personas, scripted matches, and choreographed movements, are athletes who put their bodies at risk with every piledriver, clothesline, and body slam.

Yet, there is no ignoring the World Wrestling Federation star who made the biggest impact of all—in more ways than one—while the television cameras rolled. Owen Hart is considered to be one of the greatest professional wrestlers of all time. He certainly was one of most charismatic and entertaining wrestlers of the 1990s, and it was in his role as entertainer, making an entrance to the ring, that he made his exit—not as an athlete but as a consummate performer.

Born in Calgary, Alberta, to a wrestling family in 1965, Owen Hart began his career in Canada on his father Stu Hart's Stampede Wrestling circuit. He went on to tour Japan and ultimately became a superstar with the World Wrestling Federation, the world's premier professional wrestling show.

On May 23, 1999, Owen Hart was one of the stars of the WWF's *Over the Edge* pay-per-view event at Kemper Arena, a 19,500-seat venue in Kansas City, Missouri. This was a wrestling spectacular, and all the WWF's biggest stars, including the Rock, Triple H, Steve Austin, and the Big Boss Man, were there.

Now, it should be mentioned again that for all the drama and real-life brutality they contain, WWF wrestling matches were not legitimate sporting events but choreographed, scripted playlets. For an event of this magnitude, the WWF scriptwriters wanted to ensure that Hart made a spectacular entrance that not only demonstrated his comedic skills but also kicked off a very serious battle between good and evil.

His scheduled opponent was WWF Intercontinental champion the Godfather. The Godfather character was played by African American wrestler Charles Wright as a hulking "pimp daddy" who'd often enter the ring surrounded by "hoes"—usually women from local strip clubs—whom he'd offer to an opponent in exchange for forfeiting the match. The Godfather was the "evil."

For his part, Hart had resurrected his character, the Blue Blazer, a spoof superhero in electric blue tights, a feather-lined cape, and a blue, silver, and red face mask. The Blue Blazer would make his entrance as an actual superhero might—descending into the ring from high in the rafters of the arena.

He wouldn't actually fly, of course. The script called for him to be lowered on a grapple line connected by a harness. Attached to the harness would be midget wrestler Max Mini, wearing an identical Blue Blazer costume. When Hart was a few feet above the ring, he'd drop Max Mini, pretend to become entangled in the line, then release himself and fall flat on his face in the ring. The Godfather would proceed to beat the daylights out of him. The Blue Blazer would recover, turn the tables, and take the title. "Good" would prevail.

Owen Hart had run into difficulties when he carried out a version of this superhero entrance at a *WWF Sunday Night Heat* event in 1998. After he descended toward the ring, the release clip on the safety harness took too long to disengage, leaving him hanging a few feet off the floor outside the ring. While he fumbled and twisted in the air, his opponent stepped out of the ring and kicked and punched at him like he was a piñata. The scene was ridiculous enough, but it was agreed that the long delay didn't make for good television. The WWF brass insisted that Owen Hart needed to separate himself from the cable much more quickly.

A rigger from Orlando, Florida, was hired to coordinate the stunt. Bobby Talbert had worked on a similar drop of the wrestler Sting of the rival World Championship Wrestling organization. Talbert's solution was simple. This time, the harness would be attached to the line with a nautical clip—a hair-trigger, instant-release mechanism designed for use on a sailboat mast. Hart would just have to give it a touch and he'd fall from the rappelling line.

Several stunt coordinators allegedly refused to test the new method, saying it was "crazy," but despite the reservations, Talbert and his assistants moved forward with the complicated rigging high above the arena floor. They supposedly performed two tests with a 250-pound sandbag. Meanwhile, Hart was very nervous about the entire stunt and refused to carry another stuntman on the way down. The fact that Max Mini didn't speak English and was in need of a translator to explain the dangers of hitting that nautical clip too early led to the scrapping of the double drop.

Owen Hart did a solo rehearsal at 3:30 PM. The drop worked well enough, but he forgot to pull the release cord and moved around the ring with the line still attached. He said he realized his mistake and would get it right when it counted.

Showtime for Owen Hart was forty minutes into the *Over the Edge* event. He was positioned, along with Talbert and his assistants, on a catwalk just under the eighty-five-foot-high roof of the arena, above the southwest corner of the ring. He was fitted with the harness and release cord that, when pulled, would open the nautical clip and free him from the rappel line.

The house lights dimmed. Owen Hart climbed over a four-foot railing. Talbert checked the tension of the line by dangling the wrestler a few feet beneath the catwalk. A forty-second video profile of the Blue Blazer began to play on the giant TitanTron screen below. While the referee cleared debris from the ring following the last match, Hart let go of the catwalk railing, placed his hands on his harness, and dangled, suspended, waiting to be lowered.

He extended his elbows to adjust the cape that was attached to his hands by elastic bands and kept getting in his way. Then there was the sound of a snap.

The nautical clip had somehow released prematurely. Owen Hart plunged toward the wrestling ring. His 229-pound body dropped seventy-eight feet before slamming chest-first on the top rope of the ring. Hart flipped backwards, landed on his back in the ring, and bounced a foot off the canvas. His arms continued to bounce on the springy floor of the ring before settling.

The crowd, not realizing what it was witnessing, cheered. A fan in the stands offered testimony on an Internet forum:

> Since it was my first pay-per-view, I was anxiously looking around the arena, rather than watching the boring pre-taped promo on the TitanTron. As I was looking around, I noticed something blue out of the corner of my eye. I quickly looked over and saw the Blue Blazer's body falling to the ring. He didn't kick his legs or flail his arms. He didn't scream or make any sound. It looked as if it was just a stiff lifeless mannequin that was dropped as a stunt.
>
> Most people in attendance actually thought it was a dummy at first, which caused a lot of laughs and confusion in the audience until everyone saw the EMTs rushing to the ring. Then everyone gasped and there was an eerie silence.

Wrestlers and WWF commentators climbed into the ring, cut off Hart's tight facemask, and saw immediately that he wasn't breathing. Within minutes, his skin turned ashen grey. There were no vital signs. His eyes remained open, staring at nothing. Emergency personnel attended to him. His fellow wrestlers called out encouraging words as he was loaded into an ambulance.

Owen Hart was transported to Truman Medical Center, but there was no chance. The impact had severed his aorta, filling his lungs with blood and killing him. Owen Hart was thirty-four.

As the fan reported, the fall took place while a video was being projected, so it wasn't seen on the WWF pay-per-view special, which went on as scheduled. Wrestling commentator Jim Ross announced Hart's death to the pay-per-view audience, but nothing was said in the arena.

———————

The day after the tragedy, the WWF celebrated the fallen star on its weekly *RAW* program. Wrestler Mark Henry read a poem in Owen Hart's honor, which included the following lines:

> *When Owen left, it felt like hands across my throat . . .*
> *My heart is heavy, this is why you get the burn when you cry.*
> *It digs down deep, you cannot sleep.*
> *You toss and turn in your sheets.*
> *Awaken with sobs and wet pillowcases.*
> *You wander aimlessly, looking to the sky.*

The event was never released on home video like other WWF spectaculars, but fifteen years later, *Over the Edge 1999* was aired on the new streaming WWE network (the World Wrestling Federation had been rebranded World Wrestling Entertainment in 2002, after a lawsuit from the World Wildlife Fund). All footage of Owen Hart was cut from the show, which was preceded by a photo tribute and the words:

> In Memory of Owen Hart May 7, 1965–May 23, 1999
> *who accidentally passed away during this broadcast.*

WWE officials claimed the only copy of the video of the tragedy remained locked away in its headquarters, never to be shown.

13

Radio

dead air (noun): a period of silence
especially during a radio broadcast

—Merriam-Webster Dictionary

RADIO IS ILLUSION, and the sound of a voice can hide many things, as
exemplified by all those radio deejays from the 1960s who soldier on with
programs on oldies or classic rock stations today, sounding very much as
they did in their heyday, their voices the one element of their beings able to
resist the ravages inflicted on their corporeal forms. Think of the scene in
American Graffiti in which Richard Dreyfuss's character, Curt, walks into
the radio station to visit the legendary Wolfman, and doesn't recognize that
the Wolfman is the fat guy in the Hawaiian shirt sitting right in front of him.

Radio is often able to disguise and distract what's actually going on
in the studio. Alexander Woollcott, the critic, commentator, and member of the group of cultured wits known as the Algonquin Round Table,
was on the air in CBS Studios in Manhattan on January 23, 1943. He
was part of a nationally broadcast panel discussion about Hitler when
he passed a note to a fellow participant that read "I'm feeling sick."
The broadcast continued, and the radio audience was unaware that he'd
suffered what would be a fatal heart attack at fifty-six—although a few
listeners did call the station to ask why he was suddenly, unusually

quiet. (One of Woollcott's most memorable quotes was, "You haven't lived until you died in New York.")

Kid Canfield

What appears to have been the first death on the air behind the radio microphone took place in the studio of radio station WHIS in Bluefield, West Virginia, on the evening of March 12, 1935.

Kid Canfield, a former gambler and conman and current star of vaudeville stage and silent movie screen, was in town for two days of shows at the Rialto Theatre and making his first-ever appearance on the radio. The ads that ran in newspapers as he made his way through theaters in the South summed up the show:

> *The notorious gambler*
> *On our stage and on the screen*
> *Kid Canfield who has cut cards with noted gamblers*
> *such as Arnold Rothstein, Al Capone and Legs Diamond*
> *will bare to the public all the crooked devises of the underworld.*
> *He will convince you that you cannot win!*

The notorious former gambler—a reformed self-professed *cheating* gambler, one should add—had an arsenal of loaded dice, marked cards, and an ability to deal from the bottom of the deck.

Born George Washington Bonner, the Kid worked as a shell gamesman at circuses and an expert at the unwinnable three-card monte before setting off from sweet home Chicago at seventeen to travel the country in search of big card games, facing down the most extravagant and feared gamblers and always, in his telling, coming out on top. Among his pigeons was Arnold Rothstein, the New York City mob kingpin who'd go on to fix the 1919 World Series. Kid Canfield claimed he took the racketeer for $350,000 in one sitting. He said it was no gamble—the cards were marked. The only chance he took was making it out of the room with his ill-gotten pot of winnings.

According to the legend he recounted so many times, Kid Canfield's notorious gambling career came to an end after he cheated several thousand dollars out of a sucker at a poker game in San Francisco. The beaten, depleted sap stood up from the table, pulled out a gun, placed the barrel to the side of his head, and pulled the trigger. That mark, Kid Canfield would reveal, turned out to be his brother.

The remorse led the Kid to turn his life around, denounce his past, and dedicate the future to exposing his crooked, crooked ways. He hit the vaudeville circuit with a warning about the fruitlessness of gambling, an exposé of underworld gambling houses, and a demonstration of all his best cheating methods. It turned out to be a pretty entertaining show.

In 1912, Kid Canfield starred in a silent two-reel short, split between the story of his gambling days—ending with that brother suicide scene—and a demonstration of his dishonest methods and gimmicks. Ten years later, he directed and starred in a full-length silent western. *Kid Canfield, the Reform Gambler* told very much the same tale.

In 1935, Kid Canfield was on the vaudeville circuit with that movie and his stage show. Now, instead of stopping into taverns or backrooms to bilk some of the local mutts out of their hard-earned cash, he'd stride into the newsroom of the local daily paper and challenge the assembled journos to give him a write-up if he proved to be good at his game.

That's what he did on Saturday afternoon, March 9, at the *Bluefield Daily Telegraph*. He went on to flummox the ink-stained wretches with three-card monte, then dealt a game of poker after letting one of the reporters shuffle. The first man drew four tens. The next drew four Jacks. Kid Canfield drew four aces.

The Kid threw in a demonstration of his loaded dice. After everyone rolled snake eyes, the paper gave him a write-up. "Kid Canfield," one of those reporters wrote, "with his long tapered fingers, resembling a piano player's, could manipulate a deck of cards so fast that the eye was unable to follow his movement."

The following Tuesday night, he was at WHIS to promote his Thursday and Friday shows at the Rialto. Kid Canfield had faced brutal mobsters on the other side of a hand of marked cards, spoken to crowds numbering in the thousands, and held hundreds of theater audiences in thrall, but this was his very first appearance on the radio. With twenty or thirty spectators watching, and that big microphone looming in front of him, he was feeling a little nervous. He told announcer Mel Barnett so, but then the red light flashed and something lit up in Kid Canfield. He went into his stage patter.

"Boys of Bluefield, take it from the man who has gambled with the best of them. It is a crooked game, and the sucker has no chance!" He roared the words, so loud that the microphone kicked back with over-modulation. The engineer at the transmitter lowered the volume. The Kid was off and running. "Gambling does not pay! It is a game run by professional crooks. Boys, let me tell you a story—"

And with that, Kid Canfield fell over like a stack of poker chips. He managed to pick himself up, but then he dropped like a marked card onto the scarlet rug of the studio floor. The microphone came crashing down with him.

Mel Barnett jumped up. Staffers ran in and carried the Kid to a couch while somebody called a doctor. Kid Canfield continued to breathe for about a minute. Then he stopped breathing altogether. Kid Canfield was dead of a heart attack at fifty-seven.

Meanwhile, after a brief period of confusion, the producers threw on a record—dance music played by an orchestra. WHIS listeners knew something had interrupted Kid Canfield at "Boys, let me tell you a story—" They had no idea it was death, but they knew something was wrong at WHIS. The same song kept playing, over and over again, until midnight.

Carlton KaDell

Carlton KaDell was an all-American boy from Danville, Illinois, who got his first radio job at WJJD in Chicago in 1931 and became a radio star a few years later after migrating west and joining NBC's Pacific Coast staff in Hollywood. He announced or acted in radio shows and serials, including *Amos 'n' Andy*; *Big Town*, with Edward G. Robinson; *Mayor of the Town*, with Lionel Barrymore; the Jack Carson and Edgar Bergen shows; *Chesterfield Time*, with the Hal Kemp Orchestra; and *Jack Armstrong, the All-American Boy*. He even played the title role on *Tarzan*.

In 1949, he was forty-three and announcing NBC Radio's popular *Sealtest Variety Theater* starring Dorothy Lamour when his career almost came to a sudden, embarrassing halt. The crisis began in a bar on Vine

Street in Hollywood, one of those bars that were frequented by all kinds of characters, most specifically men of a certain persuasion that in 1949 needed to be kept under wraps.

Carlton KaDell got to talking to a fellow in that bar. The two of them seemed to hit it off, and in the code that those men of a certain persuasion used in those days, Carlton supposedly asked the chap if he wanted to have a good time.

The gentleman replied that he certainly did. The pair got into KaDell's car and headed toward his home in Reseda, about seventeen miles away in the San Fernando Valley. They got as far as Cahuenga Boulevard, about a mile and a half north of the bar, when the fellow instructed KaDell to pull over. It wasn't for a roadside quickie. The fellow, it turned out, was Officer T. C. Lindholm of the Hollywood vice squad, one of a squad of undercover LAPD officers who posed as gay men for the purpose of entrapment.

Many of these vice officers were muscular, handsome, even pretty young men who couldn't find acting roles in Hollywood. The LAPD trained them to take on the mannerisms and language of the homosexuals and then sent them into bars and other gathering spots like Pershing Square with a quota to trap "perverts."

Typically, these vice boys would offer someone a ride or accept a ride. Sometimes, they didn't even wait for the gay man to make a pass. It didn't matter. Once he slapped on the handcuffs, the cop's word would be taken as gospel. The gay man would be desperate to avoid publicity and get this thing over with, and agree to pay a fine.

That was the case with Carlton KaDell. Officer Lindholm claimed he'd made "improper suggestions" inside the auto. KaDell protested that he'd only offered the fellow a ride home to the Valley. Lindholm and his partner J. C. Parslow, who was following KaDell's car, busted him on a morals charge.

The arrest made the papers. Lindholm was quoted, alleging that KaDell had moaned, "The publicity will ruin my career. Drinking is probably responsible for the whole thing."

Ten days later, Carlton KaDell had more of the publicity he dreaded and his photo on page three of the *Los Angeles Times*. The paper reported that Municipal Judge Edward Guirado had ordered KaDell to pay a fifty-dollar fine or serve twenty-five days in jail for "disturbing the peace." He paid the fine.

Carlton KaDell's career survived. He continued to work as an announcer and star on big radio shows, though it's not clear whether his arrest and the ensuing publicity led to his move back to Chicago in the 1950s, where he starred, somewhat ironically, in WMAQ's (NBC Chicago) 1954 dramatic radio series *Case Dismissed with Carlton KaDell*. It was developed as a public service to lay out "the story of your legal rights."

More than twenty years later, he was still behind the microphone in Chicago, hosting the 3:00–7:00 PM *Classical Kaleidoscope* show at WEFM. On Friday evening, March 14, 1975, the station's general manager George Stone stopped into the booth to say goodnight, just after KaDell had finished the 6:00 PM news spot. The announcer was definitely in distress.

"He told me he would appreciate it if I would call another announcer because he had had some chest pains," Stone told the *Chicago Tribune*. Stone assigned a station staffer to accompany the announcer in a taxicab to Northwestern Memorial Hospital. They never made it. The chest pains he'd experienced were signs of a heart attack. Carlton KaDell had another heart attack in the cab. He was dead at seventy.

The *Tribune* article mentioned KaDell's past glories, but not his 1949 arrest. He was quoted saying, "I've done what I wanted to do. I've had a good life." The *Trib* described him as "a bachelor."

Scotty O'Neil

They called Scotty O'Neil "Las Vegas's own Ed McMahon." For more than a decade, the veteran radio deejay was the announcer and sidekick on *The Dennis Bono Show*, a live radio variety show taped onstage before a big audience in a real Vegas showroom. First broadcast in 2000 from Club Madrid at the Sunset Station Hotel & Casino, about ten miles southeast of the Vegas Strip (and actually in the town of Henderson), the show moved five years later to Sam's Town Hotel & Gambling Hall (only seven miles east of the Strip on the edge of the desert on Boulder Highway), and five years after that to the South Point Hotel Casino and Spa on the

Las Vegas Strip—well, on Las Vegas Boulevard, at least, but far out on the edge, a little over six miles south of the Mandalay Bay Resort and Casino, where the Strip officially begins. The edges are where old-school Vegas performers worked in the first decade of the twenty-first century (Jerry Lewis broadcast his last five Muscular Dystrophy Association telethons from the South Point), and *The Dennis Bono Show* was definitely an old-school Vegas show.

Bono's show was a throwback to the days of Merv Griffin and Mike Douglas, or even *The Frank Rosenthal Show*, the late-1970s TV program hosted from the Stardust by mobbed-up casino exec Frank "Lefty" Rosenthal. *The Dennis Bono Show* consisted of interviews, music, and comedy acts, all featuring the Vegas performers who played the remaining lounges, afternoon shows, and small rooms in off-market casinos downtown or off the Strip, and occasionally showrooms that had a decidedly old-Vegas feel.

When a top headliner did visit, it was a star along the lines of old-guard performers like Rich Little, Steve Lawrence, Tony Orlando, and Charo. Bono, a standards singer who was once managed by Frank Sinatra's pal Jilly Rizzo and opened for Don Rickles, launched each episode with a song and a monologue, followed by some repartee with his second banana, Scotty O'Neil.

Scotty was well suited for the role. He was a longtime radio personality in Los Angeles and Las Vegas. He'd left his last deejay gig at KJUL-FM six years earlier, when the station changed format from standards to country, but maintained a large, if elderly, fan base.

Corrie Sachs was the third component of the on-air team. The vivacious singer was a veteran performer who, as a teen with the group the Lemon Twist Showstoppers, often opened for Dick Shawn. She had a regular gig impersonating Reba McEntire in the *Country Superstars Tribute* at the Golden Nugget. Sachs describes the show: "It was a lot like the old Johnny Carson *Tonight Show* but without the desk. We all just kinda clicked off each other, and most of the time we winged every show. We'd maybe have a few things we knew we wanna talk about, but then we'd just go for it. Once it's showtime, we'd just kinda ad-lib our way through, just try to have fun."

Everything was copacetic, swinging, and fun leading up to the taping of *The Dennis Bono Show* on March 24, 2011. "The day started out normal," Sachs tells us. "We had our usual rehearsal, which usually starts around eleven. Everything went smooth. We always have a buffet before the show, and as a matter of fact, Scotty joined us for lunch. Everything was fine, normal, the usual."

As showtime approached, five hundred folks, most of them on the north side of sixty-five, settled into seats in the South Point Showroom, while in a dressing room backstage, Scotty and Bono went over the monologue, finding funny bits to add and good moments to riff on. The two old pros liked the spontaneity and played off each other. Scotty was in particularly good form. The show, which would be aired that evening on various radio stations around the country, kicked off on time, at 2:00 PM.

Scotty announced the guests. Dennis Bono came out and sang a number backed by Bob Rosario's band, then headed toward the couch for some banter with Scotty. "Then I came on," says Sachs. "I sang my song and sat over on the couch next to Scotty. It was about fifteen minutes into the show. I sat down, said hello to everybody—said hello to Dennis, said hello to Scotty. And Dennis, I vaguely remember saying some bad joke or whatever. I looked at Scotty, and he looked at me like he was gonna ask me a question. You know how you kinda look up, like you're trying to think about something? Well, he looked up to the sky, kind of like he was thinking about what he was gonna ask me next. And that's when it hit him. He just slumped backwards on the couch.

"His head was back. And at first we thought he was just kidding, or reacting to a bad joke that Dennis might have said. We all started laughing, and then I leaned over and I realized he wasn't breathing, and so I immediately started pressing on his chest. I looked at the audience and I said, 'Is there a doctor in the house?'"

Scotty let out a snoring sound. The director cut to a commercial break for the Bootlegger Bistro. The Italian restaurant, nightclub, and performer's hangout on Las Vegas Boulevard was two and a half miles closer to the action on the Strip and owned by Bono's wife, singer and former Nevada lieutenant governor Lorraine Hunt-Bono.

Hunt-Bono was also in the room. "Everyone thought he'd fainted," she told *Las Vegas Sun* columnist John Katsilometes. "Even Dennis thought he might have been doing it as a joke, a comedy bit. Everyone was just in shock."

Corrie Sachs continues: "The way the stage was built at the time, we couldn't close the curtains. So we proceeded to pull him off the couch and have him lay on the floor. We pulled him onto the floor and had the cast surround his body. We all stood around his body to cover him from the audience. And fortunately, one of the stagehands was a paramedic, and so he was immediately right there on hand, and he knew right away. He just looked at all of us and shook his head."

Comedian John Padon was backstage waiting to make his first appearance on the show. "Somebody came backstage screaming, 'Call 911!' he told the reporter from the *Las Vegas Review-Journal*. "I poked my head around the corner and there's Scott laying on the floor. Security is with him."

"And meanwhile I'm telling the audience, 'I'm sorry, we're not gonna continue with the show,'" Sachs says. "It was so funny. People were like, 'What do you mean you aren't gonna finish the show?' It's like, 'Uh, no. We're not.'" Scotty was gone. The show did not go on.

"Scotty was very well-respected in the broadcast industry," the former lieutenant governor reflected. "And he was a great sidekick, the perfect Ed McMahon." Dennis Bono released a statement that evening. It read, in part, "Scotty passed onstage doing what he loved."

"There's always been a hole, ever since he's been gone," Corrie Sachs says. "You always go straight ahead but we're always gonna miss him. I enjoyed being around him, and I think everyone felt that way. He was just an all-around great guy. And his voice was gorgeous. He had this beautiful radio announcer–type voice. I never heard him make a mistake. He was a real pro—and irreplaceable. As a matter of fact, we didn't replace him. Once Scotty was gone, it was just Dennis and myself."

Scotty O'Neil was sixty-nine.

14

Social Media

THANKS TO THE INTERNET, SOCIAL MEDIA, and outlets like YouTube, Facebook, Snapchat, and Instagram, everybody's a star, all the world's a stage, and many performers are dying on it. Travel vloggers fall off cliffs and waterfalls while taking selfies or making cell phone videos. Amateur daredevils die while live-streaming stunts. Social media graduate Christina Grimmie, a YouTube singing star who entered the mainstream when she competed on NBC's competition series *The Voice*, was shot to death by an "obsessed" stranger on June 10, 2016, while meeting fans after a show in Orlando, Florida. (Her murder has almost been forgotten, overshadowed when, less than two days later, a terrorist gunman killed forty-nine people at the Pulse nightclub in the same city.)

Then there's Prentis Robinson, a musician and self-described "Art & Intertainment Director & Producer" from Wingate, North Carolina. As "Cowboy//Django," the fifty-five-year-old African American performed for thousands of his Facebook friends via the Facebook Live streaming feature. His Facebook page was filled with videos of him wearing a cowboy hat, playing acoustic guitar and singing, and also walking the streets of his town with a cell phone selfie stick, pointing out criminality in his neighborhood.

He was taking one of those walks on the morning of Monday, February 26, 2018, live-streaming with his selfie stick, when he encountered someone off camera and called out several times, "You on live!" The person responded by firing four shots. Prentis Robinson fell dead on the social media stage. The cell phone on the end of the stick landed camera lens up and streamed someone jumping over his body. Facebook Live allows viewers to post comments in real time. A few seconds after the shots rang out, someone commented, "Omg."

Alison Parker

It was known as "America's first social media murder": the killing of a television news reporter and cameraman, recorded by the gunman's own POV cell phone camera, posted on his Facebook and Twitter accounts, and spread worldwide—and broadcast live on television to thousands of viewers.

The unlikely incident occurred on the morning of August 25, 2015. Alison Parker, a twenty-four-year-old general-assignment reporter for WDBJ-TV Channel 7 News in Roanoke, Virginia, and videographer Adam Ward, twenty-seven, were "going live" at Bridgewater Plaza, an outdoor shopping center on the popular Smith Mountain Lake recreation area.

Outdoors, on a wooden walkway, Parker was interviewing Vicki Gardner, director of the local chamber of commerce, about events marking the fiftieth anniversary of the lake's creation. Ward had the camera on his right shoulder, with a portable light shining on his two subjects as the interview aired live on the *Mornin'* program, the local lead-in to the national *CBS Morning News*.

At 6:46 AM, in the middle of the interview, at least eight gunshots rang out. Alison Parker screamed and ran; the camera fell and, for a flash, captured the image of the gunman holding a Glock 19 9 mm pistol. The control room cut back to the studio and a shot of *Mornin'* host Kimberly McBroom, open-mouthed in shock.

The shooter got away. He was soon identified as Vester Flanagan, a former WDBJ reporter who was holding a grudge against Parker and others at the station. At 11:14 AM, Flanagan uploaded a fifty-six-second phone-camera video, shot from a first-person perspective, to his Twitter and Facebook accounts.

The video reveals his point of view as he walks up to the scene of the live interview and shows that he is holding a handgun for approximately fifteen seconds without Ward, Parker, or Gardner noticing. Cameraman Ward moves off the interview to pan across the shopping area, and Flanagan appears to wait until the camera is again pointed at Parker to ensure the shooting is shown live to the television audience.

Flanagan later shot himself during a car chase with police officers and was pronounced dead at a hospital. The state medical examiner determined that Parker died of "gunshot wounds of the head and chest"; Ward of "gunshot wounds of head and torso." Vicki Gardner was shot in the back. She lost her right kidney and part of her colon but survived.

The killings occurred amid a rash of mass shootings in the United States and a national debate over gun violence and led to conspiracy theories that the shooting of Alison Parker and Adam Ward was a hoax, cooked up by the mainstream media to gain support for stricter gun regulations.

Armin Schmieder

Today you fly with me!

Armin Schmieder was at the forefront of entertainment technology on August 26, 2016. He was before a worldwide audience via his cell phone camera and the latest social media gimmick. Facebook Live had been introduced on April 6 in a Facebook post by the network's founder, Mark Zuckerberg: "Live is like having a TV camera in your pocket. Anyone with a phone now has the power to broadcast to anyone in the world . . ."

Seven weeks before Schmieder's event, Diamond "Lavish" Reynolds took out her cell phone and used Facebook Live to broadcast the death of her boyfriend Philando Castile in the front seat of a car, moments after he was shot by a police officer during a traffic stop in Falcon Heights, Minnesota. On this day, Schmieder would take the feature to new heights, with the TV camera literally in his pocket.

Schmieder was allowing his Facebook friends and others to join him on a flight—a wingsuit flight through the Swiss Alps—in real time. Schmieder propped up his cell phone—unfortunately making the amateur mistake of positioning it vertically rather than horizontally—to stream the video, which ultimately would run for seven minutes and eleven seconds.

The sequence begins with Schmieder on a mountaintop near Kandersberg, a popular spot for BASE jumpers. He is climbing into his wingsuit and, oddly, perhaps in nervousness at being the star, gives the middle finger to those watching, laughing as he gets his gear and equipment together. He zips into the suit, which contains fabric between the legs and under the arms that allows him to lift from a vertical drop into flight, before a parachute is deployed for landing.

He laughs while he narrates in German, putting on his sunglasses and a helmet, fitted with a GoPro camera and light, then turns the cell phone camera to reveal a view of the jagged peaks and lush valley he's about to fly into. He waves goodbye with a "ta ta" and puts the cell phone in his pocket.

The picture turns to a blurry pink-orange; the Facebook friends are now looking at the inside of his wingsuit pocket. They'll only be able to hear—not see—the flight in real time. "The viewer sees nothing but . . . the sound," reported *Blick*, Zurich's daily German-language newspaper. "But this is all the more disturbing."

Schmieder makes his jump at around the six-minute mark. He's heard to say, "Today you fly with me!" He says "one, two" in German, and then there is the loud rushing of air—and, about twenty-five seconds later, a scream. Next comes the sound of tumbling and a brutal impact.

"Then," *Blick* reported, "there is silence—only the bells of cows can be heard." Armin Schmieder, the newspaper reported, died "live on Facebook." Schmieder, an Italian citizen, was twenty-eight and had a young child. According to a friend, "He was an experienced skydiver but flew only a year with the wingsuit."

Once the tragedy was publicized, the video made its way swiftly to YouTube, where it began to generate hundreds of thousands of views.

Interlude

Tragic Kingdoms

Deborah Gail Stone

Deborah Gail Stone was a beautiful and talented California girl, an excellent student and star athlete in track and swimming at Santa Ana High School. In June 1974, she was poised to blossom into adulthood. She turned eighteen and graduated with top honors and that year's Principal's Award for academic excellence. In the fall, she'd travel seventeen hundred miles from home to begin her freshman year at Iowa State University. Until then, she'd be residing in "the Happiest Place on Earth," because shortly before her birthday she'd landed a job in Disneyland.

Petite, blonde, and from a devout Christian family, Deborah was the perfect match for the squeaky-clean theme park. Soon after she arrived for training, her superiors saw her as ideal for the role of hostess for a brand-new attraction that was about to replace the Carousel of Progress located in Tomorrowland.

America Sings would feature a cast of audio animatronic animals warbling songs from America's musical history. Although the show didn't really fit into Tomorrowland's theme, which was an optimistic look into the future, America Sings was designed in anticipation of America's Bicentennial. The twenty-four-minute program featured the voices of Burl Ives as Eagle Sam and Sam Edwards (who voiced the adult

Thumper in the Disney film *Bambi*) as Ollie Owl, and made use of the Carousel building's unique layout.

The large circular structure contained an outer ring of six theaters, connected by divider walls that revolved mechanically around six fixed stages about every four minutes. Two of the theaters were used for loading and unloading the guests. The walls revolved clockwise for the Carousel of Progress. For America Sings, they'd turn in the opposite direction.

As the theaters rotated, each theater audience would experience each song in sequence. Between each act, the lights blacked out, and the theater was illuminated with flashing stars. During the rotations, Eagle Sam sang about the next era the audience was about to enter, reprising the chorus of "Yankee Doodle."

America Sings opened to the public on Saturday, June 29, 1974. Debbie worked the prime evening shift, standing at the left of each stage, using a microphone to welcome and say goodbye to the guests during every turn.

On July 8, the ride had been in operation for just over a week, and the rotating theaters, animatronics, and hostesses were working in precision. This was also a very exciting and special day for Debbie Stone. Her boyfriend asked her to marry him, and before she began her shift, she called her parents to ask their permission. Permission was granted.

Deborah had so much to look forward to. Around 11:00 PM, at the end of the 10:30 show, and near closing time at the park, there was another forty-five-second period in which the audience cleared out and the stage moved into position for another cycle.

Then came the scream. It was described by a guest in an adjacent theater as "a blood-curdling scream," and the sight he saw resembled a child being pulled between the moving walls and a stationary one.

That "child" was the five-foot, five-inch, one-hundred-pound Debbie Stone being pulled between two hard walls without enough space in which to fit. By the time the ride operators rushed over and the wall stopped moving, beautiful Debbie had been crushed into a bloody, shattered pulp and dismembered. No one was sure exactly how it happened—whether she was leaning in to the adjacent stage to talk to a fellow cast member, trying to jump from one stage to the other, or simply distracted.

Debbie's parents got word of the tragedy a few hours later, in the middle of the night. "It was around two o'clock in the morning," her father Bill told the *Omaha City Weekly* thirty years later. "It was somebody who lived in another street saying the deputy sheriffs were looking for us. Just about the time I hung up, they pulled up to the house."

The memory was fresh as yesterday to Debbie Stone's mother Marilyn. "I can picture the two guys that were here," she told the Omaha reporter. "I can pretty well picture what they said and what I said. Of course, when you hear that, you go into shock. The feelings are there, but they're dulled to a point that you really aren't feeling anything.

"When the deputy left, my husband and I knelt down and thanked God he gave her to us for eighteen years."

Bill Stone remembered his last conversation with Debbie. "The night of her death, she asked us if it would be okay if she got married. She really got engaged that night, so she was calling to ask our permission. I think the hardest thing that I had to do during that whole thing—other than go through it—was call her fiancé in the morning to tell him."

The America Sings attraction was closed for two days after Debbie Stone's death while sensor lights were installed to warn the operator if someone went too close to the walls. Later, breakaway walls were constructed, in case the sensors failed. The attraction remained in operation until 1988.

The Disney corporation never memorialized its first fallen cast member anywhere in Disneyland. Her high school renamed a pool, and her friends created a scholarship award, in her honor.

Although there have been more than a dozen deaths, including at least one homicide, in the world of yesterday, tomorrow, and fantasy (not to mention a number of suicide jumpers from the Disneyland Hotel and the more recent Mickey & Friends parking structure), Debbie Stone is, as of this writing, the only performing "cast member" (the term used to refer to all Disneyland employees) to have died while performing on the big stage called Disneyland in more than sixty years of operation.

Walt Disney World, the resort in Orlando, Florida, envisioned and designed by Uncle Walt, opened in 1971, five years after his death. The place encompasses four theme parks and 43 square miles, as opposed to Disneyland's 500 acres and two parks (the Disneyland Resort also includes California Adventure theme park). As might be expected due to its size (and the addition of "Florida" to the equation), the Walt Disney World death toll (which includes drownings, ride mishaps, car accidents, suicides, and an alligator attack) is much greater than Disneyland's. Yet, like its classic cousin in Anaheim, it has so far lost one performing cast member in the line of duty, in front of an adoring crowd. That tragedy occurred thirty years after the death of Debbie Stone.

———————

Javier Cruz, a thirty-eight-year-old former park custodian, was divorced, the father of two children, and living with his mother at the Mystic Pointe apartments not far from the resort. On the afternoon of Wednesday, February 11, 2004, he was dressed as Mickey Mouse's dog, Pluto, and participating in the Share a Dream Come True Parade, a spectacular display of moving floats, giant snow globes, and costumed characters that worked its way from Splash Mountain toward Main Street, USA.

Javier was passing through the backstage gate into view of the crowds that lined the road between Frontierland and Adventureland when he stumbled. Before he could raise his front paws and get out of the way, he was run over and crushed to death by a three-section, three-ton Princess float. Disney workers needed a forklift to raise the float and peel off Javier.

Megan Long, who played Winnie the Pooh at the park, said the bulky headpieces worn by the character actors made it difficult to navigate around the floats. "Sometimes, it's tough to see when the sun is glaring right on you," she told the *Orlando Sentinel*.

The Disney corporation paid dearly for the death of Javier Cruz. It was fined $6,300.

15

Vaudeville

VAUDEVILLE, THEY SAY, IS DEAD, killed by the Depression, the advent of cinematic sound, and the retrofitting of vaudeville houses into movie palaces. Once, though, vaudeville was very much alive. For fifty years, from its rise in the 1880s through the 1930s, vaudeville was the most popular form of American entertainment. Every major and mid-sized city had a vaudeville theater, and performers worked several circuits, traveling by train, on constant tour throughout the country.

A vaudeville show was variety, usually consisting of eight or more unrelated acts on a single bill, each getting at least ten minutes of stage time. Singers, dancers, magicians, comedians, animal acts, acrobats, jugglers, mentalists, actors—you name a show business specialty and you could probably find it on a vaudeville bill. Vaudeville theaters popularized the tunes that would fill the Great American Songbook. Ethnic-comedy acts told jokes that solidified the toxic racial and ethnic stereotypes that live on to this day (*Pop quiz: What ethnic group is thought of as lazy? As dumb? As cheap?*). Vaudeville was television before there was television, and vaudeville stars became the first stars of early film, radio, and television.

Yes, vaudeville lived, and on vaudeville stages across time and America, vaudevillians died. Some are celebrated, some forgotten. The group of talents, specialties, and demises is not unlike an average vaudeville bill, though research shows that when performing, it is prudent to remain as close to the stage floor as possible.

Gladys Kelly

A comedian had the matinee audience roaring with laughter at the Eighty-Sixth Street Theatre in Manhattan on Tuesday, October 21, 1913. While he worked hard in front of a drop curtain, the stage was being set behind the curtain for the Six Diving Belles.

The Belles were a variety act who performed their feats in a big water tank. The curtain would rise and the six girls would be revealed in a row about thirty feet above the tank. Each wore a long one-piece swimsuit, each stood on a diving board. Once the curtain was up, they'd all dive in. It was impressive and not a little dangerous. With a few minutes to go until their cue, some of the girls took their positions on the diving boards. They had to walk and balance lightly, because the spring under each board was powerful enough that the slightest movement could start the board and launch whoever was standing on it.

Gladys Kelly was one of the girls. As the comic kept 'em laughing, she inched out onto a board at one end of the row of six. She was just getting into position, into the pose that would be revealed when the curtain rose, when she suddenly lost her balance. She tried to right herself, but it was too late. She fell, head first.

Gladys's head smacked into the edge of the water tank. She then bounced ten more feet before her body slammed to the floor of the stage. Some of the other girls climbed down and rushed to her side. The stage manager, Harry Abbott, ran to the box office to get someone to call an ambulance.

Gladys was carried off into the wings. The comedian took his bows. The girls got back in place for the rise of the curtain. Only now there were five. Harry whispered encouragement, and, though they were nervous, the other Diving Belles completed their act without anyone else getting hurt. Gladys, meanwhile, was taken to Flower Hospital on East Sixty-Fourth Street. Two hours later, she was pronounced dead. She'd fractured her skull and broken her neck.

The other five girls weren't told about the seriousness of Gladys's injuries until they were back in their dressing rooms—hold on. Did we say there were *five* other girls?

Actually, there were three. Not all the diving "belles" were women. Two of them were boys, seventeen-year-old Ted Healy and his sixteen-year-old partner, Moe Howard. Decades later in his memoir, Howard would recall the death of "a pretty young lady named Gladys Kelly," writing that she "misjudged the tank and landed on the artificial waves made of papier-mâché and two-by-fours that decorated the side of the tank. She had broken her neck and died instantly." Howard wrote that the tragedy led him and Healy to quit the act.

Ted Healy went on to become the highest-paid performer in vaudeville in the 1920s, with a comedy act featuring Howard, Howard's brother Shemp, and Larry Fine as his "stooges" (supposed audience members who'd act as comic foils). After Shemp was replaced by his younger brother, Moe, Larry, and newcomer Curly went off on their own. In 1934 they began performing as the Three Stooges.

Joseph E. Howard

Joe E. Howard's last words were "I'm in love with you."

Howard was a vaudeville legend. Born in 1878, he made his first vaudeville appearance as an eleven-year-old boy soprano and was still a teen when he formed a headlining act with his second wife, Ida Emerson. Along with Ida and a series of other collaborators, he was a prolific songwriter, creating Broadway shows and composing some of the most enduring Tin Pan Alley standards of the early twentieth century, including "Goodbye, My Lady Love," "I Wonder Who's Kissing Her Now," and "Hello! Ma Baby" (the best-known rendition of which was sung by the Warner Bros. *Merrie Melodies* cartoon character Michigan J. Frog).

As vaudeville died out, Howard carried on as a nostalgia act. He was host of *The Gay Nineties Revue*, an early live television series that ran on ABC from 1948 to 1949. In 1956, he published his autobiography, *Gay Nineties Troubadour*.

After eight decades in the business, Joe E. Howard was still going on the evening of May 19, 1961, when he appeared onstage at Chicago's Civic Opera House in a benefit concert for the Marmion Military Academy. The house was filled to capacity that Friday night with an SRO audience of thirty-eight hundred who'd coughed up twenty-five dollars a head.

Everyone loved the old vaudevillian. After his set, he returned for an encore, leading an audience sing-along of "Let Me Call You Sweetheart":

Let me call you sweetheart, I'm in love with you . . .

With those words, he blew a kiss to the twelve-year-old who was accompanying him on organ—then he stumbled, grabbed the microphone stand for support, and fell to the boards. The microphone and stand came down on top of him.

The stage manager called for a quick curtain drop. The audience assumed it was part of the show. The rest of the program continued while, backstage, five doctors from the audience worked to revive the old-time song man. Howard's ninth wife, Miriam, pitched in with mouth-to-mouth resuscitation. She was at his side when the doctors gave up.

Joe E. Howard was dead of a heart attack at eighty-three.

Tiny Tim

Tiny Tim was an oddball entertainer, a musician born out of time who emerged from the Greenwich Village folk scene with a ukulele and became briefly famous in the late 1960s for his falsetto rendition of "Tiptoe Through the Tulips." He was born Herbert Khaury in Manhattan in 1932 and, had he been born twenty-five years earlier, could have been a sensation on the vaudeville circuit.

Musically, he was a human depository strained through a gramophone speaker, a strange effeminate man with a repertoire of forgotten Tin Pan Alley numbers and lost classics from the early twentieth century. Physically, Tiny Tim was a bizarre amalgam of Bob Dylan, Howard Stern, and Margaret Hamilton's Wicked Witch of the West. Tall and lumpy, with a hook nose and a shoulder-length rat's nest of scraggly hair, he dressed in mismatched sport coats and ties and carried his instrument in a paper shopping bag.

To be blunt, the man who performed under such names as Emmett Wink, Judas K. Foxglove, and, at a Times Square freak show, "Larry Love, the Singing Canary" would seem upon initial examination to be a put-on. The *New York Times* wrote that initially that possibility was the subject of great debate among critics and journalists, but "it quickly became clear that he was genuine, a lonely outcast intoxicated by fame, a romantic in pursuit of a beautiful dream."

Tiny Tim became a national novelty star in 1968, with a role in the film *You Are What You Eat*, an album produced by Richard Perry (on which he also showed off his baritone and range), and, most important to his acceptance by the mainstream, appearances on the television series *Rowan & Martin's Laugh-In*. Tiny Tim also proved to be a dependably amusing and strange talk-show guest. On December 17, 1969, he married an attractive—and seventeen-year-old—fan, "Miss Vicki" Budinger, on *The Tonight Show Starring Johnny Carson*. The wedding was watched by forty-five million people, the show's largest audience.

His popularity was bound to fade. Tiny Tim and Miss Vicki had a child they named Tulip before divorcing in 1977, and he carried on along the edges of the national spotlight, a man who only needed the ukulele in his shopping bag to find a stage and audience.

Many would say that Tiny Tim was born decades too late, that his act was made for vaudeville. That may be the case, but that doesn't mean he missed out on the experience. Throughout the 1970s and into the early 1980s, he was a featured act in various versions of *The Roy Radin Vaudeville Revue*, a variety show that played small cities and backwater towns across America, matching circus-type acts with oldies groups such as the Shirelles and Danny & the Juniors, and forgotten headliners including George Jessel, Donald O'Connor, and Frank Fontaine. (Fontaine and Addie "Micki" Harris of the Shirelles would suffer fatal heart attacks while performing onstage in 1978 and 1982, respectively; Danny Rapp of Danny & the Juniors shot himself during an engagement in Arizona in 1983; Donald O'Connor did not die onstage—but his father did in 1927, dancing in a vaudeville show while two-year-old Donald watched from the wings. Roy Radin was shot in the head and blown up with dynamite over a soured movie deal in 1983, in what would be known as the Cotton Club Murder. George Jessel died of a heart attack in 1981, at eighty-three.)

Tiny Tim received a surge of attention in the 1980s when several hipster bands recorded albums with him, some using him as an object of ridicule, others with purer musical intentions. In the 1990s, Tiny (as his friends and fans called him) began showing up on Howard Stern's radio show, amusing and sometimes disgusting Stern's audience with his odd phobias, conservative Christian values, and professed penchant for wearing adult diapers instead of underwear. In 1996, he filmed a cameo appearance for Stern's movie *Private Parts*.

Tiny Tim took his third wife, Susan Marie Gardner ("Miss Sue"), at the Immaculate Heart of Mary Church in Minnetonka, Minnesota, on August 18, 1995 (apparently a chick magnet, Tiny Tim had married Jan Alweiss—"Miss Jan"—in 1984). The couple lived in a nice two-story house on tree-lined Zenith Avenue South in Minneapolis, and shared what Miss Sue described as "a very traditional marriage.

"He was the head of the household and made the decisions. I looked up to him, as an older person, as a man," she wrote to the website Findadeath.com. "I pledged to love, honor and obey. It was okay, because I know the Bible says it's supposed to be that way, and he was so wise and so kind. Not a bully. I knew he would never oppress me, and he didn't."

Tiny did stay on the road for three-hundred days of the fourteen months they were together and, according to Miss Sue, spent most of the rest of the time at home, flat on his back in bed. For in the fall of 1995, Tiny Tim had developed congestive heart failure. Add that to the diabetes and other ailments for which he had never sought proper treatment, and Tiny Tim's days surely were numbered.

Yet he continued to venture out to perform. A milestone on his journey took place on September 28, 1996, when Tiny was featured at the Ukulele Hall of Fame Museum's first Uke Expo at the Montague Grange Hall in Montague, Massachusetts. He stepped up to the microphone and announced, "I'm not feeling very well, so if I happen to cough or anything, that's why."

His backing band struck up the first note, and, as if on cue, Tiny Tim collapsed. He fell forward off the stage, down another two feet, and smashed his head on the concrete floor.

Tiny had suffered a heart attack. He fluttered back to consciousness as he was carried out and managed to wave to his fans. He spent three weeks at the Franklin County Medical Center, where doctors warned that if he didn't want to die, he shouldn't work for the next year.

He convalesced at home in Minneapolis for only two months and still managed to work in several local appearances before accepting an invite to perform at a Woman's Club of Minneapolis gala on November 30, 1996. His wife's stepmother was a prominent member.

Tiny was feeling very dizzy on the day of the show. He almost fell climbing into the hired limousine, and when he and Miss Sue arrived at the Woman's Club building on Oak Grove Street, he could barely make it up the eight stairs to the front door. Once inside, he sat through a dinner in the elegant ballroom but didn't feel well enough to eat very much. He confessed to Miss Sue that he hadn't been taking his medications.

When it neared showtime, the leader of what Tiny had expected to be his backup band claimed to be unaware that Tiny had been booked that night and refused to perform with him. He said his combo didn't know the songs. Tiny was appalled. "You don't know 'I'm Looking Over a Four Leaf Clover'?"

So Tiny Tim would perform solo. He was scheduled to go onstage at 9:00 PM. At 10:00, the band was still going strong. When they finally left the stage, Tiny Tim was feeling even worse, and the gala was winding down.

According to Miss Sue, the bandleader refused to follow show business protocol and introduce the headliner, so the woman in charge of the event did the honors. Tiny Tim faced a room that was mostly empty. His ukulele was out of tune, but he was a trouper and performed his set. The last song he played was "Tiptoe Through the Tulips."

At the show's end, as he always did, Tiny Tim waved and blew kisses to what there was of the audience. Miss Sue could see he was shaking, so she hurried to him and took his arm.

"Are you all right?" she asked.

"No," he replied. "I'm not."

With those last words, Tiny Tim once again collapsed onstage. A doctor who happened to be in the house began CPR. An ambulance arrived within minutes, and EMTs worked on him on the floor for half an hour. After he was transported to the Hennepin County Medical Center, doctors there gave it a go for another hour and fifteen minutes before calling it.

Tiny Tim was dead at sixty-four. He was buried with his ukulele.

16

The Circus

IN SHOW BUSINESS, THE TERM *death defying* is most often used in description and promotion of circus stunt artists who work above the crowd, often without a net, in routines that at the least appear to be a step away from disaster. Circus performers are, for the most part, professionals who know the dangers and the safety precautions to avoid them, but there are some who might be better described not as "death defying," but "death inviting."

Massarti, the One-Armed Lion Tamer

On January 4, 1872, the Bolton correspondent for the London *Daily Echo* tapped out this dispatch, which was picked up and carried in the weeks to come by newspapers around the world: "Last night, Massarti, the lion tamer at Manders' Menagerie, now exhibiting in this town, was torn to pieces by the lions with whom he was performing." That didn't tell the half of it.

Thomas Maccarte, better known as Massarti the Lion Tamer, was no ordinary animal trainer. He was one of the rare one-armed lion tamers. He lost the appendage ten years earlier, when he was mauled while working with the Bell and Myers Circus in Liverpool. Sarah Manders, who ran the traveling show, was herself a former "lion queen." She hired Maccarte to replace Maccomo, "the negro lion tamer" who died in

January 1871, to star along with the most grand traveling collection of wild and exotic animals in the United Kingdom. She hired him although she'd been warned that Maccarte was a bit of a loose cannon, with a reputation for not only being bold and adventurous but also taking too many unnecessary risks.

On this January 3 in Bolton, the traveling troupe was performing an extra, unscheduled 10:30 PM show as a farewell to the folks in the town outside Manchester before pulling up stakes and moving six miles down the road for a stand in Bury.

There were five hundred spectators in the stands and five lions in a cage waiting for Massarti to make his entrance. Usually, the keepers and workers had red-hot iron rods and scrapers fired up to use on the animals if they got out of hand, but since this show was not on the schedule, the usual safety precautions weren't in place.

Massarti himself may not have been in the best condition to face down the wild beasts. Two nights earlier, one of the lions, an African with a black mane, bit him on his surviving hand, and he told his wife he was afraid of the cat. So before he made his way into their den, he fortified himself with some hefty shots of liquor. One witness said he wasn't exactly drunk, but had downed enough alcohol to be foolhardy.

Massarti was dressed as a one-armed Roman when he entered the lion's den. Waving his Roman falchion—a one-handed sword, of course—he put the giant cats through their motions, to the delight of the audience. He kept the lions in their corners, careful not to cross what the animals were trained to recognize as the imaginary line that separates their space from the tamer's "office."

Maccarte noticed that the African, the one who'd bitten him, was getting uppity and insubordinate. He stared the lion down, and in doing so, took his eyes off an Asiatic lion named Tyrant. Still staring intensely, Maccarte moved to slide his sword back into its sheath. That's when he slipped and fell on his one arm.

He must have crossed that imaginary line when he hit the ground. Tyrant pounced and bit into Maccarte's haunches. The African hopped down and chomped down on his armless shoulder. Blood spurted.

Maccarte screamed for help, for the hot iron rods, for the guns, all the while stabbing at Tyrant's eyes, nose, and mouth with his tiny sword.

The crowd was in a panic. The animal keepers scrambled to get metal partitions in place in the cage to separate the lions from the tamer, but audience members were jammed up against the cage and in their way. The keepers fired guns, but they were blanks. One of them began slamming the iron rods and scrapers into the fire, heating and weaponizing them.

The uproar and the blood pouring out of Maccarte incited the other lions. Now a third lion, an Abyssinian, chomped onto his ribs. A five-year-old lion, Maccarte's favorite of them all, scampered down from its perch, put its big jaws around the tamer's head, and chewed down, scalping him. The flesh hung down his neck. The tamer's pet returned to his corner.

There was more gunfire, and the lions began to back away. Two of the keepers entered the cage with the hot rods. They beat back the lions, and just as they were getting the attackers under control, the fifth, last lion, decided to have one last bite of the body in the dirt. The divider was in place, and three of the lions were separated thanks to the hot irons. The black-maned African was edged into a corner. It seemed the fifteen-minute attack was over.

It wasn't. The remaining lion grabbed Maccarte by his leg, just above the boot, and dragged him toward the others. The mauling and flesh feast went on for another five horrific minutes, until more men with more hot iron rods got into the cage. They finally forced all the lions to the other side of the divider and were able to carry out the destroyed body. Maccarte uttered a few incoherent words. A coworker said he asked to forget about getting him to a doctor; he knew he was a goner.

They set him down in the infirmary. He died minutes later. Maccarte was thirty-four. A reporter for the *Bolton Evening News* listed an inventory of his wounds:

> The only arm the deceased had was streaked with deep gashes from the shoulder to the hand; the scalp was torn right back, and from the hips to the knees, where he was seized from behind, the muscles are completely torn out. There are pieces of flesh

gone from the ribs, and the bones of the pelvis, which are the strongest in the human frame, have had pieces bitten clean out.

At the inquest, the coroner placed no blame on anyone, and even stated that Maccarte's drinking wasn't a factor, because once he was down, he defended himself as a sober person would. The jury returned a verdict of death by misadventure but showed themselves to be far ahead of their time when they added this statement: "The jury feel it to be their bounden duty to express their entire disapprobation of the reckless custom of so-called lion tamers performing in dens where ferocious animals are caged."

The Two Cliff Greggs

A statistically hazardous performing occupation is that of the human cannonball, the individual as projectile, fired from a cannon into the air toward a net, airbag, or body of water—anything that will provide a survivable impact upon landing. The "cannon," of course, does not operate like a regular cannon, which would blast a human body to smithereens. Fireworks, gunpowder, or smoke might be added to simulate the firing of an actual weapon, but the launch mechanism is actually compressed air or a simple spring that propels the human cannonball through the cylinder toward the target. The "cannonball" can travel up to seventy miles per hour, to an altitude of seventy feet, as far as two hundred feet—and of course, it's not the flight but the landing that can hurt the most.

The first recorded human cannonball was a fourteen-year-old girl. Rossa Matilda Richter, known professionally as Zazel, was launched about thirty feet at the Royal Westminster Aquarium in London on April 2, 1877. Judging by photographs at the time, a key to Zazel's popularity and the popularization of the human cannonball stunt was the fact that "she had to shed most of her Victorian clothing" to fit into the cannon barrel. Zazel went on to a career with P. T. Barnum's circus until, according to one report, she was launched into a "rotten net" and broke her back.

Zazel was a lucky one. Human cannonball historians have counted upward of thirty deaths of human cannonballs since that first flight—including two Cliff Greggs.

———————

Now what are the odds that there were two Cliff Greggs who were human cannonballs, both killed in a human cannonball stunt, not related by birth or marriage, with deaths separated by four years?

There is a very logical answer, and it begins with Cliff Aeros, a well-known German acrobat who, between 1926 and 1929, built and owned three human cannonball cannons. In 1930, one of the Aeros cannons was sold to Fred O. "Fearless" Gregg, a circus performer famous for his loop-the-loop double auto act (the type of mechanical thrill act that until then had replaced the human cannonball in the United States).

Fearless Gregg booked his human cannonball act into the Robbins Brothers Circus. He wasn't about to have himself shot out of the cannon, so he hired men to do it for him—roustabouts, thrill seekers, and desperate types who could use the money. Each of them took the name Gregg.

———————

On Monday, September 28, 1931, the Robbins Circus had set up camp at the Oklahoma State Fairgrounds in Oklahoma City. That afternoon, Fearless Gregg's Aeros cannon was mounted on a large truck. A human cannon fodder calling himself "Major" Will Gregg was fired toward the large net, ninety feet from the cannon's mouth. He landed just short of the net.

Will Gregg escaped with minor injuries but had to sit out the next show. The following afternoon, a German immigrant named Wladyslaus Kruck, who'd taken the name "Captain" Cliff Gregg and was advertised as Will's older brother, was launched by the same cannon. This time, this Gregg flew high into the air, with tremendous velocity. There was not enough velocity, unfortunately, to reach the net. Cliff Gregg landed four feet short. He landed on his head, breaking his neck and dying.

As the Associated Press would report, "'The show must go on,' the old adage of show people, was demonstrated very forcibly"—as was the notion that human cannonballs can't take a hint—when, twenty-four hours later, Will Gregg donned a leather helmet and slid feet-first back into the cannon, despite its obvious faulty firing mechanism. This time, he was launched, flew the entire ninety feet, and landed safely in the net.

Two hundred performers filed into the Hahn Funeral Chapel in Oklahoma City on Friday morning to pay tribute to the twenty-five-year-old German Cliff Gregg. His pallbearers were members of the Hamid Troupe of Arabs ("the Whirlwind Acrobatic Sons of the Desert") in full stage costume.

At the time of his death, Cliff Gregg had been scheduled to perform the human cannonball act twice daily at the Louisiana State Fair, beginning October 24. The fair's booking agent assured everyone that the show would go on, with Will Gregg or another Cliff Gregg ready to give one last wave to the crowd before sliding feet first into the mouth of a cannon and being blasted off into the unknown.

An altogether different Cliff Gregg was shot from a cannon at the Ocean Park Pier in Santa Monica, California, on July 26, 1935. A huge and boisterous crowd watched as Cliff Aeros's cannon catapulted the human cannonball into the sky and over the Pacific Ocean in what seemed to be a perfect 125-foot arc toward the water—perfect, until he hit the water.

Crew members said other Cliff Greggs usually straightened out at the end of their flights, but a slight wind blowing that day made it difficult to do so. That may be why, according to witnesses, instead of striking the water in a diving position, this Cliff Gregg kept his body rigid. He slammed into the surf at the exact moment a comber—a long, curling wave—roared in. He hit the comber, face first, and was knocked unconscious. His body rose to the surface once, then disappeared.

Ed Unger was in a boat offshore, waiting to fish the cannonball out of the drink and take him back to the pier. "I could see him under the water, still not moving," Unger told a reporter for United Press.

"I grabbed at his hair, but lost hold. Then I dived after him, but he was gone."

This Cliff Gregg's body was found under the pier the following day. His identity was confirmed on that Saturday as well. He was William C. Miller, a twenty-two-year-old from Newtonville, Massachusetts, and New York City. Miller didn't work for the Fearless Gregg show. Pier attendants said he'd simply showed up at the pier that Friday. Appearing to be out of work, he volunteered to be shot from the cannon.

The manager of the show, who also called himself "Captain Cliff Gregg," said Miller had claimed to be an experienced diver and to have performed as a human cannonball back East. Miller's friends, though, said he was just looking for a thrill. Will Miller died on his first-ever attempt.

Sarah Guyard-Guillot

With its mix of acrobatics, music, character-driven plots, fantastical costumes, and advanced technical innovations—and lack of animals—Cirque du Soleil offers far more than the "nouveau cirque" it represents. The entertainment company, based in Montreal and founded in 1984, has expanded through every continent except Antarctica, with more than twenty productions touring, playing Broadway, or settled permanently in Las Vegas. Each show presents a mash-up of circus styles and performers from around the world, synthesized into a theatrical experience very different and far more refined and awe-inspiring than the traditional sawdust three-ringers.

Volta was Cirque's forty-first production. Billed as "a story of transformation . . . inspired in part by the adventurous spirit that fuels the culture of action sports," the show opened in April 2017 in a new, environmentally correct Big Top in Montreal and went on to engagements in Gatineau, Toronto, Miami, and, on Valentine's Day 2018, the parking lot of the Tampa Greyhound Track in Tampa, Florida.

Yann Arnaud was among the cast. The thirty-eight-year-old French aerialist had been with Cirque for more than fifteen years and was featured in *Le Rêve*, its long-running spectacle at the Wynn resort in Las Vegas. Four days into the Tampa run, Arnaud posted on his Instagram account that he was ready to unveil an intricate new routine that evening: "After so much work and training and staging, our straps duo act is finally in the show tonight. It's time to go for it."

A "straps duo act" is a complicated specialty in which two aerialists perform muscular acrobatics while hanging from long leather straps. Arnaud and Pawel Walczewski "went for it" around 9:52 PM that Saturday night for the crowd that filled the twenty-six-hundred-seat tent. While a line of drummers banged out a beat below them, the men performed spins and aerobatics, each clutching a long red strap. When the straps were raised, Arnaud and Walczewski linked their free arms and performed in tandem, then separated, flying off in opposite directions above the crowd. As gravity swung him back toward the center of the circular stage, Arnaud lost his grip. He flew into the air and then dropped thirty feet, smashing to the stage, on his head.

There was a collective gasp from audience. Someone shouted, "Oh, Lord!" Several Cirque crew members rushed to the stage where, according to audience member Ben Ritter (a former US marine confined to a wheelchair), Arnaud was "out cold and not moving." As Walczewski dangled above, watching helplessly, an announcer noted that "the show has been temporarily interrupted." By the time paramedics got to him around 10:00 PM, Arnaud was unresponsive and in a coma. He had fractured his skull and suffered severe brain damage.

The audience was asked to leave—the show did not go on. Around 3:30 AM on March 18, during surgery at Tampa General Hospital, Yann Arnaud was pronounced dead. Two more performances of *Volta* had been scheduled for that Sunday before the troupe moved on from Tampa. Those final shows did not go on either.

———————

The tragedy of Yann Arnaud, the second onstage death of a Cirque performer, was horrifying, but not as shocking, or with effects as far reaching, as what had happened in Las Vegas during Cirque du Soleil's performance of *Kà*.

From its first preview at the MGM Grand Resort and Casino on November 12, 2004, the show *Kà* was by all measures the most elaborate and technologically sophisticated Cirque production yet. The title was "inspired by the ancient Egyptian belief in the 'ka,' an invisible spiritual duplicate of the body that accompanies every human being throughout this life and into the next." The plot (*Kà* was the first Cirque show with a storyline) about imperial twins—a boy and a girl—on a quest to reclaim their Far East palace from evil warriors, played a distant second to the $165 million production. *Kà* was an awe-inspiring presentation that included pyrotechnics, puppetry, martial arts, multimedia, a digital audio system that included a pair of ear-level speakers in each of the 1,950 seats, and a performance space unlike any before.

Where there should have been a stage was an abyss, a pit, fifty-one-feet deep, with a series of moving decks, platforms, and lifts that seemed to float above and through a bottomless void. The decks could move in front of, behind, above, and below each other. Above the stage level, a performance grid turned nearly vertical, extending ninety-eight feet. In all, there was a total of fifteen stories of performance space.

"Indeed, this show, which is also said to need around $1 million weekly to operate, may well be the most lavish production in the history of Western theater," wrote Mark Swed in the *Los Angeles Times*. "It is surely the most technologically advanced."

That didn't mean that *Kà* lacked the human component. The crew numbered three hundred; eighty were cast members.

Sarah Guyard-Guillot was among the cast. A veteran acrobat and aerialist who was born in Paris and graduated from the famed Annie Fratellini Art & Circus Academy in Saint-Denis, she joined *Kà* in 2006. She was known by her stage name, Sasoun.

Seven years later, she was still with the show, while also running a children's acrobatic fitness school on West Flamingo Road called Cirquefit. She was divorced, with two daughters, aged five and eight, and involved in an unusual yet comfortable backstage triangle. Her ex-husband Mathieu Guyard, the girls' father, was also a *Kà* performer. So was his new wife, Kelly Tucker Guyard.

There were two performances on Saturday night, June 29, 2013, both bound to be overshadowed by the official premier of Cirque's latest concoction, *Michael Jackson ONE*, two blocks south at the Mandalay Bay. *Kà's* final scene in the second show disrupted those assumptions.

Everything in *Kà* led to this, a battle in which the forces of good and evil squared off as the stage platform slowly tilted until it was almost vertical and the audience viewed the action as if from above. The warriors, flying, flipping, and fighting close to the spectators, were all acrobats, wearing harnesses attached to thin cables that allowed them to move in all directions.

Sasoun was playing one of the bad guys, a Spearman warrior. She was hoisted up the side of the vertical stage to a height of at least ninety-four feet (some eyewitnesses said it may have been over a hundred feet), when her harness apparently slipped from its safety wire and she fell. One of the other acrobats reached out to catch her, but just missed. She was too far away and dropped too quickly, like a stone into the abyss below the stage. It was a ten-story fall that ended in a landing out of the audience's view—but not earshot.

If anyone in the crowd thought for a flash of an instant that Sarah Guyard-Guillot's spectacular fall was part of the choreography—and gravity- and reality-defying stunts were a hallmark of the Cirque brand— the sound that followed the fall was all too real. Everyone could hear the screaming, then Sasoun's anguished moans and groans and the sound of a woman crying.

The first news flash came from audience tweets: "Wire snapped. Performer on far stage left side of stage." "He/she fell fast & awkwardly at LEAST 50 feet into pit."

The fall was from twice that height. The show was stopped. A recorded voice asked the audience to leave and said refunds would be offered. The other acrobats watched from above as they dangled in the air. One by one, they were lowered to safety.

Sarah Guyard-Guillot was pronounced dead in the ambulance on the way to the hospital. She was thirty-one. Hers was the first onstage fatal accident in Cirque du Soleil's twenty-nine-year history. The Clark County coroner ruled that she "died from multiple blunt force trauma suffered Saturday when she fell approximately 90 feet during a performance of 'Kà' at MGM Grand."

The production was shut down. It resumed on July 16, without the final battle scene.

Three months later, the Nevada Occupational Safety and Health Administration completed its investigation into Sarah's death and concluded that she "flew up at a higher rate of speed than normal toward the grid without tucking in her feet or legs" and collided with the grid. "This collision caused a shock load to the winch; the wire rope came out of the sheave/pulley and scraped against a shear point cutting numerous wires in the wire rope. The wire rope broke apart."

OSHA cited Cirque du Soleil Nevada Inc. for six safety violations, including improper training in the use of equipment, improper assessment of hazards, improper record-keeping, and the removal of Sarah's thirty-eight-foot-long wire before investigators arrived. The citations added up to a fine of $25,235. MGM Grand Hotel and Casino was cited for three violations, including exposing employees to hazards caused by Cirque's deficiencies, a $7,000 fine.

Interlude

The Great Wallendas

Karl Wallenda

The patriarch of the Kennedys of the circus world (in terms of often avoidable tragedy), Karl Wallenda was born in Magdeburg, Germany, in 1905, into a circus family whose history of high-flying acrobatics could be traced back to the eighteenth century. He began performing at age six and at seventeen put together a high-wire act with his brother, Herman, a man named Joseph Geiger, and the teenage Helen Kreis, whom he'd later marry. The Great Wallendas performed across Europe and around the world. John Ringling saw them perform in Cuba and hired them to perform at the Ringling Bros. and Barnum & Bailey Circus in the United States. When they made their debut at Madison Square Garden in 1928, the Wallendas added a new degree of difficulty to their high-wire routine: they performed without a net. They had no choice. The net they worked with had been lost in transit. Their determination that the show would go on led to standing ovations at the Garden. From that point on, the Great Wallendas were the aerial daredevils who worked without a net.

The Great Wallendas became known as the Flying Wallendas—a play in their native German on the title of the Wagner opera *The Flying Dutchman*—after the term appeared in a news article following their fall from the wire in the 1940s. It stuck.

In the years to follow, the troupe would leave such an impressive trail of injuries and death in its wake that, to some, the title "Falling Wallendas" was more fitting.

———————

When the Ringling Bros. and Barnum & Bailey Circus train rolled in to Hartford, Connecticut, on July 5, 1944, the trains were so late that one of the two shows scheduled for that day had to be canceled. Missing a show is very, very bad luck among circus folk, and although the evening show went on as planned, many superstitious roustabouts, clowns, and performers were aware that some calamity could be in the offing.

The next day was a Thursday; on this very humid July 6 afternoon, nearly eight thousand people, mostly women and children, crammed into the five-hundred-foot long big-top tent on a field at the Barbour Street Show Grounds in the city's North End. Whip-cracking lion tamer Alfred Court had finished his act and the Great Wallendas were about twenty minutes into their own, when the circus bandleader Merle Evans spotted flames. They were licking the southwest wall and crawling toward the roof of the tent.

Evans had a signal known to all the circus folk that alerts them to an emergency. He immediately directed the band to play "Stars and Stripes Forever." At the orchestral sound of the universal distress code, the Wallendas scrambled down ropes and poles.

Ringmaster Fred Bradna tried to address the crowd, tell them to keep calm, and get them to leave in an orderly fashion. It was too late. Within seconds, hundred-foot flames were chewing through the tent and spreading quickly across the canvas, waterproofed with a mixture of gasoline and paraffin. There was panic and a stampede to the exits. Within eight minutes, the tent collapsed, trapping hundreds beneath it.

(Charles Nelson Reilly, the actor, director, and 1970s television game show panelist, was among the survivors. He told the story in his one-man stage show: "A little girl went past me, and her face had been burned away. And she kept screaming, 'My mommy's gonna kill me, my mommy's gonna kill me, my—' She was already dead. Her mother wasn't gonna kill her. The circus did that.")

The Hartford Circus Fire was one of the worst fire tragedies in American history. The cause was never determined; neither was the exact body count. Official tallies run from 166 to 169, but there were probably more. Many bodies were never identified, and some smaller bodies may have been lost. Seven hundred people were injured.

None of the Wallendas, however, were hurt.

This wartime era proved very important to the Wallendas' legacy. While they'd always be associated with the Hartford circus fire, Karl Wallenda was developing a new aerial high-wire act that was not only unique but most definitely death-defying: the Seven-Person Pyramid. This marvel of design and physics included three levels of performers: two pairs of men walking the wire, each pair yoked by shoulder bars and supporting another person on a tier above them. Those two aerialists, above the four, carried a pole upon which the seventh member of the troupe balanced in a chair. The walk, three stories above the ground, without a net, put the Wallendas on the map. They were fearless. They were indestructible.

The Great Wallendas performed the Seven-Person Pyramid for decades, hundreds of times, safely and death-defyingly, until January 30, 1962, when they performed with the Shrine Circus at Detroit's State Fair Coliseum. Seven thousand children and adults watched as they performed their act three stories above the concrete floor.

The bottom level of the moving pyramid consisted of two pairs of men. Leading the way across the wire was Karl's nephew Dieter Schepp, a twenty-three-year-old refugee from East Germany. Dieter had been in the United States for only four months; this was his first appearance with the troupe. Following was Richard Faughnan, twenty-nine, the only American in the group and husband of Karl's daughter Jenny, who watched from a platform at the end of the wire. Karl's twenty-one-year-old son Mario Wallenda and nephew Gunther Wallenda, forty-two, were the second pair.

The second level consisted of Karl and his brother Herman, standing on long rods that ran along the younger men's shoulders. Dieter Schepp's sister Jana sat on a chair on a rod, balanced on the older men's shoulders. She was just seventeen.

The troupe was midway across the wire when Jenny, on the platform, noticed that Dieter didn't appear to have a good grip on the thirty-five-pound balancing bar. "It looked like Dieter didn't feel so good," she told the Associated Press.

In fact, the pole was slipping from his fingers. Dieter shouted to the others: "Ich kann nicht mehr halten!" ("I can't hold it any longer!")

"He threw the pole into the air to grip it in the center and lost his balance," Jenny said. "This threw everybody else off balance, and down they went. I screamed. I heard myself scream. I don't know nothing after that."

The pyramid collapsed, and everyone came tumbling down in a collision of flesh, bone, and rosin. Dieter, Richard, and Mario plunged thirty-six feet and slammed brutally to the hard concrete.

Amid the tangle of poles, Herman and Gunther managed to grab onto the wire. Jana tumbled out of the chair, more than fifty feet in the air, on the way to the longest fall of all, until Karl instinctively reached out and grabbed her hand. The teenager crawled onto his back and all four balanced precariously.

Panic spread through the arena. Some men tried to run into the ring. Women wept. Far too many children sat frozen, traumatized by the mayhem. There may have been a surge to the exits, or worse, if not for Blinko the Clown. Standing center ring in his greasepaint and clown costume, the clown known off-hours as Ernie Burch soothed the crowd while circus rescuers rushed into the ring and stretched a blanket as a makeshift net below the dangling performers. Jana, hanging by Karl and Gunther's hands by now, dropped to the blanket, but she hit so hard and fast that the impact tore the blanket from the men's hands. She bounced, slammed into the concrete headfirst, and wound up with a serious concussion.

Richard Faughnan died soon after the accident. Dieter Schepp died in the hospital three hours later. Mario Wallenda was left paralyzed from the waist down for life and faced years of rehabilitation. (In later years, before his death in 2015, Mario returned to the high wire strapped onto his "sky cycle," a two-wheeled electronic bike.) Karl Wallenda suffered pelvic injuries.

The fall did not deter the Great Wallendas. The night after the tragedy, Herman and his son Gunther, the only ones not injured, returned to the wire. Gene Mendez flew in from Stockholm to be the third man. They improvised a performance to deafening cheers.

———————————

Karl's sister-in-law Yetta had left the act about a dozen years earlier and on April 18, 1963, was performing a solo aerial act with the Shrine Circus in the Omaha City Auditorium. She was billed as "Miss Rietta, skirting on the borderline of eternity." She performed in a very scanty, sexy outfit—and also performed without a net.

On this evening, 4,666 spectators craned their necks to watch Yetta in the spotlight, atop a swaying, forty-five-foot-tall fiberglass pole. Yetta was beginning to attempt a headstand when she paused to adjust a footstrap. She slipped, fell backward, and plummeted toward the floor. The spotlight followed her down as she dropped thirty feet, struck a guy wire, and spun around. Yetta smashed onto the floor, facedown in the green sawdust. The spotlight widened around her crumpled body. Then children and adults alike began to scream.

A United Press International reporter wrote, "A clown act which followed in the Shrine Circus performance came on as scheduled. But most of the eyes in the audience, many of whom were school children, followed an ambulance crew as they put the broken performer on a stretcher.

"She was dead on arrival at a hospital." Yetta Wallenda was forty-two.

———————————

On November 5, 1963, a television crew from NBC's *Show of the Week* was filming at the Wallendas' winter headquarters in Sarasota, Florida.

The surviving Wallendas were going to attempt the Seven-Person Pyra-mid for the first time since the tragic fall in Detroit less than two years earlier. Three of the group, Karl, Gunther, and Herman, were part of that doomed pyramid. Jenny Faughnan, who watched her husband die that day, was in the chair at the top this time. The wire was only twelve feet above the ground. That's a good thing: as the television camera rolled and the Wallendas' pyramid began to move across, the wire that was stretched between two trees gave way with a loud *twang*. The pyra-mid came tumbling down. Gunther received deep face lacerations and lost four teeth. Karl again injured his pelvis and went to the hospital for X-rays.

"We wanted to do the pyramid once more to show we weren't afraid," Karl told the *Tampa Bay Times*. "It was to be a farewell to Herman and Gunther before they retire."

On November 20, 1963, in Fort Worth, Texas, the Wallendas per-formed the Seven-Person Pyramid once more. This time, they used a net. After the engagement, Karl announced his family would never again perform the routine.

In the years after the Detroit disaster, Karl Wallenda continued to per-form with a smaller troupe and gained new attention for his "sky walks" between buildings and across stadiums. He was sixty-five when he crossed the Tallulah Gorge in Georgia on a high wire on July 18, 1970. The thousand-foot, eighteen-minute walk, 750 feet above the ground, included two handstands. When he stepped off the wire, his wife handed him a martini. (A friend once asked Wallenda why he risked his life on the high wire. He replied, "To get to the martini on the other side.")

The Wallenda-Leontini Circus had rolled into Wheeling, West Virginia, on Friday night, July 28, 1972. It was opening night and a benefit for local Shriners. Six thousand people spread out through the twelve-thousand-seat open-air Wheeling Island Stadium, most all of them looking upward to watch legendary Karl walk a high wire strung between two light towers, sixty feet off the ground.

Stories of Wallenda tragedies and of course the deaths in Detroit had only added to his mystique and the drama every time he set foot on the wire. Potential disaster was certainly on the minds of many spectators. For sixty-seven-year-old Karl Wallenda, though, this was a breeze. Holding his balancing pole, he navigated the dangerous walk and was reaching the end. There was but one hitch.

"I was pretty steady," he told the Associated Press, "but I didn't know how to get down."

Son-in-law Richard Guzman was on his way to help. Guzman was twenty-nine and also performing that day. Married to Karl's daughter Carla, he'd been a Flying Wallenda for the past six years. Everyone called him "Chico."

Now he was climbing one of the light towers to take Karl's pole so the old man could get off the wire. Chico reached the top and was just about to grab the balancing pole when he touched a live electrical wire. The shock was massive. Thousands of volts burned through his nervous system in a flash, knocking him back into the air. He fell backward and landed ten feet below on a pair of electrical wires. For a moment he lay there, enough time for a police officer to run beneath him to try to catch his fall. Then, Richard "Chico" Guzman dropped another fifty feet. He landed on the cop.

A nurse at the scene managed to revive him, but Guzman died at a local hospital. Death was attributed not to electrocution but to head injuries.

His wife Carla and three of their four kids were at the circus. The next day, Carla was supposed to join her father on the wire, and the kids were going to do their bicycle act.

Interviewed that next afternoon, Karl Wallenda noted that Chico Guzman had fallen from a wire seven years earlier and spent nine months in the hospital. "Our life is show business," he said. "Without show business, we don't survive. And we have to exist." Karl Wallenda returned to the wire for Saturday's show.

"The only place I feel alive is on the wire," Karl said. "To be on the wire is life. The rest is waiting." It was March 22, 1978; Karl Wallenda was seventy-three years old. Four members of his immediate family were dead, and his adopted son was paralyzed from the waist down, but nothing was going to stop him from walking the high wire without a net. He'd first walked the wire in 1920, and this morning he was about to walk a high wire strung ten stories over a street between the two towers of the beachfront Condado Plaza Hilton and Condado Holiday Inn hotels in San Juan, Puerto Rico.

The ocean breezes were kicking up. It really was a bit windy for such a walk, but two hundred people had gathered below and news cameras were rolling. Local television station WAPA was broadcasting the event live. This was a splendid promotion for the Pan American Circus, in which the Great Wallendas were the featured act. Karl, his seventeen-year-old granddaughter Rietta, and two nephews performed each show on a wire, fifty feet in the air. So, in long-sleeved white shirt and red trousers, with a long balancing pole in his hands, the old man prepared to take his steps 121 feet above the pavement.

Gary Williams had a bird's-eye view, perched on the rooftop, above the spot Karl Wallenda intended to reach. A photographer for *El Nuevo Día*, the local newspaper, Williams had been invited by Wallenda the previous day. The old man wanted as much publicity as possible for his circus appearances. "I set up my camera on the chimney that was right above the wire, and I put on a wide-angle lens," Williams tells us, recalling the moment like it happened yesterday. "I was going to get up there when he got close to me and take the picture with the crowd down below.

"So he starts walking. I take my pictures. I'm shooting with a very long lens. A 300 millimeter lens. And he's walking, walking, walking to me. And then the pole starts going back and forth. Up and down. And he's having trouble controlling the pole. And people were going, 'Ooh! Ooh!' And one of the people who work with him in the act was watching from the roof. He yelled, 'Sit down! Sit down!' And he takes what they call—I found this out later—he took what they call a 'three-point position,' where he sits down. He can hold that position for hours. But he had no strength."

Karl Wallenda had made it more than halfway across the wire. The winds suddenly picked up, gusting to 30 knots (about 34.5 miles per hour). "And soon as he grabbed that three-point position, he spun," Williams says. "And he fell. And he went all the way down. My finger froze on my motor drive. Thank God I had a motor drive. There were two other photographers on the roof with me. But they didn't have a motor drive, so they didn't have anything of the fall."

Victor Abboud, an accountant from Montreal, was also a witness to the horror. "I saw him go down on his knees on the wire and I thought he was kneeling to rest," he said in a report filed by the Associated Press. "But then I saw he was shaking, the winds blew him off and he went all the way down, head first."

Karl Wallenda had made a desperate grasp for the wire before plunging to the driveway of the Holiday Inn below. His head smacked against a parked taxi before he smashed to the pavement. The sight led to some hysteria among the spectators. Several fainted or collapsed.

"I couldn't see the hit, because there was a ledge sticking out from the first floor where the casino was, and it was covering the entrance of the hotel," Williams continues. "I heard a hit. And then, I think it was a family member to the left of me, collapsed on the roof. And she started wailing. I took another camera and I shot a picture of that and then I ran downstairs. And I saw some people there. I took a couple of pictures of a woman and I realized that I didn't have my wide-angle lens. It was up on the roof. So I had to go back up to the roof and get the lens, came down, and I took the wide-angle picture of him lying on the ground. And there's a woman from the hotel praying over him and the crowd around him."

The police were concerned about the crowd, Williams says, but local law made it difficult to simply move the body to a secure location. "In Puerto Rico you're not allowed to remove a body from a crime scene or an accident until the district attorney shows up." But one of them hit on a solution. "A policeman yells, 'He's still alive!' And they moved the body. They put it in the backseat and they took it to the hospital. The policeman there used his head, because there were so many people there—threw him in a cab and got him out of there."

Karl Wallenda was pronounced dead at Presbyterian Hospital at 10:20 AM.

In the aftermath, the obvious question was whether Wallenda thought of calling off the stunt because of the winds. James B. Harrington, manager of the circus, said he didn't. "He thought it was fine. He tested and installed the wire himself." Ultimately, the wind and faulty wire rigging took the blame for the tragedy (others cited Karl's age and health as factors; Gary Williams says a doctor friend informed him that his photos indicate a heart attack).

When news of his uncle's death reached him at home in Sarasota, Florida, Gunther Wallenda told United Press International, "If Karl would have had a choice, this would have been the way he wanted it." Gunther, who had retired in 1962, after the Seven-Person Pyramid collapse in Detroit, insisted, "The show will definitely go on, in the finest of circus tradition. That's the way Karl would have wanted it."

His prediction proved to be very accurate, for on the afternoon of Karl's death, granddaughter Rietta and the Great Wallenda nephews went on with the show. "My editor said, 'You got to go to the circus. The Wallendas are going on,'" Gary Williams recalls. "I said, 'They just lost Karl Wallenda. What do you mean they're going on?' 'The show must go on.' And so I went to the circus. And sure enough, I get there, I'm standing right under the high wire act. I'm still in shock, I guess. And she was up there doing something like a small pyramid. The girl. Two guys with a pole go on top. And I thought she was going to fall. And she got down and stepped into the spotlight. The same girl [who'd collapsed] on the roof overlooking the wire. And as she's taking the bow, she just breaks down in tears."

———————

On June 4, 2011, Karl's great-grandson Nik Wallenda and his mother Delilah returned to the Condado Hilton to attempt the same 135-foot walk in Karl's memory. Mother and son started at opposite ends of the wire. When Delilah reached the middle, roughly where Karl had fallen, she sat down and Nik stepped over her before the two continued to opposite ends. Before completing the walk, Nik knelt on the wire and blew a kiss in honor of Karl's memory.

While several branches of the Wallendas continue to perform today, it's Nik who's inherited Karl's mantle as the Great Wallenda of the twenty-first century. Born in 1979, Nik holds a dozen world records and has walked the high wire where no one had been allowed before, including Niagara Falls and the Grand Canyon. He also prefers to perform without a net.

"The myth is when you use a net, just because you have a safety device, it means that you're safe," he tells us. "I wore a tether over Niagara Falls because it was mandated by my partner at the time, ABC. I was more worried that that was going to tangle up and kill me than actually just walking without it."

Nik supersized the Wallenda legacy when he added one more body to the infamous Seven-Person Pyramid. Nik and his troupe were rehearsing their *eight-person* pyramid under the Circus Sarasota Big Top in Sarasota, Florida, on February 8, 2017. Nik and three others were on the bottom, two, including Nik's sister Lijana, were the next layer, and the man above them held Nik's fifty-six-year-old aunt Rietta on his shoulders. They were rehearsing without a net.

When Lijana lost her balance, the pyramid collapsed. Five of the troupe fell to the ground. Rietta plummeted forty feet from the top. Nik and two others managed to hang on to the wire. No one was killed, but Lijana, who landed on her face, was injured most severely.

"Yes, it was the roughest day of my life," Nik says. "After our fall, I've chosen that when we do the big pyramid, we'll use an airbag. I think that pride plays a role in what we do, and it was tough on me to put an airbag under us, but I felt like it was the right decision. I feel like society is changing. I don't think anyone who comes to a circus wants to see someone die. We toured for the last year, and everywhere we went, we used [an airbag]. And to be honest, the audience's response was no less than it was without one. Now, when I'm walking alone, it's a little different. I'm not responsible for the others, I don't have people on my shoulders, so I prefer not to use a net or wear a safety device.

"But I think wisdom has to play a role in our lives and you can't be arrogant, cause that'll kill you."

Nik explains he doesn't intend to die on the wire and takes no comfort knowing that his great-grandfather died "doing what he loved." "No, I don't think anyone in the family wanted to see that. We did learn from my great-grandfather's death that there is a time to retire. And I think I will retire. The challenge is when it's your life and passion—and this is our passion—but I've already begun to prepare myself for that."

Epilogue

Audience Participation

Everybody wants ta get inta da act!

—Jimmy Durante

IN THE 2007 IRISH MUSICAL film *Once*, Glen Hansard and Markéta Irglová portrayed two struggling musicians in Dublin, Ireland. Their characters wrote and performed songs that told the story of their romance. The pair, who performed in real life as the Swell Season, also composed the film's score, including a number titled "Falling Slowly" that won the 2008 Academy Award for Best Original Song. So it was somewhat ironic when, on August 19, 2010, their concert was stopped by someone who fell very quickly onto their stage.

The duo and their backing band were playing an outdoor show at the Mountain Winery in Saratoga, California. The twenty-two-hundred-seat amphitheater is perched high on a mountain with views across the Santa Clara Valley and is built around the facade of the original winery. The winery building is the backdrop to the stage.

It was a perfect setting for the duo's intimate, romantic folk pop, and many of the nineteen hundred people in the audience recalled the night as "magical"—magical, that is, until it turned into a horror show.

Shortly after 10:00 PM, the group took an intermission of sorts. Most of the musicians left the stage to the fiddler player, who performed a traditional Irish song in the balmy breeze. When the ensemble returned, Hansard sang "When Your Mind's Made Up" from the *Once* soundtrack.

He followed that intensity with some levity, teasing the lead guitarist about the first song he ever wrote. Hansard began to lead the audience in a sing-along, getting another big laugh when he promised to be "rocking out to the maximum."

It was around then that some people in the amphitheater, high above the performers, noticed the figure on the roof of the winery behind and above the stage. It was a person in dark clothing. They saw him run across the tile shingles and then leap into the sky, as if taking off from a diving board. He descended rapidly and silently near the lighting rig, flipped head over heels in midair, and, after a forty-foot drop, smashed with a loud thud onto the stage, about five feet away from Glen Hansard.

Some people assumed that the figure was a dummy. The way the body fell certainly looked as if it could have been thrown off the roof. One witness thought he was seeing a black cape or sheet falling. Some assumed a speaker or lighting rig had fallen. Some thought the jumper was part of the show, that he had something to do with Hansard's routine with the guitarist. Others knew immediately.

Hansard rushed over to the fallen man, knelt next to him and looked toward the wings. "Quickly!" he shouted.

By then, people in the audience were already punching 911 into their cell phones. Doctors and paramedics from the audience ran to the stage and began CPR. A crew member stepped up to a microphone and asked if anyone could help identify the man. Then he asked that everyone remain seated, so as not to clog the narrow mountain roads used by the ambulance that was already on its way.

Everyone watched the doctors, EMTs, and firefighters work on the man for a good half hour. Eventually a black curtain was placed around them to block the view. A doctor who'd been in the audience declared the man dead on the stage.

The man was identified as Michael Edward Pickels. He was thirty-two, from nearby San Jose. Pickels had arrived at the show with a friend. Around 10:00 PM, he'd left all of his personal belongings on his seat and disappeared. A short time later, he was seen on the roof. Apparently, he'd gone around the back of the building, where it was easy to climb up.

If there was no apparent reason for his public suicide, there were at least indicators. On New Year's Day, Pickels had gotten into a violent argument with his girlfriend. He'd tied up her hands and legs, pointed a loaded shotgun at her, and threatened that he was going to kill her and himself. Somehow, the girlfriend convinced him to let her go. She ran to another house and called police, who negotiated with Pickels for ninety minutes before he gave up the gun and surrendered.

He was arrested and charged with assault with a firearm, domestic violence, and false imprisonment. The night of the Swell Season show, he was free on $150,000 bail and facing a court appearance in October.

The morning after, the Swell Season extended its sympathies in a MySpace post: "Our hearts go out to the victim who decided to take his own life at last night's gig . . . and to his friends and family."

"We are just in shock and grief and full of bewilderment," Howard Greynolds, the band's manager, told the local *Mercury News*. "Clearly, next year, we are going to come back to the area and do a show for a suicide prevention or something, if it turns out to be a suicide. Maybe at the Warfield [in San Francisco] or someplace—I don't think we'd want to go back to the Mountain Winery."

The Swell Season played as scheduled that Friday night at the Oregon Zoo in Portland. They later promised to pay for group grief counseling sessions for hundreds of fans who witnessed the suicide.

The Mountain Winery did not offer refunds to the traumatized concertgoers, many of whom told their stories in the readers' comments section of the *San Francisco Weekly*:

> The ghastly image in my head still won't let me sleep. What a horrific abrupt ending to a sublime concert. . . . The adorable Marketa made a comment earlier in the show that she will always remember Saratoga because it was her first ever "costume change" (she was cold and changed from her dress to jeans and a sweater). Now she will remember Saratoga for an entirely different reason. What a nightmare.
>
> Honestly, I'm really pissed that this jerk ruined an evening for so many. This was a fantastic show up until this point, and

how many of us (not to mention the bandmembrs themselves)
will remember this selfish dead man when we listen to their
music?

As the audience response made clear, there's a big difference between
an amateur trying to steal the spotlight and performers who dedicate,
and ultimately give, their lives to their art onstage.

Acknowledgments

THE AUTHORS GIVE SPECIAL THANKS to Alison Holloway, our executive producer, without whom this book could not have been written; our editor Yuval Taylor, developmental editor Devon Freeny, and copyeditor Joseph Webb, and the team at Chicago Review Press, without whom this book would not have been published—and whose work improved upon it along the way; Robert S. Bader, who was always a source of inspiration and assistance, and above all a man of his word; and many others who were important to the research and completion of this project, including Laurie Abkemeier, Cindy Adams, Glen Alai, Robert M. Angel, Alan Bisbort, Dan Bowen, Michael Braverman, Lisa Lew Brennan, Peter Brennan, Paul Brownstein, Joseph Burrus, Mike Caveney, Dick Cavett, Bruce Charet, John Cox, Michael Custer, Donato Di Camillo, Tony Douglas, Dave Edison, Cliff Einstein, Mark Evanier, Kriss Famous, Wayne Federman, John Fisher, Vic Garbarini, Tracey Goessel, Danny Gold, Dara Gottfried, Gilbert Gottfried, Chuck Granata, Howard Green, Bob Greenberg, Joe Gunches, Tom Hearn, Ricky Jay, Penn Jillette, Lori Jonas, John Katsilometes, Sally Jade Kearns, Sam Kearns, Dianna T. Kenny, David Koenig, Michael Kurth, Norman Lebrecht, Matt Lubich, Mark Malkoff, Gillian McCain, Don McGlynn, Legs McNeil, Mónica Aunión Monroy, Kliph Nesteroff, Greg Otto, Billy Riback, Ricky Riccardi, Ray Richmond, Jay Ruttenberg, Corrie Sachs, Frank Santopadre, Glenn Schwartz, Michael Sells, Carmine Sesto, Adam Shawn, John Shetler, Randy Skretvedt, Jim Steinmeyer, Zach Stork, Nik Wallenda, Dean Ward, Karen Wheeler, Spats

White, Gary Williams, Elli Wohlgelernter, Danny Wolf, and, of course, Al Dvorin, and all those who lived to perform and died doing what they loved.

Appendix

Fifty More Who Died Onstage—a Chronological Selection

Americo Sbigoli was singing second tenor in a quintet led by Domenico Donzelli in January 1822 when he had to match Donzelli's powerful voice in a climactic phrase during a Rome performance of Giovanni Pacini's opera *Cesare in Egitto*. He strained too hard, burst a blood vessel in his throat, and died.

Sam Patch, recognized as the first American daredevil, died on Friday the Thirteenth of November 1829, after jumping 125 feet from the High Falls of the Genesee River in Rochester, New York. Eight thousand people witnessed the leap. His frozen body turned up downriver the following spring. He was twenty-two. Somebody placed a wooden board over his grave that read SAM PATCH—SUCH IS FAME.

Romanian actress **Matilda Pascaly**, wife of acclaimed actor and director Mihail Pascaly, was playing an angel and flying over the stage in a production of *Don Juan de Marana* in 1873 when stagehands bungled the wires that were holding her up and sent her crashing, upside down, into a wall.

Alfred Glanville Vance, a popular British music hall pantomimist, comic, and singer known as the Great Vance, was onstage at the Sun Music Hall in Knightsbridge, London, on Boxing Day, December 26, 1888. Wearing the robe and wig of a judge, he was on the third verse of a number called "Are You Guilty?" when he suddenly left the stage and collapsed in the arms of his agent (cutting his face on a partition as he fell). He was dead on arrival at St. George's Hospital. A postmortem revealed that the Great Vance had heart disease. He was believed to be fifty.

Aerialist **Eva Gilbert**'s specialty was swinging from a trapeze, flying through the air, and catching her foot in a loop, thirty-five feet above the stage. At the Powhatan Theatre in Newport News, Virginia, on February 11, 1902, her foot slipped. She dropped headfirst to the floor, broke her neck, and was dead within ten minutes.

An Algerian dancer known as **Princess Turkait** was performing a ballet at a "Russian amusement concession" at the Panama-Pacific International Exposition in San Francisco on March 18, 1915, when a man rushed into the theater and began firing a pistol. The princess was shot in the heart. The shooter was identified as Isaac Lizraki, another dancer and the victim's own brother. He refused to say why he killed his sister.

Otto Kline, known as the best horseback rider in America, was performing with the Barnum & Bailey Circus at Madison Square Garden on the afternoon of April 21, 1915. Five thousand people saw the cowboy swinging over the sides of his galloping horse when he slipped, was flung into a box, and fractured his skull. Kline was twenty-eight.

Adolphe Blind, a Swiss magician who performed as Professor Magicus, showed off his sleight of hand at a charity event in Bogis-Bossey, near Lake Geneva, on August 23, 1925. He placed an egg in a little black bag and explained that he was about to make it vanish into thin air. Then he collapsed, silently, to the floor. The audience applauded politely. Professor Magicus was fifty-three.

Vaudeville balancing and tumbling act the Wille Brothers were working with a twenty-six-foot steel pole during an afternoon show at the Harris Theatre in Pittsburgh, on January 31, 1927. "Brother" **Matt Untermeyer** was balancing the pole on his shoulder, and Henry Wille was hanging from the top by a foot rope, when the rope broke. The pole slipped and Untermeyer broke his neck. He died on February 6, at fifty-two.

Charles Rowan was a South African magician and escape artist who performed as Karr the Mysterious. On October 9, 1930, he was in the street outside Springfontein Town Hall, promoting a show by attempting to escape from a straitjacket before a speeding car ran him down. He was too slow.

Royden Joseph Gilbert Genesta, who performed magic as **Genesta, the Wizard of Wonders**, attempted to escape from a water-filled barrel at a vaudeville theater in Frankfort, Kentucky, on November 9, 1930 (his version of Houdini's "milk can trick"). On this day, the secret lid that he'd usually slide off was bent. He drowned at fifty-two.

Mary A. McLaughlin died suddenly on November 16, 1931, while playing Desdemona in a burlesque and comedy version of Shakespeare's *Othello* at the South Congregational Church in Hartford, Connecticut. The young woman was in the middle of a song when she sat down in a chair, dead from heart disease. According to witnesses, the audience and actors assumed she was adding an extra comedic touch, and they allowed her to remain in the chair until the situation became embarrassing.

Mary Larkin de Phil performed with her husband Charles de Phil as the Flying Phillips aerial cycling act. On October 17, 1934, they were wrapping the second show at the Roxy Theater in New York City's Times Square. Charles had climbed down to the stage and was waiting for Mary to take their bows when she slipped while dismounting from her unicycle and plunged forty feet to the boards. She was twenty-six.

Actor **Frank Allworth** died of a heart attack onstage at the Broad Street Theater in Philadelphia on September 2, 1935, opening night of the comedy *Portuguese Gal*. He was dancing with star Lenore Ulric when he collapsed to his knees, then fell to the stage, all the while with his hands locked in a death grip with hers. He was thirty-five.

Walter Edwin Floyd was the first magician on the Lyceum Circuit, a nineteenth-century lecture circuit that was an early form of adult education. On August 21, 1940, Floyd performed for an audience of about a hundred men at a dinner in his hometown, Chelsea, Massachusetts. He was in the middle of a routine called the Miser's Dream, making coins appear out of thin air, when he dropped dead of a heart attack at seventy-nine. (When his body arrived at the undertakers, a coin was found clutched in his palm.)

Operatic tenor **Aroldo Lindi** died of a heart attack on March 8, 1944, while performing Leoncavallo's *Pagliacci* at the War Memorial Opera House in San Francisco. He was holding the final note of "Vesti la giubba," one of the most moving and well-known operatic arias of all time, when he sank to the floor and fell flat on his face as the curtain rang down. The audience gave him a standing ovation. He was fifty-five.

Swedish contortionist and escape artist **Bernhard Eskilsen**, a.k.a. **Bernardi**, staged a publicity stunt in Rønne, Denmark, on April 22, 1946, for the opening of a new circus season. He was shackled and tied in a sack, and the sack was set on fire and thrown in a river. Bernardi did not emerge from the sack. The coroner ruled that the stunt had aggravated a preexisting heart condition, producing a clot that traveled to Bernardi's brain. He was forty-four.

Isabel Bonner had the leading role in her husband Joseph Kramm's play *The Shrike* when the drama opened in Los Angeles at the Carthay Circle Theatre on July 1, 1955. During a scene set in a hospital room, she fell forward onto the bed and across the lap of actor Dane Clark. "Speak to me," Clark ad-libbed. "Is something the matter? What's wrong, darling? I love you." When the actress failed to respond, he commanded, "Ring down the curtain." Isabel Bonner was dead of a cerebral hemorrhage at forty-seven.

Gareth Jones was portraying a character who died of a heart attack in a live television play when he died of a real heart attack on November 30, 1958. Jones was appearing in the science fiction play *Underground*, on the anthology series *Armchair Theatre*, broadcast on Britain's ITV network. The other actors improvised to make up for his absence. The following year, production moved from Manchester to London, where shows could be prerecorded on videotape. Jones was thirty-three.

Actor **Louis Jean Heydt** completed act 1, scene 1, in a pre-Broadway performance of *There Was a Little Girl* at the Colonial Theatre in Boston on January 29, 1960. Then he took a step into the wings and dropped dead from a heart attack. He was fifty-six and starring opposite Jane Fonda in what would be her Broadway debut.

Actor and singer **Nelson Eddy** was best known as the stolid Royal Canadian Mountie serenading Jeanette MacDonald with "Indian Love Call" in the 1936 film *Rose-Marie*. On March 5, 1967, at age sixty-five, he performed in the nightclub of the swank Sans Souci Hotel in Miami Beach. Eddy was introducing his second song when his voice failed and he became confused. "My face is getting numb," he said. "Something's wrong. I can't see! Is there a doctor here?" He'd suffered a stroke, caused by a cerebral hemorrhage. He was pronounced dead in the early hours of March 6. The Associated Press reported that a week earlier, Eddy promised to continue working "until I drop," because "I love it."

Actor **George Ostroska** collapsed from a heart attack while playing the title role of *Macbeth* at the Crawford Livingston Theater in St. Paul, Minnesota, on January 8, 1970. He was thirty-two. Some believe he fell to the "curse of Macbeth."

Predrag Jovičić, vocalist of the Yugoslav rock band San, died from an electric shock during a February 2, 1975, concert in Čair Hall in Niš.

Los Angeles country musician **Skinny Dennis Sanchez** (so called because he had Marfan syndrome, standing six foot eleven and weighing just

135 pounds) played upright bass and was best known for his work with Texas music legend Guy Clark. (He was immortalized in Clark's song "L.A. Freeway.") Skinny Dennis collapsed and died of heart failure on March 20, 1975, while backing singer John Malcolm Penn at Sunset Beach in Orange County, California. He was twenty-eight.

Canadian country, folk, and gospel singer **Marg Osburne**, nicknamed "the Girl from the Singing Hills" and a regular on the television show *Don Messer's Jubilee*, suffered a fatal heart attack during a concert in Rocklyn, Ontario, on July 16, 1977. She was forty-nine. Her co-star on *Jubilee*, balladeer and step-dancer Charlie Chamberlain, had died of heart failure exactly five years earlier, two weeks after he'd collapsed during a television rehearsal. Charlie was sixty-one.

Mindru Katz, the brilliant pianist who was born in Romania in 1925 and emigrated to Israel in 1959, died onstage on January 30, 1978, during a recital in Istanbul, Turkey. He was performing "Tempest," Beethoven's Piano Sonata No. 17 in D Minor. Katz was fifty-two.

Miguelito Valdés, the Cuban singer known as "Mr. Babalú" (and a friendly rival to Desi Arnaz, who made the song his signature on the 1950s sitcom *I Love Lucy*), died onstage in Bogotá, Colombia, on November 9, 1978. He was performing a medley of his hits, including "Babalú," when he collapsed from a heart attack at sixty-six.

Joe E. Ross, the burlesque comic turned star of sitcoms including *Car 54, Where Are You?*, suffered a fatal heart attack while performing his act in the clubhouse of the Oakwood Apartments in Burbank, California, on August 13, 1982. He was sixty-eight. His wife Arlene reportedly collected only half the promised one hundred dollar fee because Joe E. only completed half a show.

Sylvester "Papa Dee" Allen, who played conga, bongos, and other percussion for War, the multi-ethnic funk outfit from Long Beach, California, suffered a cerebral hemorrhage onstage at the Talk of The Town nightclub in Vallejo, California, on August 30, 1988. He died at fifty-seven.

Bill Cerri, longtime classical music announcer on Washington, DC, public radio station WETA-FM, was behind the microphone on July 17, 1990, when he began garbling his words, got up, and walked out of the studio, leaving four minutes of radio silence. He had suffered a stroke and died that day at age sixty, a month away from retirement.

Country Dick Montana, singer, drummer, and guitarist for the Beat Farmers, the influential cowpunk band from San Diego, died on November 8, 1995, during a show at the Longhorn Saloon and Grill in Whistler, British Columbia. According to a report in the *Lake Tahoe Review*, he suffered a heart attack resulting from a blood clot in his leg, possibly the result of the six-foot-four musician traveling "thousands of miles sitting bent-kneed in a van." He was forty.

Rhythm and blues and funk guitarist **Johnny "Guitar" Watson** was performing his hit "Superman Lover" at the Ocean Boulevard Blues Cafe in Yokohama, Japan, on May 17, 1996, when he fell to the stage, dead of a heart attack, at sixty-one.

British actor **Anthony Wheeler** was playing Judas in an open-air production of *Jesus Christ Superstar* at the Sani Beach Hotel on Greece's Halkidiki peninsula on August 17, 1997, when he failed to attach his safety harness and hanged himself during his climactic scene. He was twenty-six.

Unlikely reggae music star **Judge Dread** was actually the large, blond-haired, and balding Anglo Saxon Brit named Alexander Minto Hughes. With smutty double entendre ditties like "Big Six," he racked up more UK chart hits in the 1970s than any other reggae artist—including Bob Marley (and holds the Guinness World Record for the most banned songs of all time—eleven). When he appeared at the Penny Theatre in Canterbury on March 13, 1998, Dread closed the show by exclaiming, "Let's hear it for the band!" He then collapsed and died of a heart attack at fifty-two.

Mark Sandman, bassist and lead vocalist for the Boston-based alternative rock band Morphine, died onstage at the Nel Nome del Rock festival outside Rome, Italy, on July 3, 1999. Sandman was performing with the guitarless (bass-saxophone-drum) trio when he suffered a heart attack and collapsed in front of several thousand spectators. He was forty-six.

Aerial artist **Eva Garcia** was dressed as sexy *Tomb Raider* adventurer Lara Croft on August 1, 2003, when she made an entrance from the ceiling of the Hippodrome Circus in Great Yarmouth, England. She had thirty feet to go when the cable jammed. Seven hundred people, including many families with children, watched her be flung to a bloody death. She was thirty-eight. (Eva's brother-in-law, French aerialist Gilles Antares, died at forty-seven on February 7, 2006, the day after he fell at the Cirque d'Hiver-Bouglione in Paris. He'd been suspended from a belt held by his brother Bruno on a trapeze. The belt snapped.)

Popular, award-winning gospel pianist **Anthony Burger** was performing on a Gaither Homecoming gospel music cruise in the Caribbean on February 22, 2006, when audience members noticed he wasn't moving and that his hands had clenched into fists over the keyboard. He'd suffered a massive heart attack at forty-four. His official biography said that "his heart burst."

Miriam Makeba, the South African singer and social activist known for her worldwide hit "Pata Pata," sang the song at a benefit concert in Castel Volturno, Italy, on Sunday, November 9, 2008, forty-one years after its Top 20 success. When the song ended, she collapsed while walking offstage. She died of heart failure at seventy-six.

Icelandic rock 'n' roll hero **Rúnar Júlíusson** died on December 5, 2008, after suffering a heart attack while reaching for his guitar onstage at the Ráin restaurant in his hometown of Keflavík (known as "Beatletown" for the number of rock musicians who hailed from there). He was sixty-three and promoting a CD retrospective, *Söngvar um lífið 1966–2008*. The title translates to "Singing About Life."

Rapper **MC Daleste** was playing a free concert in a public housing project in Campinas, São Paulo, Brazil, on July 7, 2013, when two shots rang out from the audience, killing him. Police investigators said the shooting was likely a professional hit, possibly by a vigilante death squad with links to the police. One of the twenty-year-old's songs included the line "Matar os polícia é a nossa meta," which translates to "Killing the police is our goal."

Singer **Agustin Briolini**, lead singer of the Argentinian rock band Krebs, was electrocuted on November 23, 2014, when he touched a microphone during a soundcheck before a sold-out show at the Teatro del Sol in Villa Carlos Paz. He was twenty-two. Pico Moyano, singer for the band Iceberg, also on the bill that night, said the accident left him "shocked."

Dancer and choreographer **Kulwinder Kaur** and her troupe were performing at a wedding celebration in the town of Maur Mandi in Punjab, India, on December 3, 2016, when a friend of the groom blasted her in the face with a 12-bore shotgun. She was twenty-two and two months pregnant. Video of the killing went viral.

Venezuelan singing star **Memo Morales**, known as "the King of the Pasodoble," collapsed onstage from a heart attack at the Hermandad Gallega Hall in Caracas on January 1, 2017. He was seventy-nine. His daughter Alicia, who performed with him in two New Year's Eve concerts, said, "He left as he wanted to go, singing, doing what he liked. . . . He died happy."

Sib Hashian, former drummer for the band Boston, died aboard MSC Cruises' cruise ship *Divina* on March 22, 2017. He was performing "the hits of Boston" on a Legends of Rock cruise of the Caribbean when he collapsed over his drums from a heart attack. He was sixty-seven. Hashian's daughter Lauren, a singer-songwriter, has had a long relationship and two children with Dwayne "the Rock" Johnson. In an Instagram post, Johnson called Sib Hashian "my second dad."

Ryan Nunez, a member of the San Francisco Gay Men's Chorus, collapsed onstage at the Herbst Theatre on March 31, 2017, during intermission of the group's annual spring concert. Doctors, nurses, and paramedics from the chorus performed CPR. Nunez was thirty-nine.

French singer and songwriter **Barbara Weldens** revived the *chanson réaliste* tradition popularized by Édith Piaf. While performing with her duo in a medieval church turned concert hall in the village of Gourdon on July 19, 2017, her heart stopped beating. She'd been electrocuted when she stepped on a defective electrical device. Weldens was thirty-five. She always performed barefoot.

Laudir de Oliveira, a Brazilian percussionist who was a member of the band Chicago from 1975 to 1982, suffered a fatal heart attack on September 17, 2017, while performing in Rio de Janeiro. He was seventy-seven.

Russian-Jewish classical pianist **Mikhail Klein** performed with the Irkutsk Philharmonic Orchestra on October 3, 2017, in Irkutsk, Siberia, where he'd lived for the past forty-five years. He was playing his jazz composition "This Is All Russia" when he slipped from the bench and wound up in a heap at the foot of the grand piano. He was seventy-two.

DJ Kaleb Freitas was killed before a crowd of five thousand at the Atmosphere Festival in Esteio, Brazil, on the afternoon of December 16, 2017. He was performing in heavy winds when a gust ripped down the massive rigging above the stage, sending steel, columns of speakers, lights, and a giant video screen crashing to the stage. He was thirty.

British stand-up comic **Ian Cognito** sat down and died onstage during the Lone Wolf Comedy Club event at the Atic bar in Bicester, England, on April 11, 2019. Shortly after joking about having a stroke "and waking up speaking Welsh," he sat on a stool, breathed heavily, and went silent. The audience thought it was part of his act. Born Paul Barbieri, he was sixty.

Index